RABBINIC THOUGHT IN THE TALMUD

BY THE SAME AUTHOR

Jewish Prayer

A Guide to Rosh Ha-Shanah

A Guide to Yom Kippur

Jewish Values

Studies in Talmudic Logic and Methodology

The Palm Tree of Deborah
(Translated from the Hebrew of Moses Cordovero, with Introduction Notes)

Tract on Ecstasy
(Translated from the Hebrew of Dobh Baer of Lubavitch, with Introduction and Notes)

Principles of the Jewish Faith: An Analytical Study

A Jewish Theology

The Talmudic Argument

Helping with Inquiries

God, Torah, Israel

Religion and the Individual

We Have Reason To Believe
(Fifth revised edition)

Their Heads in Heaven: Unfamiliar Aspects of Hasidism

Judaism and Theology: Essays on the Jewish Religion

Jewish Preaching: Homilies and Sermons

RABBINIC THOUGHT IN THE TALMUD

LOUIS JACOBS

VALLENTINE MITCHELL
LONDON • PORTLAND, OR

First published in 2005 in Great Britain by
VALLENTINE MITCHELL & CO. LTD
Suite 314, Premier House, 112–114 Station Road,
Edgware, Middlesex HA8 7BJ

www.vmbooks.com

and in the United States of America by
VALLENTINE MITCHELL
c/o ISBS,
920 NE 58th Avenue, Suite 300, Portland, OR 97213-3786 USA

British Library Cataloging-in-Publication Data
have been applied for

Library of Congress Cataloguing in Publication Data
has been applied for

ISBN 0 85303 564 4 (cloth)
0 85303 568 7 (paper)

Printed in Great Britain by
MPG Books Ltd, Bodmin, Cornwall

Contents

For Geoffrey Paul, with
thanks for his constant help
and encouragement

Preface

Although most of the essays in this book have appeared previously in print, they are presented here as having a unified theme: the way the Babylonian Talmud came to be presented by its final editors and the way in which Talmudic authority was discussed and applied in post-Talmudic Rabbinic literature. The essays are technical and, I hope, will be of interest to academics in the field. I have tried also for the presentation to be sufficiently popular to be of some relevance to the general student of Talmudic-Rabbinic thought.

The four opening chapters are based on the lectures I gave to the Oxford Centre and were intended to serve as an introduction to the Babylonian Talmud, hence the perhaps somewhat unusual form, in which the text is more general with the notes describing the state of the art in modern Talmudic studies. In the section on the Talmudic *sugya* my chief concern has been to develop further the idea, stated forty years ago in my book *Studies in Talmudic Logic and Methodology*, to point out the contrived nature of the Babylonian Talmud. I still maintain that the nature of the Talmudic *sugya* is misunderstood without this element of contrivance, in which the student is intentionally directed to follow the arguments as leading skilfully to the conclusion, as in any work of literature. It is impossible to see the Talmud as a simple record handed down orally from generation to generation. In the other chapters on the general topics of Talmudics I have tried to be original without being unhistorical.

In the section on Rabbinics, I try to show how the great post-Talmudic Rabbis went about their task, including, in the final chapters, how the famous Halakhists were often influenced by their social background as well as their individual temperament. The same applies, I would maintain, to the Talmudic heroes themselves. As I wrote in my book *A Tree of Life*, behind the mind of the most objective and sober Halakhist there lies the heart of a poetic Aggadist.

THE ORIGINAL HOMES OF THE ESSAYS

Chapters 1, 2, 3 and 4 have not hitherto been published but were delivered as lectures at the Oxford Centre for Postgraduate Hebrew Studies (The Jacobs Lectures). Chapter 5 has not hitherto been published. Chapter 6 was published in *HUCA*, Vol. XLII, 1971, pp. 185–96. Chapter 7 appeared in *Hebrew Annual Review*, ed. Reuben Ahroni, Vol. 7, 1983, pp. 137–49. Chapter 8 appeared in *Studies in Aggadah, Targum and Jewish Liturgy in Memory of Joseph Heinemann*, Jerusalem, 1981, pp. 32–44. Chapter 9 appeared in *Ish Bi-Gevurot: Studies in Jewish Heritage and History, Presented to Rabbi Alexandre Safran*, ed. Moshe Hallamish, Jerusalem, 1990, pp. 29–33. Chapter 10 appeared in *Tribute to Geza Vermes*, ed. Philip R. Davies and Richard T. White, Sheffield, 1990, pp. 193–205. Chapter 11 appeared in *The Tel Aviv Review*, ed. Gabriel Moked, Vol. 2, Fall 1989/Winter 1990, pp. 32–83. Chapter 12 appeared in *Bulletin of the School of Oriental and African Studies*, Vol. XXXV, Part 2, 1972. Chapter 13 appeared in *Journal of Semitic Studies*, Vol. 2, No. 4, October 1957, pp. 349–59. Chapter 14 is a Claude Montefiore Lecture, London, 1962. Chapter 15 appeared in *The Jewish Law Annual*, Vol. VI, pp. 94–108. Chapter 16 appeared in *Essays in Jewish Historiography*, Wesleyan University, 1988, pp. 66–77. Chapter 17 appeared in *Perspectives on Jews and Judaism: Essays in Honor of Wolfe Kelman*, ed. Arthur A. Chiel, New York, 1978, pp. 189–214. Chapter 18 is a lecture published as the Third Jewish Law Fellowship Lecture, The Yarnton Trust, London, 1991.

ACKNOWLEDGEMENTS

Vallentine Mitchell has now published, in the space of just over a year, four volumes of my collected essays, each volume standing on its own but with a uniform style. My thanks are due to Frank Cass, who has encouraged the project and seen it all through as he has done with other works of mine over the years. Toby Harris has done a good job on the publicity and distribution side, for which I am grateful. My special thanks to Sian Mills, whose care and skills in editing the difficult texts has been of enormous help.

Part One
The Nature of the Babylonian Talmud

— 1 —

The Babylonian Talmud: A Composite Work

The Babylonian Talmud, in all the splendour of its over thirty folio volumes in the standard editions, gives the surface impression of a gigantic, unified work compiled at one time, like the great encyclopaedias and dictionaries. The truth is, however, as every student of the Talmud knows, that the work is composite with material deriving from different periods. In the twentieth century, the suggestion was made that a 'Rainbow Talmud' be published in which the various strata would be identified by special coloured type rather like the famous 'Rainbow Bible', though such a suggestion was never taken up because the cost of such an enterprise would be prohibitive, to say nothing of the difficulty of correctly assessing the different dates of the materials. For all that, in outline, at least, it is possible to detect the different strata with a fair degree of success.[1]

The earliest material in the Talmud consists of the numerous Biblical verses quoted throughout the work, introduced generally by *dikhtiv* ('it is written') or *de-amar kera* ('the verse says') or *sheneemar* ('as it is said') or *rahmana amar* ('the All-merciful says'). There are more than eight thousand quotes from Scriptural verses in the Babylonian Talmud.[2]

Next comes the material from the Tannaitic period, the first two centuries of the current era – the Mishnah, the Tosefta, the Halakhic Midrashim (Mekhilta, Sifra and Sifre) and the many other Baraitot from the same period. A major part of the Babylonian Talmud consists of commentaries and discussions on these works of the Tannaim, especially on the Mishnah, by the Babylonian (and Palestinian) teachers, from the beginning of the third to the end of the fifth centuries, known as the Amoraim. A problem with regard to the terms Tannaim and Amoraim is that these terms are employed in the Talmud in two quite different senses. There are frequent references to two functionaries, one of whom (the Tanna) rehearsed Baraitot before his teachers, the other (the Amora) whose task it was to make explicit the cryptic sayings of a sage. But these two terms are also used in a different sense. A Tanna is, in this sense, a teacher belonging to the Mishnaic (hence Tannaitic) period and an Amora, a teacher of the later period, hence the term Amoraim i.e. those who expounded the earlier Tannaitic material. The plausible suggestion has been made that originally both sets of teachers (those of the Mishnaic and the post-Mishnaic periods) were called simply *hakhamim* ('sages') or *talmidey hakhamim* ('disciples of sages') and it was not until the latest stages of Talmudic redaction, of which more will be said presently, that that the sages of the first two centuries were called 'Tannaim' and the sages of the later centuries 'Amoraim', both terms being adopted from the earlier usage in the sense of the two functionaries.[3]

It is clear that the sayings of particular Amoraim are presented in the Talmud as part of the *sugya* in which their teachings are discussed. The conventional term for the framework of the *sugya* is *stama de-gemara* ('the anonymous part of the Gemara'), that is, the framework into which the opinions of the various teachers are inserted. Another conventional term, for those who provided the framework, is *mesaderey ha-Gemara* ('those who gave order to the Gemara' or the editors of the Talmud). David Weiss-Halivni has coined the useful term *Stamaim* ('The Anonymous Ones') to denote the authors of the framework. It must be realized that this framework is provided for all the material in the Talmud and it uses throughout the same vocabulary and has throughout the same style, structure and form, suggesting that it all came from the same hands. Judging by the Talmudic evidence, the final editors of the Talmud managed successfully to conceal their identity. Nowhere in the Talmud is there any definite statement about the process of redaction and how it was done and by whom. In the Middle Ages, however, on the basis of a somewhat obscure Talmudic reference, the editors of the Talmud were said to be the fifth-century Amoraim Rav Ashi (d. 428) and Ravina (d. 499). The Talmudic statement in question is in tractate *Bava Metzia'* 86a. Here it is said: 'Rabbi [Judah the Prince] and R. Nathan were the end ot the Mishnah. Rav Ashi and Ravina were the end of teaching [*sof horaah*].' It is far from certain what 'the end of teaching' means but, on the analogy of the statement about Rabbi Judah the Prince and R. Nathan, it was concluded that just as Rabbi Judah the Prince was the editor of the Mishnah, Rav Ashi and Ravina were the editors of the Babylonian Talmud. This cannot possibly be taken at its face value. The framework embraces the opinions of Rav Ashi and Ravina themselves in exactly the same style as the rest of the framework of the Talmud. This very passage – even if it means what it is said to mean, that these two Amoraim were the editors of the Talmud – must have been supplied by those who came after Rav Ashi and Ravina. Consequently, it is now generally recognized that in the framework we have yet another and very late stratum of the Babylonian Talmud.[4]

We have then three strata in the Babylonian Talmud: 1) that of the Tannaim; 2) the actual teachings of the Amoraim whose names are given; 3) the late framework into which the other two strata are incorporated. From Sherira onwards it has been noted that a fourth stratum can be detected, that of the Savoraim (*rab banan savorai*), the 'Expounders' or 'Theorizers'. Sherira states that he has a tradition to the effect that the opening passage in tractate *Kiddushin* is a Savoraic addition and other mediaeval commentators have declared the opening passage in tractate *Bava Metzia'* to be Savoraic. The style in these two passages is, in fact, different from the usual style of the framework as can easily be seen when the two are compared. Abraham Weiss has gone so far as to argue that practically every opening passage of the Talmudic tractates is Savoraic. The Savoraim were also responsible for other additions to the completed Babylonian Talmud such as mnemonics at the beginning of some passages and the final rulings at the end of lengthy debates in the form *ve-hilkheta* ('the ruling is'). The point to be noted here is that the Savoraic additions are precisely that; they have been *added* to an already complete work and in a style different from that of the framework. Investigation has thus detected four strata in the present text of the Babylonian Talmud: 1) that of the Tannaim; 2) that of the named Amoraim; 3) the all-pervading framework; 4) the Savoraic additions.[5]

In some circles, nowadays, under the influence of Kaplan, there is a tendency to apportion a good deal of the framework material to the Savoraim but this is to ignore the clear stylistic differences between the framework and the acknowledged Savoraic material. There are difficulties in deciding how much of the framework material is original with those who provided it, the Stamaim, and how much is the work of the Amoraim recorded by name in the framework material, but there can be no doubt that there are four distinct strata in the Babylonian Talmud, dating from different periods: 1) The Tannaitic material; 2) the actual words of the named Amoraim; 3) the Stamaim, those who provided the framework to the whole; 4) the Savoraim. The framework, comprising a major part of the Talmudic material, was, in all probability, added after Ravina, which means that the Babylonian Talmud assumed its present form not earlier than the beginning of the sixth century.

At the other end of the scale, there is no need to reject the supposition of Abraham Weiss and others that earlier portions of anonymous material were used by the final editors, the Stamaim. This may well be the case but it was all apparently recast in a sustained framework; the final editors using this earlier material as they used the actual words of the Amoraim to produce carefully organized units. For instance, the opening passage of tractate *Bava Kama* (2a–3b) discusses the question of main categories of damage and their derivatives. The main categories are called *avot* ('fathers') and their derivatives *toledot* ('offspring'). Here some of the *toledot* seem already to have been delineated and described in a language different from that used in the rest of the passage (*mai hi* as distinct from mai *ninhu*). Yet a careful study of the whole passage demonstrates that it has all been reworked so as to provide a sustained and contrived narrative.[6]

There is a good deal of material stemming from Palestine in the Babylonian Talmud. The leading early-third-century Palestinian teachers, R. Johanan and Resh Lakish, for instance, are mentioned very frequently in the Babylonian Talmud though they never visited Babylon. But this fact does not permit the conclusion that there are units of shaped Palestinian material in the Babylonian Talmud, only that the opinions of the Palestinian teachers were used and recast by the Babylonian editors as they used the opinions of the Babylonian Amoraim for the same purpose of providing a sustained narrative. Even if the editors of the Babylonian Talmud had copies of the earlier Palestinian Talmud (a very dubious proposition in any event), they never refer to these. In fact it can be shown that occasionally, at least, the Babylonian editors were not averse to putting their own opinions into the mouths of the Palestinian teachers they quote, all for the purpose of creating the *sugyot* in their own contrived style.[7]

A number of modern scholars have purported to detect in the Babylonian Talmud editorial work from different Babylonian centres and not only in different tractates but even in the same tractate, explaining in this way the existence of duplicate *sugyot* and especially contradictory *sugyot*. In many instances, however, it is possible to explain the duplicates and contradictory passages as due not to different editors but to the same editors shaping the material they had in different ways. The point to be noted in this connection is that the style of the framework is the same throughout and since there is no internal evidence of a redaction in different places the existence of duplicates and contradictions can adequately be explained without the hypothesis of editing in different centres. Attention has been called, however, to the different style in the framework in tractates *Nedarim, Nazir, Me'ilah, Keritut* and *Temurah*, which would seem to suggest that these tractates have been edited in different places. Yet the differences are slight, the use of some different words and the like, and again, this needs to be stressed, the overall style is the same for the framework of all the tractates in the Talmud, including these five. This very close similarity of style throughout has largely been overlooked in modern scholarship so that, at the most, even if different centres were at work there is a unifying pattern which they all followed.[8]

Even after the Savoraim, some few additions were made to the text of the Babylonian Talmud. Rav Hai Gaon (B. Lewin: Otzar *ha-Geonim* to *Bava Kama*, Jerusalem, 1943, p. 37) remarked long ago that here and there marginal notes were incorporated into the text and it is well-known that some of Rashi's notes managed to slip into the text from the margins. But this is not really a matter of additions to the Talmud but belongs rather to the different question of the history of the Talmudic text.[9]

NOTES

1. For the nature and composition of the Babylonian Talmud see the article 'Talmud' by W. Bacher in the *Jewish Encyclopedia*, Vol. XII, pp. 1–27; the article 'Talmud, Babylonian' in *Encyclopedia Judaica*, Vol. 15 , pp. 755–68; H. Albeck: *Mevo ha-Talmud* ('Introduction to the Talmud'), Tel-Aviv, 1969; M. Mielziner: new bibliography by Alexander Guttmann, New

York, 1968; H. L. Strack and G. Stemberger: *Introduction to the Talmud and Midrash*, translated by Markus Bockmuehl, Edinburgh, 1991; J. Kaplan: *The Redaction of the Babylonian Talmud Introduction to the Talmud*, New York, 1933, J. N. Epstein: *Mevuot le-Sifrut ha-Amoraim* (Latin title: 4th edition with 'Prolegomena Ad Litteras Amoraiticus'), ed. E. Z. Melammed, Jerusalem, 1972; J. Neusner, ed.: *The Formation of the Babylonian Talmud: Studies in the Achievements of Nineteenth and Twentieth Century Historical Researches*, Leiden, 1970; B. De Freiss: *Mehkarim be-Sifrut ha-Talmud*, Jerusalem, 1968; Shamma Friedman: *Perek ha-Ishah Rabbah be-Bavli*, Jerusalem, 1978, and the bibliography cited there; Judith Hauptman: *Development of the Talmudic Sugya*, Lanham, New York and London, 1 988; H. Klein: *Collected Talmudic Scientific Writings of Hyman Klein*, Introduction by A. Goldberg, Jerusalem, 1979; S. M. Rubenstein: *le-Heker Siddur ha-Talmud*, Kovno, 1932; J.Shachter: *The Student's Guide Through the Talmud*, London, 1952; M. A. Tenenblatt: *The Formation of the Babylonian Talmud* (Heb.) Tel-Aviv, 1972; Abraham Weiss: *Hithavut ha-Talmud Bishlemato* (English title: 'The Babylonian Talmud as a Literary Unit'). New York, 1943 and *le-Heker ha-Talmud* (English title: 'The Talmud in its Development'), New York, 1954; David Weiss-Halivni: *Midrash Mishnah and Gemara*, Cambridge, MA, 1986; David Kraemer. *The Mind of the Talmud*, OUP, 1990. (The name for a complete unit of the Talmud is *sûgyā*, from the root *segi*, 'to go', hence the layout of a passage, the way it 'goes'.)

2. For the Biblical verses quoted in the Babylonian Talmud see the Index volume in the English translation of the Talmud under the editorship of Dr I. Epstein, Soncino Press, London, 1952, and the work by M. D. Rubin: *Kol ha-Mikraot she-be-Talmud Bavli*, Jerusalem, 1985.
3. For the transformation of the terms see A. S. Amir: *Mosedot ve-Toarim be-Sifrut ha-Talmud* (English title: 'Institutions and Titles in the Talmudic Literature'), Jerusalem, 1977; see especially pp. 11–17 on the Tannaim and pp. 176–7 on the Amoraim. Amir (p. 191) suggests, on grounds of greater accuracy, instead of speaking of the Tannaitic and Amoraic periods or of the Tannaim and the Amoraim, we should rather speak of the period of the Sages of the Mishnah and the period of the Sages of the Talmuds (the Babylonian and the Palestinian). This suggestion has not been widely accepted by scholars since, after all, the terms Tannaim and Amoraim do appear in the second sense in the framework of the Talmud, at least, as Amir admits. For examples of the term Tanna as rehearser of Baraitot see *Berakhot* 5a; 12a; 57a; *Shabbat* 66b; *Sotah* 22a; and in the other sense of Tannaitic teacher *Berakhot* 2a; 9a; 24a; *Shabbat*, 53b, *Betzan* 19a; *Makkot* 2b; *Gittin* 32a. Examples of Amora in the sense of 'expounder' of the words of a sage are: *Yoma* 20b; *Ketubon* 106a; *Sotah* 40a; *Hullin* 15a; and in the sense of Amora as a later teacher *Shabbat* 112b and see especially *Megillah* 15b; 'like all the Tannaim and all the Amoraim'. The interchange of terms is so frequent that possibly, *contra* Amir, they were used in both senses from the beginning.
4. The major mediaeval source for the question of the redaction of the Talmud is the famous Letter of Sherira Gaon (d. 1006), the Gaon of Pumbedita from 968–1006, in reply to a question on this very problem sent to him by Jacob b. Nissim of Kairovan in 981. The best edition of the Letter is that of B. Lewin: *Iggeret de-Rav Sherira Gaon*, Jerusalem, 1972 (photocopy of the Haifa edition of 1921). R. Sherira (Lewin ed., p. 69) accepts that the passage in *Bava Metzia'* does mean that Rav Ashi and Ravina were the editors of *a* Babylonian Talmud but this probably refers to the core material of our present version not to the present version itself. The whole question of redaction has been discussed at length in the modern works mentioned above, especially by Kaplan, Epstein, Abraham Weiss, David Weiss-Halivni, Neusner Strack/Stemberger and Kraemer, but I here pursue my own views.
5. For the Savoraim see B. Lewin: *Rabbanan Savorai ve-Talmudam*, Jerusalem, 1937; Strack/Stemberger, pp. 222–5; Abraham Weiss, Kaplan, and article 'Savora, Savoraim' in *Encyclopedia Judaica*. Vol. 14, pp. 920–1. Sherira's reference to the Savoraim is in the Lewin edition, p. 71.
6. This passage is quoted by Weiss in his *le-Heker ha-Talmud*, pp. 98–100 and see the discussion in my *Studies in Talmudic Methodology*, London, 1961, pp. 132–151, where I have taken issue with Weiss's contention that we have here a double process of redaction. It is not without significance that the usual expression for the derivatives of contamination (*tumah*) mentioned in the *sûgyā*, is not *toledot* but *rishon* or *sheni* or *vlad* (see e.g. Mishnah *Pesahim* 1:6). It would seem that in our passage the term *toledot* is used throughout so as

to make it fit in with the other *toledot* (those of 'damages' and 'Sabbath') presented and discussed.

7. In tractate *Megillah* 10b, R. Johanan is quoted as saying that when Israel crossed the sea and the Egyptians were drowning God declared to the angels: 'The work of My hands are drowning in the sea and you wish to sing' i.e. God cannot rejoice and allow His angels to sing when His creatures, the Egyptians, are drowning. But, as J. Heinemann (*Aggadot ve-Toledotehen*, Jerusalem, 1974, pp. 175–9) has shown, in Palestinian sources R. Johanan refers not to the Egyptians but to the Israelites as 'The work of My hands'. According to Heinemann, the Babylonian editors used the saying of R. Johanan in an Introduction to the Book of Esther (as the passage states) but, living in the lands where the events of the book took place, were more circumspect so that the Babylonian 'R. Johanan' is made to say that God is aggrieved at the destruction of Israel's foes. Another example is the different treatment of a saying by the third-century Palestinian teacher, R. Eleazar, in the Palestinian Talmud, *Ketubot* 1:1 (24d) and in the Babylonian Talmud *Ketubot* 8b–9a. In the Palestinian version R. Eleazar says: 'She is forbidden to him' whereas in the Babylonian version R. Eleazar says: 'He is believed'. This is because the Babylonian Talmud is concerned in the passage with the question of belief in the man's testimony so that R. Eleazar is made to say what the particular *sûgyā* requires him to say. There has been much discussion on whether or not the editors of the Babylonian Talmud possessed a copy or copies of the Palestinian Talmud, see Y. J. Greenwald: *Harau Mesaderey ha-Bavli et ha=Yerushalmi?*, New York, 1954; Strack/Stemberger, pp. 218–9, and J. N. Epstein *Mevuot* pp. 290f. Epstein (p. 291) rightly concludes that there was no text of the Palestinian Talmud in the hands of the editors of the Babylonian Talmud and no earlier version of the text of the Babylonian Talmud in the hands of the editors of the Palestinian Talmud. For the *nanotey* ('descenders'), the Palestinian scholars who conveyed the teachings of their native land to the Babylonians, see the Letter of Shenira Gaon, ed. Lewin, p. 61 and Strack/Stemberger, pp. 198 and 219.

8. The hypothesis of redaction in different centres has been advanced especially by J. N. Epstein: *Mevuot* and by N. Aminoah: *The Redaction of the Tractate Qiddushin in the Babylonian Talmud* (Heb.), Tel-Aviv, 1977. See for example Aminoah's analysis (pp. 163–6) of the *sugya* in Kiddushin 50b–5la. The whole passage can be explained quite adequately on the grounds that the final editors put it all into its present form in a contrived manner and there is no need to invoke the notion of dual redaction. On the five different tractates see Strack/Stemberger, pp. 213–5. In support of my contention that the differences can be explained without the hypothesis of redaction in different centres, *Rosh ha-Shanah* 34a should be compared with *Avodah Zarah* 43a–b and *Sanhedrin* 52b compared with *'Avodah Zarah* 11 a (where the style in both is exactly the same but the material has been arranged so as to arrive at different conclusions). If different editorial hands were at work why should they have used exactly the same style? Cf. *Sanhedrin* 27a, where two different versions have been woven into a single 'narrative and see *Bava Kama* 72a–b where the same basic material receives further elaboration. To be noted in this connection is the way the Talmud itself accounts for duplication e.g. in *Kiddushin* 50a. A good illustration of different editorial aims in the presentation of the same material is provided when the three passages in *Berakhot* 20a, *Ta'anit* 24a–b and *Sanhedrin* 106b are compared. In all three passages Rava seeks to account for the fact that while R. Judah's prayers for rain were answered immediately his, Rava's, prayers were not. It cannot be because R. Judah had greater proficiency in learning since Rava was convinced that his ability in learning was greater. In all three passages the material is presented in more or less the same way but in each Rava is made to give a different reply. In *Berakhot* R. Judah's superiority is said to be because he exhibited a greater willingness to sacrifice his well-being for his religion. In *Ta'anit* Rava's failure is said to be due to the unworthiness of his generation. In *Sanhedrin* Rava attributes his failure to the fact that the All-merciful desires the heart i.e. R. Judah was more sincere than Rava. It would be absurd to explain the difference on the grounds that the three passages were edited in three different centres. The differences are obviously due to the three different concerns in these passages. In the *Berakhot* passage the concern is with self-sacrifice, as the whole passage demonstrates. In *Ta'anit* the whole section, of which this is a part, deals with fasting when the rains fail to come and with the merit required both by the one who prays for the community and the community itself if the prayers are to be answered. In

the *Sanhedrin* passage the theme is that of unworthy but learned men like Doag and Ahitofel, men who knew a good deal but had no 'heart' i.e. it does not follow that all learned men are sincere and Rava proves this from his own experience, believing that he was less sincere, though more learned, than R. Judah.

9. Finally, reference must be made to passages, originally in the Talmud, that have been omitted from the current texts out of fear of the censor e.g. the few references to Jesus (see Strack/Stemberger, pp. 225–7) but this, too, belongs to textual criticism and is beyond the scope of this lecture.

— 2 —

The Babylonian Talmud: A Literary Work

In the Middle Ages, Rashi and other French commentators held that originally the Babylonian Talmud was not a literary work but was compiled, in all its intricate detail, in the minds of its editors and then transmitted orally until it was eventually recorded in writing at a much later date. According to this school of thought, the Mishnah, too, was originally compiled in oral form and was only recorded in writing at this later date together with the Talmud. Many of the Spanish authorities, on the other hand, held, as Maimonides states, that Rabbi Judah the Prince compiled the Mishnah in written form and the Babylonian Talmud was compiled by its editors as a written work.

The basic problem is that there are Talmudic references (*Gittin* 60b, *Temurah* 14b) to a prohibition against writing down the 'Oral Torah' just as there is a prohibition against rehearsing by heart the 'Written Torah'. The Talmudic editors, it is argued, would not have disregarded their own rules against writing down the 'Oral Torah' and the Talmud was only written down later as an emergency measure 'lest the Torah be forgotten from Israel'. Against this, it can be argued, the Talmudic injunction against writing down the actual laws, rules and discussions, permitting this only in an emergency, was never intended as forbidding making a written record of the whole activity, that is, of the present text of the Babylonian Talmud. The actual *study* of the 'Oral Torah' was undoubtedly undertaken verbally but this has nothing to do with a record in writing of the whole corpus. During the post-Talmudic, Geonic period, when the written record certainly was in existence, the study of the Talmud was still engaged in verbally and it was considered *infra dig* to consult the written text. It follows that a clear distinction must be made between the study of the Talmud, which had to be undertaken verbally, and the writing down of the Talmud as a record of the original studies. Since the distinction has to be made, in any event, there is no cogent reason for denying that the Talmud was compiled originally in written form.[1]

Since eventually the Talmud was written down[2] the essential question is whether the present written text is no more than a literary record of a previously composed verbal text or whether the text came from the hands of its editors as a literary creation right from the beginning. Now the Babylonian Talmud displays all the signs of a literary work – the careful arrangement of the material in dramatic form in which one argument leads naturally to another until a climax is reached and the like, all of which is entirely appropriate in a literary work, the aim of which is to hold the attention of the reader as well as to instruct, but inappropriate, if not impossible, in an oral composition. Even elements of humour and what appears to be sheer entertainment are also apparent in this extraordinary work. The material is often arranged in numbered sequence and contrived patterns constantly emerge to catch the eye of the experienced student. It is astonishing that practically all the modern scholars who have discussed with great learning the problem of Talmudic redaction have overlooked entirely this element of contrivance. It is very hard indeed to imagine that all this kind of creative activity was all made up entirely in the mind. A poem, for example, seems on the surface to be a spontaneous creation but this is the result of the poet's skill by which the constant revisions, reordering of the words and recollecting in tranquillity his original emotions all take place before the final form of the poem is completed.[3]

It is true that, even nowadays, there are to be found Talmudists who know the whole Talmud by heart but what they have memorized is a given text. How is it possible for the text itself, of such magnitude and complexity, to have emerged spontaneously out of the head of a series of authors? The thought processes of the creators of the Talmud may have been very different from our own but they cannot have been all that different, especially since we can think their thoughts after them as we study their creation. Moreover, since there did emerge eventually a written Talmud, why should it be postulated, except on dogmatic grounds, that the 'literary' style was not the form the Talmud took right from the beginning?

It is important to appreciate that what we have in a typical Talmudic *sûgyā* is not the actual opinions of the named Amoraim but rather what the final editors state as being the opinions of the Amoraim. With regards to the great debates among the Amoraim, for instance, there are hardly any references to these actually taking place face to face. The debates, to give an obvious example, between Palestinian and Babylonian Amoraim were not real debates since in most cases the two participants did not live in the same country and never actually met one another and debates are also recorded between one Amora and another who did not live at the time. What happens in the Talmud is that known opinions attributed to one teacher and known contradictory opinions attributed to another teacher are arranged and discussed as if the debates are taking place before our eyes so that when the Talmud states 'Rabbi A says … but Rabbi B says … ', the meaning is: 'Rabbi A *would* say … but Rabbi B *would* reply …'; all arranged in an artificial and therefore a more dramatic way by the editors. The comparison of the Talmud to a 'Hansard' is way off the mark; as if someone was sitting there busily taking notes of an actual debate that was taking place at the time. A closer analogy would be to a novel constructed round a historical, Parliamentary debate but with the event told so that every statement and every interruption and even every 'loud laughter' comes in at just the right moment, something that would rarely, if at all, happen in real life. It seems overwhelmingly certain that a contrived work of this kind can only have been compiled in literary form.[4]

Among the numerous examples of sheer contrivance in the Babylonian Talmud, a cogent example is that of the phenomenon '*ta shema*' ('Come, hear'). Throughout the Talmud the discussion of a problem very often proceeds by a series of quotations from earlier sources, usually from a Mishnah or a Baraita, each of which is announced by the formula meaning: 'This seems to be relevant to the issue.' A careful examination of this phenomenon demonstrates that the series is usually progressive, without this being stated explicitly. That is to say, the Talmud is implying: 'You have dealt adequately with A in the series but come and hear B where your reply has no force' and so on through all the attempted proofs or replies.[5]

A phenomenon I have not seen noted is that of 'as Rabbi A has said…' introduced *before* Rabbi A actually says it later on in the *sûgyā*. This seems to be a purely stylistic device and a token of literary arrangement of the material.[6]

There are a number of actual poems in the Babylonian Talmud but my contention is that, in a sense, the whole of the Talmud is a kind of poem; not to be sure of words and with rhyme and rhythm, but of ideas symmetrically arranged as in a poem. Other easily spotted literary devices are the use of Biblical expressions for effect and of puns. These two can, of course, be explained even if the Talmud is not a written work but their ubiquitousness does lend support to the theory of the Talmud as compiled in literary form from the beginning.[7]

If our contention is correct, the final editors of the Talmud, the Stamaim,are really the creative authors of the Talmud as we now have the work. They reworked all the material they had to hand to produce a new and complete literary work. Nowhere is this stated explicitly but then the Talmud is in any event silent on how, when and where it was compiled. We do know however that at one period the Talmud was committed to writing and already in the early Middle Ages the Talmud existed in written form. Since, as has been noted, there is so much in the Talmud that bears all the marks of a literary composition, the best explanation of how the Talmud came to be is that it was compiled right from the beginning as a literary work.

NOTES

1. On the whole question see especially the summary in Strack/Stemberger, pp. 35–40. For the 'French' school, that the Talmud was not originally a written work, see Rashi to *Shabbat* 13b; '*Eruvin* 62b; *Bava Metzia*' 33a; Tosefot to *Megillah* 32a. For the 'Spanish' school, that the Talmud was originally compiled as a written work, see: Samuel ha-Nagid: lntroduction to the Talmud, printed in the Vilna, Romm editions after tractate *Berakhot*; Abraham lbn Daud: *Sefer ha-Kabbalah*, edited Gerson D. Cohen, London, 1967, p. 27, where he says that Rav Ashi began to *write* the Talmud; Maimonides in his Introduction to his Commentary to the Mishnah and his Introduction to his *Mishneh Torah* Menahem Meiri in his *Bet ha-Behirah* to tractate *Avot*, ed. B. Z. Prag, Jerusalem, 1964, p. 49, who also says that Rav Ashi *wrote* the Talmud, and on .50 that in the days of Savoraim they still studied by heart because the Talmud, although already in writing, was not yet widely known;and see I.H. Weiss: *Dor Dor ve=Doreshav*, N.Y. and Berlin, 1924, vol. ll, pp. 216f. and Vol. III pp. 243–8. For the Geonim studying by heart even though they had a written text of the Talmud see I. Halevy: *Dorot ha-Rishonim*, Vol. III, Berlin, 1920, p.1 12a and Lewin's Introduction to his edition of the Letter of Sherira Gaon, pp. 26b–27a. Lewin and many others hold that there are two versions in the Letter of Sherira on the question of writing down

but Epstein, *Mevuot*, pp. 610–15, takes issue with this. Although in all the discussions on the question it is assumed that the question concerns both the Mishnah and the Talmud, there is, in fact, no reason why it should be assumed that the two are interconnected. It may be the case that even if the Mishnah was compiled verbally, itself very doubtful, the much more complex Talmud must have been compiled in writing.

2. For reference to the complete Talmud written by R. Natronai Gaon in 773 see Lewin: *Otzar*, Vol. 1, p. 20 and see note on p. 19; *AZ* ed S. Abramson, JTS, NY, 1957, p.13; Nahmonides, *Milhamot* on BK 856 in *Rif* BK p. 310 in Vilna and Romm edition.
3. In the discussion on this lecture Professor Littman objected that in Homer, for example, or in African poetry, although these were produced in verbal form, there is a good deal of sophisticated arrangement of the material and thus detailed creative activity is no evidence of literary form. But, in the Talmudic arrangement, much earlier material has been used throughout in the construction, unlike in the examples given by Littman. The Talmud is a kind of poem of ideas but it is not in itself a unified saga dealing with one type of material, as shown in the first lecture and will be shown in the following lecture. An epic poem, in ancient cultures, can well be said to have been constructed solely in the mind. It is quite otherwise where, as in the Talmud, diverse (often literary) materials have been shaped to form a unit in sophisticated form. That this could have been composed solely in the mind of the editor or editors is highly improbable.
4. The comparison of the Talmud to a 'Hansard' is made by Herbert Loewe in his Foreword to Dudley Wright's *The Talmud*, London, 1932, p.10. On the element of 'contrivance' in the typical Talmudic *sugya* see my books: *Studies in Talmudic Logic and Methodology*, London, 1961, Part II, pp. 53–164; *The Talmudic* Argument, CUP, 1984; *Structure and Form in the Babylonian Talmud*, CUP, 1991. For a critique of my view that a good dealof the Babylonian Talmud is pseudepigraphic see Sacha Stern's review of the latter book in JJS, Vol. XLIV, No. 1 Spring 1993, pp. 147–8. While agreeing with the basic contention that the Talmudi *sûgyā* does not represent the transcription of actual debates, though Stern believes that my analysis is too sketchy. Stern in his article: 'Attribution and Authorship in the Babylonian Talmud', Vol. XLV, No. 1, Spring 1994, pp. 28–51, is much more critical of my stance but confuses the final editing of the Talmud with statements attributed to the Amoraim themselves. For the use of a contrived numbered sequence see the article by Shamma Friedman '*Mivneh sifruti be-sugyot ha-Bavli*' in Proceedings of the Sixth World Conference of Jewish Studies, Jerusalem, 1977, pp. 387–402 and my elaboration in 'The Numbered Sequence as a Literary Device in the Babylonian Talmud' in the *Hebrew Annual Review*, Vol. 7, edited Reuben Ahroni, Ohio State University Press, 1984, pp. 137–40.
5. Example: In *Bava Kama* 27b–28a the *ta shema*' from Mishnah *Bava Kama* 3:1 is not introduced until later in the *sugya*, where the progressive form requires it, even though it is to this Mishnah that the *sûgyā* is appended. For further examples see especially the series of *ta shema*, in *Berakhot* 19b–20a; *Berakhot* 59b; *Shabbat* 36b–37a; *Shabbat* 136a; *Shabbat* 155a–b; 'Eruvin 22b; *Pesahim* 16–b; *Pesahim* 26a-b; *Pesahim* 55a–b; *Yoma* 40a–b; *Betzah* 17a–b; Megillah 22a–b; *Yevamot* 14a–1 6a (a series of ten); *Yevamot* 40b (a series of seven); *Yevamot* 90a–b (a series of five); *Yevamot* 91 b (a series of five); *Yevamot* 114a–b (a series of ten, and the Mishnah to which the *sûgyā* is appended is not quoted until the end); *Ketubot* 41a–b; *Sanhedrin* 46b–47a and many others. This method of adducing a series of proofs in progressive order, where each follows on the other, without this being stated explicitly, is found, too, without *ta shema*' e.g. in *Hullin* 11a–12a (a series of ten).
6. Examples: *Rosh ha-Shanah* 2b; *Yoma* 31b: *Megillah* 2a; *Betzah* l0b–11a; *Bava Metzia*' 21b.
7. See the article by D. Golinkin: 'The Poem in the Talmudic Literature' (Heb.) in Proceedings of the Rabbinical Assembly, New York, 1986, Heb. section, pp. 328–32. On page 332 Golinkin gives a partial list of these poems. Aaron Lewin: *Birkat Aharon* to tractate *Berakhat*, New York, 1968, No. 165, pp. 74d–75b, gives a list of Talmudic puns to which more can be added. See e.g. *Sanhedrin* 74a–b – *ketol aspasta ve-i lo katil-*

na lakh liktol vye-lo likteley – which the Soncino translation *Sanhedrin,* pp. 504–5 has completely misunderstood through failing to note the pun. Lewin, pp. 81b–82c also gives a list of Talmudic forms of elegant language based on Scriptural verses.

— 3 —

The Babylonian Talmud: A Comprehensive Work

Even at a superficial glance it can be seen that the Babylonian Talmud consists chiefly of a commentary to the Mishnah, section by section. Around this core the editors have woven their tapestry of debate and discussion. The Palestinian Talmud, too, has the same form of Mishnaic commentary as the Babylonian Talmud but the Babylonian Talmud pursues this aim in a far more elaborate way and in its own particular style. Naturally there are often introduced into this core work many other topics but apart from this whole segments of material have been introduced as units on their own. In this lecture we must first consider the core material and then the other segments which differ from it in style and language.

The Gemara is arranged as a running commentary to the Mishnah.The Mishnah is the key text on which commentary is made in much the same way as the early Midrashim comment on the verses of the Torah. But just as the Midrashim do not constitute pure exegesis of the Biblical texts but use the texts for their particular purposes by reading ideas into them, so, too, the Gemara uses the Mishnah for its own purposes. There are thus two separate ways of interpreting the Mishnah. The Mishnah has to be understood on its own terms as a distinct work complete in itself and the Mishnah is interpreted in the Gemara in the latter's own way and special requirements. A much-discussed question is whether the interpretations of the Mishnah found in the Gemara are really a reading of ideas into the Mishnah or whether they are authentic accounts of what the Mishnah itself intended. Now students of the Mishnah in the Middle Ages noted that some, at least, of the Gemara's interpretations of the Mishnah are so far-fetched and artificial that they cannot possibly be accepted as real interpretations of what the Mishnah intends to say, which is why Maimonides and other early commentators were prepared to disregard the Gemara to interpret the Mishnah on its own terms. To conclude from this that the Gemara has, at times, 'misunderstood' the Mishnah is precarious. It is possible that the Gemara, at times, consciously departs from the plain meaning of the Mishnah in order to produce its own original work, just as the Midrashim do not always purport to explain the 'original' meaning of the Biblical texts. It can be argued that the more unconvincing interpretations of the Mishnah in the Gemara were recognized as such and were never intended as pure Mishnaic exegesis.

An excellent illustration is provided in the opening *sugya* of tractate *Bava Kama*. The Mishnah (*Bava Kama* 1:1) lists four main categories (*avot*) of damages, one of which is the *mav'eh*, an ambiguous term; the others being the fire, the ox and the pit. The Mishnah continues that the characteristics of ox and *mav'eh* are different from those of fire since ox and *mav'eh* are endowed with life (and are therefore more liable to do damage) whereas fire is not endowed with life. In the Gemara (3b) Rav understands *mav'eh* to denote a man who does damage whereas Samuel understands it as denoting the tooth of an animal which does damage by eating produce and there is a lengthy discussion of these two different interpretations of *mav'eh*. The Gemara (4b) continues that R. Zevid strongly objected, why not say that *mav'eh* denotes fire and to this the reply is given, how can *mav'eh* possibly mean fire since fire is mentioned separately in the Mishnah and, if *mav'eh* means fire, how can the Mishnah distinguish it from fire in that it is endowed with life? Now the objection to R. Zevid is so obvious that it is quite impossible to imagine that his original suggestion, that *mav'eh* denotes fire, could ever have been taken seriously by him since if that were the case, as the Gemara implies, the Mishnah makes no sense at all. The Gemara here cannot possibly be understood as an exercise in Mishnaic interpretation and the interpretation of *mav'eh* as fire cannot have been taken seriously even as a possibility. The whole discussion seems to be totally artificial and consciously so in order to provide the usual style of the Talmud in presenting its material in the form of question and answer rather than direct statement. Instead of simply stating the obvious, that *mav'eh* cannot possibly mean fire, the Gemara puts this obvious fact as if it could seriously be entertained. If this is correct it means either R. Zevid did not present his objection at all and it was put into his mouth by the editors, or he made it not as an objection but as a simple and obvious comment and it was the editors who put it in this form for dramatic effect. The same applies to the 'strong objection' by

R. Mari in the passage, why not say that *mav'eh* is water, a suggestion that is similarly rejected as nonsensical. The suggestions by R. Mari and R. Zevid are nonsensical but the two teachers are presented not as talking nonsense but as rejecting nonsense.

Another very revealing illustration is provided by the opening *sûgyā* in tractate *Bava Metzia'* (although this *sûgyā* is generally held, on stylistic grounds, to be a Savoraic addition, this only means that the Savoraim, too, employed the same methods in the matter of Mishnaic interpretation). The Mishnah *Bava Metzia'* (1:1)records the case of two men who come before the court holding a garment, each claiming that he had found it. The Mishnah formulates this as:

> Two men are holding a garment. This one says: 'I found it' and this one says: 'I found it '. This one says: 'It is all mine' and this one says: 'It is all mine'; each must take an oath that he claims not less than a half and they divide it between them. If one said: 'The whole of it is mine', and one said: 'The half of it is mine'; the one who said 'The whole of it is mine' must take an oath that he claims not less than three-quarters, and the one who said 'Half of it is mine' must take an oath that he claims not less than a quarter. And this one takes three-quarters and this one a quarter

The Gemara (2a) asks why does the Mishnah say both 'This one says, "I found it"' and 'This one says, "It is all mine"' i.e. why repeat the same claim? The reply is that the repetition is required to refer to two different cases; one where each claims that he found the garment, the other where each claims that he bought the garment. Thus the Mishnah is understood to mean that this one claims either that he found it or that he bought it and so the other. The statement 'It is all mine' does not refer to a case of both claiming to have found the garment but to a different case, where each says 'It is all mine' because he bought the garment. And the Gemara proceeds to discuss, in the case where each of them claims to have bought it, why not ask the shopkeeper to which of them he sold it.

But it is easy to see why the Mishnah says 'This one says, "It is all mine"' and there is, in fact, no repetition in the Mishnah. We can easily see what the Mishnah intends if we set it out as:

> Two men hold a garment, this one says, 'I found
> it' and this one says. 'I found it' [where]
> this one says; 'It is all mine … '
> [but where]
> this one says, 'Half is mine …'

The Mishnah deals only with the case of finding (and buying is not referred to at all) but there are two cases of finding so that 'This one says", It is all mine"' and 'This one says, "Half of it is mine"' are in the nature of headings to the two different types of claim. This is so obviously the plain meaning of the Mishnah that it is hard to imagine that the Gemara did not see it. But if, as has been suggested above, the Gemara is not bent on interpreting the Mishnah but on using the Mishnah for the sake of the new material it wishes to discuss (the case of buying and the discussion of this) in its own style of argumentation, all becomes perfectly intelligible.[1]

Although the framework of the Babylon Talmud is woven around what we have called the core material, there can also be detected a number of segments forming separate units complete in themselves. These segments must now be examined if the Babylonian Talmud is to be seen for the all-embracing work it is. As already stated, material extraneous to the normal *sûgyā* is often found, as a digression, in the *sûgyā* itself, but our concern here is with whole units that have been inserted *as units complete in themselves*.

There are, for example, a number of Midrashim in the Babylonian Talmud which bear the marks not of the conventional *sûgyā* but follow more or less the general pattern of the Palestinian Midrashim, albeit with a Babylonian slant. These segments of Midrash may well have their origin in Palestinian Midrashim but they have been adapted so as to produce a Babylonian version.[2]

Other units of material with a distinct theme are those on dreams; on the tales of the saints and seafarers' tales; on the destruction of the Temple; on demons; on magic; on popular proverbs. There are simple lists of laws presented, unusually for the Talmud, almost in the form of a Code. Of this order, too, are the list of private prayers and special sayings of particular Amoraim; the list of funeral orations delivered over various sages and the mourning songs of the women of Shokenzev; and the list of Amoraim who wept when they read a Scriptural verse.[3]

Other units of material with a distinct theme are those on dreams; on the tales of the saints and seafarers' tales on the destruction of the Temple; on demons; on magic; on popular proverbs. There are simple lists of laws presented, unusually for the Talmud, almost in the form of a code. Of this order, too, are the list of private prayers and special sayings of particular Amoraim; the list of funeral orations delivered over various sages and the mourning songs of the women of Shokenzev; and the list of Amoraim who wept when they read a Scriptural verse.

Some of these segments, different in style from the rest of the Talmud and which can easily be removed without affecting the sense of that which comes before than and that after them, seem to be interpolations, though whether by the editors themselves or by post-Talmudic teachers we cannot now determine.[4]

NOTES

1. The 'correct' understanding of Mishnah *Bava Metzia'* 1:1 is given by Israel Lipshitz in his Commentary *Tiferet Yisrael* to this Mishnah in the name of Menasseh of Ilya and it has frequently been quoted. On the whole question of how the Gemara understands the Mishnah see the following (all of whom, incidentally, ignore the possibility that the Gemara may be intentionally misinterpreting the Mishnah for its own purposes): I. H. Weiss: *Dor Dor ve-Doreshav,* Vol. III, pp. 218–27; H. M. Pineles: *Darkah shel Torah,* Vienna, 1861 see especially No. 81, pp. 97–8 (for the difficulty in the *Bava Kama* passage); Z. Frankel: *Darkhey ha-Mishnah,* ed. I. Nussbaum, Tel-Aviv n.d., pp. 343–45; B. Epstein: *Mekor Barukh,*Vilna, 1928, Vol. III, chapter 23, pp. 665–73; H. Albeck: *Mevo I a-Mishnah,* Tel-Aviv, 1960, p. 244 note 7; M. Elon: *ha-Mishpat ha-'Ivri,* Jerusalem, 1978, p. 909 note 10. For Maimonides and Yom Tov Lipmann Heller see, especially Heller's note in his *Tosafot Yom Tov* to tractate *Nazir* 5:5 and Maimonides' comment on the same Mishnah in Commentary edited J. Kapah, Jerusalem,1963, p. 128. Weiss refers to a statement supposedly made by the Gaon of Vilna that just as there is *peshat* and *derash* with regard to Scripture so there is the Gemara in relation to its interpretation of the Mishnah. If this is an authentic statement of the Gaon (Epstein does not believe it so to be) the Gaon may be hinting at the point we have noted that perhaps the Gemara never intended its comments to the Mishnah to be exegesis of the Mishnah. E. Urbach in *Encyclopedia Judaica,* Vol. 12, p. 108, quotes Saadiah Gaon who interprets a Mishnah in *Ketubot* differently from the Gemara even though the departure from the Gemara's understanding results in a change in the law. On this subject see *Otzar ha-Geonim* to *Ketubot*, ed. B. Lewin, Jerusalem, 1939, p. 310. In this connection it is worth noting that this kind of *derash* is absent from the Palestinian Talmud which is almost always much closer to the *peshat*. For instance when a Mishnah states 'All' this is always taken by the Babylonian Talmud to hint at something to be included that is not stated explicitly, see e.g. *Hagigah* 2a and very frequently. This method of Mishnaic interpretation is never used in the Palestinian Talmud. See on this M. Halevi Steinberg: *ha-Yerushalmi ha-Mevuar,* Jerusalem, 1988, *Hagigah*, p. 95
2. The main Midrashic segments are: to the book of Esther, *Megillah* 10b–17a; to Job *Bava Batra* 15a–17b; on the narratives of Samson, Jacob and the Children of Israel in *Sotah*

9b–13a; on the first Psalm, *'Avodah Zarah* 18b–19b. (When this latter is compared to Midrash Psalms, ed. Buber, Psalm 1, it can be clearly seen how material which appears there has been used in the Bavli passage for its own particular construction in its usual style). Cf. the treatment of the Biblical books in *Bava Batra* 14b–15a found nowhere else in this form in the whole of the Talmudic literature and see my chapter on this in *Structure and Form in the Babylonian Talmud*, pp. 31–41.

3. On dreams, *Berakhot* 55a–57b; on tales of the saints *Ta'anit* 19a–25b (called in the Middle Ages 'The Chapter of the Saints', *pirka de-hasidi*) and seafarers. *Bava Batra* 73a–75b; on the destruction of the Temple, Gittin 55b–58a. There is a short complete passage on demons in *Berakhot* 6a but there are numerous references to demons in the Babylonian Talmud. See Isaiah M. Gafni: *The Jews of Babylonia in The Talmudic Era* (Heb.), Jer., 1990 who points to the specific Iranian demonology e.g. in the *Berakhot* passage the demons have chicken feet paralleled by Zoroastrian beliefs that some demons have the form of birds. On magic there is the lengthy passage in *Pesahim* 109b–112b on the baneful effect of 'pairs'. On magical and other remedies the main complete unit is *Gittin* 67b–70b. M. J. Geller ('Akkadian Medicine in the Babylonian Talmud', in *A Traditional Quest*, ed. Dan Cohn Sherbok, Sheffield, 1991 'pp. 102–112 has demonstrated that many of the cures in the Babylonian Talmud can be traced back directly to ancient Akkadian usage. The series of popular proverbs (and Rabbinic sayings) which Scriptural verses support are in the form of a complete unit in *Bava Kama* 92a–93a but occasional popular proverbs are quoted throughout the Babylonian Talmud, see Kossovsky's Concordance, Vol. Five, pp. 352–4 for a list of these. Code-like forms of laws are to be found in *Pesahim* 9b–10b; *Sukkah* 3b–4b; *Bava Kama* 26b–27a. For the list of private prayers and sayings see *Berakhot* 16b–17a; for the funeral orations see *Mo'ed Katan* 25a–b and the women of Shokhenzev, 28b; and for the Rabbis who wept, see *Hagigah* 4b–5a. Reference should also be made to the segment in '*Avodah Zarah* 2a–3b on Rome, Persia and the other nations in the future and the story of Rabbi Joshua ben Hananiah and the Sages of Athens in *Bekhorot* 8b–9a. Neither of these passages occurs anywhere else in this form in the Rabbinic literature, though some of the material used by the final editors is found elsewhere in the Talmud or the Midrash.

4. Nahman Krochmal, *Moreh Nevukhey ha-Zeman*, chapter 14 (in Krochmal's *Collected Writings*), ed. S. Rawidowicz, London, Waltham, MA, 1961, pp. 238–56) put forward the suggestion that some of the Christological, obscene and superstitious passages in the Babylonian Talmud were inserted later into the manuscripts by scribes ignorant of the nature of the material they were copying. Krochmal supports his case by noting that the language in these passages is often a folk language very different from the language of the rest of the Talmud. No doubt, as it has long been suggested, the few passage in the Talmud and Midrash which seem to give support to Christianity may well have been later interpolations, as Krochmal states. But it is far too sweeping to lump together with these few the numerous passages in the Babylonian Talmud that were not to Krochmal's taste because they are obscene or superstitious. These are too numerous to be explained easily away as interpolations from without the official Talmudic circles. Krochmal's attempt at limiting the offensive passages to the Aggadah overlooks the obvious that there are Halakhic passages which deal, for example, with demonology. It is all a matter of taste and it is thoroughly unscientific to assume that the ancient Rabbis shared the intellectual andaesthetic tastes of the Maskilim. What is obscene or superstitious for a nineteenth-century scholarly gentleman like Krochmal may not have been thought so by Rabbis of the sixth century, though, with regard to magic and superstition, the Rabbis did seem to have adopted some of the beliefs of the surrounding culture.

— 4 —

The Babylonian Talmud: A Work Requiring Explication

The final editors of the Babylonian Talmud did not leave their task unfinished. The whole work was carefully structured in a complete pattern. Unlike the Palestinian Talmud, which seems to have been arrested in the middle of the editorial process, the Babylonian Talmud was 'closed', as the post-Talmudic authors call the termination of the editorial work. But this cannot be taken to mean that the ideal of oral teaching by master to disciple was abandoned. On the contrary the written text cannot be understood without detailed explication. Just as it is incorrect, as we have seen, to describe the Talmud as a 'Hansard', simply recording the debates, it is also incorrect to see it as a work in which all the necessary filling out of the material has been recorded in writing. The Talmud is a literary work but one of a very unusual kind. At every turn the text cries out for elucidation. This is why the famous Commentary of Rashi is indispensable. Rashi constantly explains not only the meaning of the words but the ideas behind them and here Rashi generally reproduces the explanations he had heard from his own teachers by word of mouth.

There is some evidence that originally the Talmud was equipped with a system of cantillation and to this day, in Yeshivot, the Talmud is 'sung' to the special Gamara *niggun*, which is really a system of punctuation. The terms *Peshitta* and *ve-hatanya,* for instance, occurring frequently, can be understood, respectively, either as a statement 'It is obvious', 'And we have learnt', or as a question 'Is it not obvious?' and 'But we have learnt [otherwise]?' Rashi generally supplies the correct meaning where necessary. The Talmud is best studied, even today, with a teacher or a colleague in which the elucidation of the text becomes, so to speak, an essential part of the text. It can be put in this way. The Talmud, in its present literary form, is a 'Written Torah' requiring, like the original 'Written Torah', the commentary provided by the 'Oral Torah', the verbal explication of the text.

A number of examples of extra-Talmudic explication being required can here be given.

In tractate *Kiddushin* 43a there is a debate concerning marriage effected through an agent. The rule is that for a marriage to be valid the act of betrothal (the man giving to the woman an object of some value and saying to her: 'Be betrothed to me with this') must be in the presence of two witnesses. Obviously the man himself cannot act as a witness since he is the person involved on whose behalf the witnesses testify. Another rule is that it is not necessary for the man himself to deliver the betrothal money or its value to the woman. He can send an agent to betroth the woman on his behalf. If, for instance, A appoints B as his agent, B declaring: 'Be thou betrothed to A' it is a valid betrothal. The question discussed in the passage is whether B, the agent, can act as one of the two witnesses required. This is formulated in the Talmud as, can an agent serve as a witness (*shaliaḥ na'aseh 'ed*). One Amora holds that he can, another that he cannot. Formulating the point at issue, the Talmud simply states that the one who holds that an agent can serve as a witness believes that it is *even better* if the agent acts as a witness (i.e. because who knows better what happens than the man who actually delivers the betrothal money to the woman). But the other holds that since a man's agent is treated as the man himself the agent cannot serve as witness any more than the man himself can serve as a witness to an act of betrothal he himself performs. The Talmud does not explain the reasoning behind the two opinions. Why does one Amora hold that is 'even better' and the other hcld that it as if he himself did it? It has been suggested that what we have here is a discussion on how the principle of agency operates. Where A appoints B as his agent to perform a certain act the act is valid because 'the agent is like the person himself'. But does this mean where A appoints B to be his agent it is only B's *act* is transferred to A or does it mean that for the purpose of the law B *becomes* A? It is easy to see that something of the sort must be supplied for the Talmudic distinction to be understood.[1]

In tractate *Hullin* 11a it is stated that there are two kinds of *rubba* ('majority' or 'probability'). These are described as 'a majority that is before us' and 'a majority that is not before us'. The first type is said to be that of the Sanhedrin, where the decision of the majority of its members is accepted, and the case of the ten shops, nine of which sell kasher meat, the other forbidden meat. Any meat found outside the shops is considered to be kasher. Just as the majority decision of the Sanhedrin is accepted as the correct decision and has to be followed, so, too, the fact that there is a majority of shops selling kasher is determinative and the meat found is kasher. An example of the second type – a majority that is not before us – is any animal that has been killed in the proper manner of *shehitah* but no examination of the animal's internal organs has been made to discover whether these had the kind of defects that would render the meat forbidden. The meat is kasher because 'the majority of animals are kasher'. Now the passage assumes that the first type – reliance on a majority that is before us – has Scriptural warrant but how do we know that the second type of majority is relied on? The Talmud proceeds to quote attempted proofs from Scripture that the second type of 'majority' is also relied on.

All the Talmud does is distinguish between these two types but the explication is left to the reader as to why the two types are distinct so that one cannot be derived from the other. All the Talmud says is that one is a case of 'a majority that is before us'and the other 'a majority that is not before us'. What precisely is this difference? But it can be seen on deeper reflection that in the case of the Sanhedrin and in that of the ten shops the probability that the decision of the Sanhedrin is correct and the meat kasher is a purely mathematical probability. The actual odds on the meat being kasher are fifty–fifty but the Torah relies on the majority principle here not because we know for certain that the decision of the Sanhedrin is correct or that the meat is really kasher but purely as a matter of procedure. The Torah relies on the majority, i.e. the decision of the Sanhedrin is 'correct' even if the majority is, in fact, mistaken in its ruling since, in law, decision is accepted. And even if the meat is from the non-kasher shop it is still 'kasher' as a matter of procedure. But in the case of 'a majority that is not before us', the probability principle has to act as a determinative factor. Since most animals are known by experience to be kasher it has to be assumed that the particular animal underdiscussion belongs to the majority and really is kasher. There is no evidence from the fact that the Torah relies on the majority principle in the first instance, *as a matter of procedure*, that the Torah also relies on the second type of probability since in this second case the question is not one of procedure but of determination. Without Scriptural warrant it may well be, in the second case, that the Torah treats the meat as only doubtfully kasher and since a doubtful case is forbidden the meat of the animal may be forbidden. Now the point here is that, while the above analysis may well convey the meaning of the distinction, it is not stated explicitly in the Talmud which simply distinguishes between a majority that is before us and one that is not before us. It is not only that the analysis is left for the reader to provide but it seems to have been left so by the editors of the Talmud.[2]

In tractate *Pesaḥim* 25b the story is told of a man who was ordered by a tyrant to kill another man otherwise he himself would be put to death. The case came before Rava who ruled: You must allow yourself to be killed and you must not kill. How do you know that your blood is redder – perhaps the blood of that man is redder?' Beyond stating that this ruling is based on pure reason, *sevara* (i.e. and is so obvious that no support from Scripture is required) , the Talmud leaves the whole matter without explaining the meaning of Rava's statement Rashi is of great help here. Rashi explains that although other prohibitions can be set aside in order to save life, the prohibition of murder cannot be set aside since murder, by definition, is the taking of a life. In the case considered it is not a question of life against a prohibition, since a life is lost in any event, but a question of a life for a life. If the man is to be allowed to murder in order to save his life it could only be because his life has greater value than the life of his potential victim and since no one can know which life is of greater value it must follow that the Torah never permits an act of murder even if it is to save the perpetrator's own life. All this is implied in the otherwise cryptic statement of the Talmud.[3]

In tractate *Makkot* 5a a statement of the Mishnah is discussed dealing with the following case. According to the Deuteronomic law (Deuteronomy 19:1 5–21) a false witness has to suffer whatever penalty he sought, by his false testimony, to impose on his intended victim. Supposing three witnesses testify falsely that A owes B three hundred zuz, then, when their offence is discovered, they have to pay him three hundred zuz in all but each of them only has to pay one hundred. Supposing, however, the three witnesses falsely testified that A is liable to thirty-nine lashes, then when their offence is discovered each of them has to undergo the penalty of thirty-nine lashes and not, as in the case of the money, a division into three. What is the difference? The Talmud simply states: 'Money can be joined to make a total but lashes cannot' without explaining the difference. But reflection shows that while three times one hundred zuz has a total of three hundred, three thirteens in respect of lashes is only three separate sets of thirteen and cannot be totalled into thirty-nine. This is because the fact that three separate persons suffer pain of the degree X does not mean that there is a total degree of pain of 3X. Unlike in the case of money, the pain of the lashes cannot be totalled together, since, in fact, none of the three would suffer more than the pain of thirteen.[4]

Or take the term *ḥazakah*, usually meaning 'presumptive state' but used in numerous different senses in the Talmud. For instance, where there is a doubt whether something has changed, it is left in its presumptive state, its *ḥazakah*, e.g. if there is a doubt whether the act of *shehitah* has been carried out properly, the meat of the animal is forbidden because, before the act, the animal was, as a live animal, in the *ḥazakah* of being in a state of forbiddenness.The term *ḥazakah* is also used for something that is repeated more than once, say, where an ox has gored three times it is assumed that it is a goring ox and, if it does damage, the owner is more liable than he would have been had the animal remained docile. Again, the fact that the onus of proof is on the plaintiff rather than on the defendant, so that if there is doubt whether the defendant is liable to pay he is not obliged to pay, is said to be because the defendant has possession, *ḥazakah*. In all these different cases the simple term *ḥazakah* is used and there are many more throughout the Talmudic literature. Indeed it can be argued that of all the themes of the Talmud that of *ḥazakah* is the most pervasive. It is very hard indeed to see that the same term, should have been used in so many different senses unless the editors understood and intended that the students of the Talmud would see for themselves in which sense the term is used and provide their own explication.[5]

Thus far we have only considered a few legal terms but the truth is that the whole of the Talmud requires the kind of amplification given to it by the Commentators throughout the ages. Not all of these were successful in recovering the plain meaning of the texts and many ideas have been read into texts which could never have been intended. Yet so many of the great mediaeval and later Commentators have succeeded so well in uncoverinci the deeper meaning of many Talmudic texts that it is hard to believe that something of the sort was not intended from the beginning. A text that lends itself so readily to explication is a text that, in all probability, was intended for the explication to be given. In other words, the editors of the Talmud have provided a structured outline but one that was intended to be filled in by those who would study it..

NOTES

1. See the comment to this passage by R. Meir Simhah Kagan of Dvinsk (*Hiddushey Rabbi Meir Simhah,* edited J. D. Greenwald, Jerusalem, 1967, Vol. 1, p. 65) who says of this kind of analysis that 'every intelligent person' will see that this is behind the debate, and see *Yalkut Perushim* to tractate *Kiddushin,* 2, ed. J. Sklar, n.p.n.d., pp. 30–2, for a more detailed analysis in the same vein.
2. On this see the keen analysis of the passage in R. Simeon Skopf's *Sha'arey Yosher,* Warsaw, 1928, Gate 3, chapter one, and see my: *The Talmudic Argument,* CUP, 1984, chapter five, pp. 50–63.
3. For a further analysis of the passage see R. Hayyim Soloveitchick: *Ḥiddushey Rabbeu Ḥiayyim Halevi* n.p.n.d., p. 1,
4. See Jacob Kamenitzky: *Emet le-Ya'akov,* New York, 1989, Vol 2, pp. 235–6 for a different analysis (in the name of J. B. Soloveitchik of Brisk). Three separate sets of lashes of thirteen are administered on three different bodies whereas the false witnesses intended that the thirty-nine lashes be inflicted on the same body so that the second thirteen would be on a body that had already suffered thirteen and the third thirteen on a body that had already suffered twenty-six. But the suggestion above seems to be the meaning of the Talmudic passage. In any event, it is clear that the bare statement of the Talmud must have been intended to be explicated.
5. See *Encyklopedia Talmudit,* Vols. 13 pp. 453–760 and Vol. 14, pp. 1–423 for a very comprehensive account of all the different kinds of *ḥazakah.* In connection with the subject of this lecture reference must be made to the Lithuanian school, originally attacked by the older Talmudists but now dominant in the majority of contemporary Yeshivot. This school is indifferent and often hostile to historical, critical investigation of the Talmud, yet its methodology of keen logical analysis often succeeds in explicating the Talmudic texts in a manner not far removed from what is probably the original meaning. The Lithuanian methodology was largely applied in verbal teaching but the following is a list of some of the more important works: R. Hayyim Soloveitchik: *Ḥiddushey Rabbenu Ḥayyim ha-Levi,* Jerusalem edition with notes by the Hazon Ish, n.d.; his son, R. Yitzhak Zeev Soloveitchik: *Ḥiddushey ha-Griz,* Jer., 1972; R. Simeon Skopf. *Sha'arey Yosher* (quoted above) and *Ḥiddushey Rabbi Shimon Yehuda ha-Kohen* Jer., 1971; R. Baruch Baer Leibovitch: *Birkat* Shmuel, New York, 1972; R. Naftali Trop: *Ḥiddushey ha-Grant,* Jer., 1989; R. Yitzhak Rabbinovitz of Poniavezh: *Zekher Yitzhak,* Jer., 1990; R. Joseph Judah Laib Bloch: *Shi'urey Halakhah,* Tel-Aviv, 1958; P. Hayyim Rabbinowitz of Telz: *Ḥiddushey Rabbi Hayyim mi-Telz,* Bene Berak, 1968; P. Jacob Kamenitzky. *Emet le-Ya'kov* (quoted above); R. Yehiel Ḥichel Rabbinowitz: *Afikey Yam.* Jer., 1989; R. Reuben Katz: *Degel Reuven,* Jer., 1991; and, espeially, the systematic treatment in R. M. A. Amiel: *ha-Middot le-Heker ha-Halakhah,* Jer., 1972.
6. Relevant to the question of Talmudic texts requiring explication are the instances in *Megillah* 2a; *'Avodah Zarah* 72a; *Yoma* 6a, where the same expression is used twice, the first in the form of a question, the second in the form of a questioning of the question. On this phenomenon see R. Samson of Chinon, *Sefer Keritut,* Part '/, No. 42, and the notes of Joel Zevi Potha to his edition of the work, Brooklyn, NY, 1961, pp. 420–1. On the

question of explication it should be mentioned that the *Entziklopedia Talmudit* (20 volumes of which have so far appeared) is good at explication but poor on historical and literary criticism and ignores completely the extra-Talmudic Halakhah. The same is true of the Art Scroll Series (to date seven volumes have appeared). The Steinsaltz edition (to date twenty volumes have appeared in Hebrew, six in English translation) is more adequate on both counts but still far from satisfactory. The Soncino translation into English is good on the historical and geographical background (especially in the notes in square brackets by the editor, Dr Epstein) but is weak on explication and virtually ignores literary criticism. On the methodology of the Lithuanian state and the influence on this of the Haskalah see Norman Solomon: *The Analytic Movement Hayyim Soloveitchi and his Circle,* Scholaris Press Atlanta, GA, 1993.

Part Two
The Talmudic *Sûgyā*

— 5 —

Havvayot de-Abbaye Ve-Rava: The History of a Talmudic Text

A statement in the Babylonian Talmud, seeming to imply that Talmudic discussions and debates are only of secondary importance, was naturally something of an embarrassment to Talmudists for whom these discussions and debates are of the essence so far as the study of the Torah is concerned. We have to look at both the history of the text itself and the fate of the text in post-Talmudic thought. For the history of the text itself we must first examine the two Talmudic passages – *Sukkah* 28a and *Bava Batra* 134a – in which the statement occurs. In reality the two passages are virtually the same but inserted, by the final editors, in each tractate where appropriate. The insertion in the *Sukkah* passage is due to the discussion of a *Sukkah* law attributed to R. Eliezer, a disciple of Rabban Johanan ben Zakkai, who, it is stated, possessed some of the same attainments as his master. The insertion in the *Bava Batra* passage is due to the story there of a man who bequeathed his property to R. Jonathan ben Uziet, who appears in the story as superior to Rabban Johanan ben Zakkai. Incidentally, the appearance by association of the same text in two different tractates throws light on the way in which the final editors went about their task.

The passage in tractate *Sukkah* is first given in English translation. 'Our Rabbis taught: Hillel the Elder had eighty disciples. Thirty of them were worthy for the *Shekhinah* to rest upon them like Moses our teacher.[1] Thirty of them were worthy for the sun to stand still for them like Joshua ben Nun.[2] Twenty of them were of average ability [*benonim*, i.e. in relation to the other sixty]. The greatest of them all was Jonathan ben Uziel. The least of them all was Rabban Johanan ben Zakkai. They said of Rabban Joḥanan ben Zakkai that he left nothing aside of Scripture, Mishnah and

Gemara,[3] Halakhot[4] and Aggadot; the careful considerations of the Torah [*dikdukey torah*] and the careful considerations of the Scribes [*dikdukey soferim*]; arguments from the minor to the major [*kalim ve-hamurim*] and arguments by analogy [*gezerot shavvot*]; cycles [*teku-fot*]; [5] *gematriot*; the speech of the ministering angels,[6]), the speech of the demons and the speech of palm trees;[7] parables of laundry-men and fox fables; a great thing and a small thing – "a great thing" refers to *Maaseh Merkavah* and "a small thing" refers to the discussions of Abbaye and Rava [*havvayot de-Abbaye ve-Rava*]. In order to fulfil what is stated: *That I may cause those that love me to inherit substance, and that I may fill their treasures* [Proverbs 8:21]. And if the least of them [of the disciples of Hillel] was so, how much more the greatest of them? They said of Jonathan ben Uziel that when he sat down to study the Torah any bird that flew over him was at once burnt.'[8]

There are what appear to be two earlier versions of this passage: in the Jerusalem Talmud (JT *Nedarim 5:7,39b)* and in *Avot de-Rabbi Natan* (ARN I, chapter 14, ed. Schechter, New York, 1967, p. 29a).

THE JT VERSION

'Hillel the Elder had eighty pairs[9] of disciples. The greatest of them was Jonathan ben Uziel. The least of them was Rabban Johanan ben Zakkai. On one occasion he [Hillel] fell sick and they came to visit him but Rabban Johanan ben Zakkai remained standing outside in the courtyard. He said to them: "Where is the least one of you? For he is a father of wisdom and the father of the [future] generations, and it goes without saying, the greatest of you." They replied: "He stands outside in the courtyard." He said: "Let him enter." When he came in he [Hillel] said to them: *That I may cause them that love me to inherit substance, and that I may fill their treasures.'*

THE ARN VERSION

'Hillel the Elder had eighty disciples. Thirty of them were worthy for the *Shekhinah* to rest upon them like Moses our teacher but their generation was unworthy of it. Thirty of them were worthy to intercalate the year. And twenty of them were of average ability.

The greatest of them all was Jonathan ben Uziel. The least of them all was Rabban Johanan ben Zakkai. They said of Rabban Johanan ben Zakkai that he left aside nothing of Scripture, Mishnah, Gemara, Halakhot and Aggadot and Toseftot; *dikduket torah, dikdukey soferim* and all the hermeneutics of the Sages, and he did not fail to study everything [*kol davar ve-davar*, of the Torah], in order to fulfil the verse: *That I may cause those that love me to inherit substance and that I may fill their treasures.*'

Given these two versions, the problem of the history of our version becomes a little less complicated than it might otherwise have been. The JT version, as the simplest of the three, would appear to be the original version. Here we have the main elements of the narrative: Hillel had eighty disciples; the greatest was Jonathan ben Uziel and the least Rabban Johanan ben Zakkai; the verse: *That I may cause* is quoted (here by Hillel). The ARN version adds, in what appears to be an elaboration of the earlier version, the following features: the division of Hillel's disciples into three groups (the members of the second group being worthy to intercalate the year); the attainments of Rabban Johanan ben Zakkai. Our version contains further elaborations (and the members of the second group are here worthy for the sun to stand still for them). First, there is the addition of: 'And if the least of them' and the reply about Jonathan and the bird. The question, at least, is clearly Amoraic and is a comment, partly in Aramaic, on the original *Baraita*. Then there is the statement we are examining about the discussions of Abbaye and Rava. This addition is obviously subsequent not only to Abbaye and Rava themselves but must date from the time when the discussions of Abbaye and Rava had become famous. Moreover, this very late Amoraic (editorial?) addition seems to be a comment on the *kol davar ve-davar* of the ARN version i.e. this is made to refer to the *davar gadol* and the *davar katan*. Thus the statement can be dated in any event as being not earlier than the end of the fourth century and may be, in fact, much later.

The actual term *havvayot de-Abbaye ve-Rava*[10] can mean either the problems set by Abbaye and Rava, as the Geonim explain it[11] or the debates between Abbaye and Rava, of which there are so many in the Babylonian Talmud. The same expression is used in the Talmud[12] of Rav and Samuel – *havvayot de-Rav u-Shmuel* and this, too, can mean either the problems raised by these two teachers or the debates between the two, of which there are also numerous instances recorded in the Talmud. Whatever the original meaning, in the course of time the term *havvayot de-Abbaye ve-Rava* came to be used as a synonym for the Talmudic dialectics as a whole, that is, for Talmudic/Halakhic studies in general.

We can now turn to the famous statement of Maimonides in his *Mishneh Torah (Yesodey ha-Torah* 4:3). In the first four chapters of this treatise, Maimonides has identified the Rabbinic *Ma'aseh Bereshit* ('The Work of Creation') and *Ma'aseh Merkavah* ('The Work of the Chariot') with, respectively, Aristotelean physics and Aristotelean metaphysics. Moreover, he understands the famous Talmudic account (*Hagigah* 14b) of the four who entered the Orchard (*Pardes*, often understood in the sense of entering Paradise) as meaning that they engaged in metaphysical studies. Maimionides then continues: 'I say that it is not right to stroll through the Orchard unless one has first filled his stomach with bread and meat. Bread and meat is a metaphor for the knowledge of that which is forbidden and that which is permitted and similarly with regard to all the other precepts.[13] Even though these matters are referred to by the Sages as a "small thing", for the Sages say: "a great thing is *Ma'aseh Merkavah* and a small thing is *havvayot de-Abbaye ve-Rava*", for all that, it is fitting that precedence be given to them for at first they promote a man's mental composure. Furthermore, they constitute the great favour that the Holy One, blessed be He, has bestowed in this world for the purpose of inheriting the life of the World to Come. And it is possible for everyone to know them, whether it be one who is great or one who is small;[14] whether it be man or woman; whether it be one whose heart is broad or one whose heart is narrow'.

This passage in Maimonides was one of many which aroused the ire of the traditionalists and it became one of the main bones of contention in the Maimonist and anti-Maimonist controversy that erupted after Maimonides' death and continued for centuries afterwards.[15] To the particular scandal of his opponents, not only does Maimonides identify Aristotelean philosophy with *Ma'aseh Merkavah*, and hence makes it a part of of the Torah, but he elevates this to the highest aspect of Torah study, in relation to which Talmudic studies are of far lesser importance. Instead of understanding the Talmudic statement, as other earlier commentators do, as meaning only that the discussions of Abbaye and Rava were a 'small thing for the powerful mind of Rabban Johanan ben Zakkai', Maimonides understands it literally that Talmudic studies, though essential, are of lesser *importance*.

Even admirers of Maimonides' Talmudic expertise, like R. Yom Toy Ishbili (d. 1330), the *Ritba*, find it hard to accept Maimonides' formulation with equanimity, striking, as the formulation seems to do, at the very basis of Talmudic studies, to which *Ritba* and his contemporaries, and, for that matter, Maimonides himself, had devoted their lives, spending laborious days and night in the study and mastery of the extremely difficult Talmudic texts, in the belief that in their studies they were doing the 'greatest thing' of all, the contemplation of the very word of God. *Ritba* writes:[16] 'A small *thing, havvayot de-Abbaye ve-Rava*, namely, a small thing in relation to the *Ma'aseh Merkavah* of which they spoke. And even in relation to this it was not the Talmud that was referred to as a "small thing". For at first it says that he did not leave aside from studying Scripture, Mishnah, Talmud, Halakhot and Aggadot, and they are the peg upon which everything hangs, but only the discussions of Abbaye and Rava, namely the difficulties raised by them and their solutions and their problems. These were unclear to them since they were less capable than the earlier sages of penetrating to the profundities of the Talmud. Since it was the result of their lack of understanding, their discussions were termed only a small thing of the wisdom of the Mishnah. But it is far greater than all the sciences of the gentiles. Every believer will see that this is the true and correct interpretation. Not as others explain it. May God forgive them.' There can be doubt that it is to Maimonides that *Ritba* refers when he speaks of 'others', avoiding any direct mention of Maimonides out of respect for the great master.[17] *Ritba* refuses to extend the 'small thing' to the whole of Talmudic studies and, naturally, refuses to identify the 'great thing' with Aristotelean metaphysics. Maimonides does both. In the subsequent debates between the Talmudists and the philosophers, the term *havvayot de-abbaye ve-Rava* was employed to denote the whole of Talmudic studies, with the statement that the subject of debate is on the question of to which prority is to be given.[18] *Ritba* is especially scathing of Maimonides' contention that the study of Gentile science is superior to Talmudic studies. 'Small thing' though even the discussions of Abbaye are in relation to the 'wisdom of the Mishnah' i.e. the whole range of Talmudic studies, yet even these are far greater than anything the science of the Gentiles has to teach us.

Similarly, the Kabbalist Shem Tov Ibn Shem Tov (d. 1441) scornfully remarks of Maimonides' identification of *Ma'aseh Bereshit* and

Ma'aseh Merkavah with Gentile science and philosophy: 'Heaven forbid that we should understand it in this way. If that were so [that the mystery of the Chariot means Aristotelean science and philosophy] these mysteries are available to everyone, to the pure and the impure, to the believer and the heretic, to the Canaanite, the Hittite, the Ammonite and the Moabite.'[19]

Even after the fierceness of the Maimonist controversy had abated and Maimonides himself had won acceptance as the supreme Talmudic authority, Talmudists continued to be puzzled by the original Talmudic statement no less than by Maimonides' understanding of it. In the sixteenth century, R. Joseph Karo's Commentary to Maimonides' Code, *Kesef Mishnah*,[20] feels obliged to quote earlier authorities, like the *Ritba*, who found Maimonides' formulation so extremely perplexing and who tried their hand at an interpretation of the Talmudic passage more in accord with the primacy to be given to Talmudic studies. Karo quotes a lengthy analysis of the Talmudic statement by R. Elijah Mizrahi (d. 1526). Mizrahi understands 'great' and 'small' in the Talmudic passage (incidentally, Mizrahi also equates the discussions of Abbaye and Rava with general Talmudic studies) as referring to the object of the studies. The Work of the Chariot concerns the Creator Himself, the supreme Object of the studies. In this sense it is undoubtedly the 'great thing', whereas the discussions of Abbaye and Rava have as their object the infinitely smaller, but no less important, aim of man's practical duties on earth. Indeed, the Talmudic studies are higher and bring in their wake far greater reward than the esoteric Work of the Chariot. In this sense nothing is 'greater' than Talmudic studies.[21] The nineteenth-century Talmudist, R. Menahem Karakowsky, goes even further[22] in understanding (though this is very forced) Maimonides himself to be saying that while the Work of the Chariot is intrinsically greater than Talmudic studies yet without the latter the former cannot be grasped at all just as bread and meat are essential even though they are surpassed by other worldly delights. The Work of the Chariot is a spiritual luxury, so to speak, but man cannot live on luxuries and can only survive by making bread and meat his staple diet.

With the rise of the Kabbalah, the Talmudic passage received a new turn. The Orchard and the Work of the Chariot now came to mean Kabbalistic studies and the discussions of Abbaye and Rava the Talmudic studies in general.[23] There was now a new rivalry, not between philosophy and Talmudic studies but between the latter and the study of the Kabbalah. None of the Kabbalists neglected Talmudic studies but for them the 'great thing' was the study of the Kabbalah.

A somewhat different form of contention for supremecy emerged in the debate between the followers of the eighteenth-century Hasidic movement and their opponents, the Mitnaggedim. For the latter, Talmudic studies remained of supreme importance while for many of the Hasidic masters the ideal was that of *devekut*, 'attachment' to God in the mind at all times. To some extent the Hasidic ideal was bound to be frustrated by severe concentration on Talmudic studies. As the Mitnaggedim said, for their part to have God in the mind while studying the Torah was to have the mind diverted from the topics studied so that Talmud study in a spirit of *devekut* was no study worthy of the name.[24] Very revealing in this connection is the attempt by the early Hasidic author, R. Meshullan Feivush Heller of Zbarazh (d.c. 1795) to have the best of both worlds. For Heller[25] the Work of the Chariot and the discussions of Abbaye and Rava refer not to two different subjects of study but to different attitudes to study. The discussions of Abbaye and Rava refer to studies of the Talmud with the aim of attaining intellectual pleasure from these. When Talmudic studies are engaged in as a purely intellectual exercise, there is little thought of God in the process and then they are, indeed, only a 'small thing', but when these very studies are engaged in as a means to *devekut* and God is in the mind at all times, then the student becomes a 'chariot' to the divine. This is the meaning, according to Heller, of the saying that the Work of the Chariot is the 'great thing'. Even the Kabbalah, when studied with a 'discussions of Abbaye and Rava' attitude, becomes a 'small thing'. Conversely, when Talmudic studies are engaged in with the proper motivation they themselves become the Work of the Chariot. Eventually, even among the ranks of the Mitnaggedim the problem arose of whether Talmudic studies were sufficient in themselves for the good life when the followers of the nineteenth century Musar movement sought successfully to demand the study of the moralistic literature as a necessary adjunct to the conventional Talmudic studies. The opponents of the Musarists declared that Talmudic studies, as the supreme form of Torah study, provided in themselves a miraculous balm for the soul, while the Musarists retorted that, at least, regular doses of the medicine provided by Musar studies could alone protect the student from the allure of worldly things.[26] But I have been unable to discover, either in the writings of the Musarists or in the literature of the anti-Musarists, any reference to our passage. This might seem rather odd in the circumstances. It might also be remarked that our passage does not seem to feature at all in the Western debate regarding Torah and Derekh Eretz, when the new rival to traditional studies was neither philosophy in the mediaeval sense nor the Kabbalah nor Hasidism but the values of Western thought and civilization. It is probable that neither the followers of Musar nor the exponents of Torah and Derekh Eretz ever thought of elevating their particular emphasis to place it above conventional Talmudic studies. Musar and Derekh Eretz, for the followers of these tendencies, were intended to add their particular relish to the standard bread and meat. It was never imagined that the bread and meat of Talmudic studies could ever be seen as anything but the supreme topic of Torah studies.

NOTES

1. See Rabbinowicz *Dikdukey Soferim, Sukkah*, that the Munich Codex omits 'like Moses our teacher' and see the marginal note in the Vilna, Romm edition, on the basis of *Sanhedrin* 11a. But Rabbinowicz, note 2, prefers the current reading.
2. Joshua 10:12f.
3. In the Munich Codex, Talmud. Gemara in the current texts is due to the fear of the censor as is well-known. Rashi's comment in the current texts that Gemara is the equivalent of Sevara is also due to the substitution of Gemara for Talmud since the term *gemara* has a quite different meaning from *sevara*, see e.g. *'Avodah Zarah* 19a and freq.
4. Rashi and Rashbam (to the *Bava Batra* passage) understand Halakhot as referring to 'laws given to Moses at Sinai' but since this term is in juxtaposition to Aggadot the meaning may be Halakhot in general i.e. he was thoroughly familiar with both the legal and non-legal aspects of Judaism.
5. Rashi, calculations of the movements of the sun and the moon but there might be an echo here of the intercalation of the year as in the version to be quoted later from ARN
6. See Meiri's rationalistic interpretation that the meaning is not that he knew the speech of the angels but that he knew how to speak about angels, Meiri: *Bet ha-Behirah, Sukkah*, ed. A. Liss, Jerusalem, 1966, p. 91.
7. See *Otzar ha-Geonim, Sukkah*, ed. B. M. Lewin, Jerusalem, 1934, p. 31 for Rav Hai Gaon's interpretation that the reference is to divination by means of the palm branches which 'speak' to one another on a windless day when a sage can discern what they are telling about future events. Cf. Angelo S. Rappoport: *The Folklore of the Jews,* London, 1937, p. 37.
8. See *Hiddushey ha-Ritba* to *Sukkah*, ed. E. Lichtenstein, Jerusalem, 1968, p. 258, who quotes the Jerusalem Talmud (but not found in our texts of the Yerushalmi) where the question is raised if the disciple was so great how much greater the master? The reply is that with the disciple the bird was only burnt if it came within his four ells whereas with the master it was burnt even outside his four ells.
9. *zug*, only in this version not in that of our passage nor in the ARN version to be quoted. Perhaps the meaning of *zug* here is not 'pairs' but 'groups' as in the other versions. Judah Halevi's *Kuzari* (III, 65), incidentally quotes the ARN version.

10. The Munich Codex has *havvayah* in the singular. Levy and Jastrow understand the root of this word as *hevi,* 'to be' hence a 'presentation' or a 'becoming'.
11. See Otzar ha-Geonim, quoted above, p. 95 and *Iggeret de-Rav Sherira Gaon,* ed. B. M. Lewin, Jerusalem, 1970, p. 9, that *havvayot de-Abbaye ve-Rava* refers to the problems discussed by Abbaye and Rava and the suggestion that all such problems in the Talmud are the work of these two teachers even in passages in which their names are not given. This is probably the beginning of the attempt to treat as synonymous the discussions of Abbaye and Rava and the whole of the Talmudic dialectics.
12. *Berakhot* 20a; *Ta'anit* 24a; *Sanhedrin* 106b. See Responsa of R. Joseph Colon, *Teshuvot Maharik,* Warsaw, 1884, No. 84, for the suggestion that Abbaye and Rava are mentioned in our passage rather than Rav and Samuel because the law generally follows the former.
13. See *Hagigah* 14a for the comparison of Torah studies with bread and *'Eruvin* 21b for the comparison with meat.
14. Here Maimonides seems to take the terms 'great' and 'small' as referring to great men and small men. On this passage in Maimonides see I. Twersky: *Introduction to the Code of Maimonides,* Yale University Press, 1980, p. 395 and pp. 493–5 and Twersky in *Jewish Medieval and Renaissance Studies.* ed. A. Altmann, Harvard University Press, 1967, pp. 85–8
15. See J. Sarachek: *Faith and Reason, The Conflict Over the Rationalism of Maimonides,* New York 1935, ed. Hermon Press, 1970.
16. *Hiddushey ha-Ritba,* ed. Lichtenstein, quoted above, pp. 257–8.
17. See Meiri, quoted above, p. 91 for a similar explanation of the passage.
18. See Isaiah Horowitz: *Shelah,* ed. Jerusalem, 1963, section *torah she-be-'al peh,* Vol. IV, p. 20a who devotes a special paragraph to Abbaye and Rava because it is right to pay homage to these two teachers in particular since 'the whole of the Talmud is called "the discussions of Abbaye and Rava"'.
19. *Sefer ha-Emunot,* Ferara, 1556, Introduction, p. 4a.
20. *Kesef Mishnah* to Maimonides *Yesodey ha-Torah* 4:13. See Hasdai Crescas: *Or Hashem,* 4:10, Jer. ed., 1990, pp. 407–10, that the Rabbis would not have called Aristotelean metaphysics a 'great thing' in relation to *havvayot de-Abbaye ve-Rava* and see the elaboration on this passage in Crescas by R. Joseph Solomon Delmedigo in *Matzref le-Hokhmah,* ed. D. Torsh, Odessa, 1965, pp. 21b–22a (47–48 in Arabic numerals).
21. See the Hasidic author, R. Eliezer Horowitz of Tarnograd in his *No'am Megadim,* ed. Brooklyn, New York, 1984 (with notes entitled *Tidrosh No'am* by S. Weiss) pp. 14–15 and 402 who quotes this explanation in the name of 'a great sage of old', obviously R. Elijah Mizrahi as in *Kesef Mishnah.*
22. *'Avodat ha-Melekh,* Jerusalem, 1971, p. 10. Isserles in *Yoreh Deah* 246:6 has adapted Maimonides' formulation, see the note of the Vilna Gaon in the standard editions.
23. See especially J. Katz's chapter on 'Kabbalah and Halakhic Studies as Rival Contenders' in his: *Halakhah ve-Kabbalah,* Jerusalem, 1984, pp. 70–101.
24. On the conflict between the Hasidim and the Mitnaggedim with regard to the study of the Torah see N. Lamm: *Torah Lishmah,* Jerusalem, 1972, and Allan Nadler: *The Faith of the Mihnagdim.* Baltimore and London, 1997.
25. *Yosher Divrey Emet* in *LikkutimYekarim,* ed. Jerusalem, 1974, pp. 103–4.
26. See Dov Katz: *Pulmos ha-Musar,* Jerusalem, 1972.

— 6 —

Are There Fictitious Baraitot in the Babylonian Talmud?

Every student of the Babylonian Talmud is aware that not infrequently in this work a ruling is given by an Amora and the very same ruling is then quoted from a Baraita in identical or near-identical words. It will be sufficient for the purpose of stating the problem to give just one or two examples.

1. *Berakhoth 12a*
   R. Judah said in the name of Samuel: "They wished to read so (the Ten Commandments daily before the reading of the Shema) also outside the Temple but they (the Sages) had already prevented this because of the insinuations of the sectarians.' We have also been taught so (i.e., in a Baraita): 'R. Nathan said: 'They wished to read so outside the Temple but they had already prevented this because of the insinuations of the sectarians.'

2. *Shabbath 58a*
   Samuel said: 'A slave may go out (into the public domain on the Sabbath) with a seal around his neck but not with a seal on his garments.' We have also been taught so: 'A slave may go out with a seal around his neck but not with a seal on his garments.'

3. *Berakhoth 40a*
   Raba b. Samuel said in the name of R. Ḥiyya: 'Eat salt after every meal and drink water after every drink and you will never come to harm.' We have also been taught so: 'Eat salt after every meal and drink water after every drink and you will never come to harm.'

4. *Kethuvoth 22a*
   Our Rabbis taught: 'If a woman said: *"I am a married woman"* but later declared: *"I am single,"* she is believed.' But did she not make herself into something forbidden? Raba son of R. Huna said, 'the case is where she gave a reasonable explanation (*amatla*) to her (former) words. We have also been taught so: 'If she said: *"I am a married woman"* but later declared: "I am single," she is not believed. But if she gave a reasonable explanation (*amatla*) to her (former) words she is believed.' And it once happened to a certain great lady, who was very beautiful, that when many men rushed to propose to her she said to them: *'I am betrothed.'* After a time she arose and married herself off. The Sages said to her: 'Why did you do this?' She replied: 'At first, when unworthy men proposed to me, I said that I was betrothed; but now that I have been proposed to by a worthy man I married myself off.' The law was brought before the Sages at Usha by R. Aha, Prince of the Palace, and they said: 'If she gave a reasonable explanation to her words she is believed.'

How is this phenomenon to be explained? If there were only a few such instances it might have been possible to attribute it all to coincidence – the Amora and the Baraita arrived independently at the same ruling, though it would be stretching coincidence too far even here to explain the identical wording in this way. In fact, there are so many instances that coincidence can be ruled out. Moreover, although one finds proofs of the correctness of amoraic views from Baraitot in the Jerusalem Talmud too one never finds the remarkable correspondence in style and language there that one finds in the Babylonian Talmud.

In order to deal with the problem I. H. Weiss[1] advances the startling thesis that suspicion is attached to many of the Baraitot in the Babylonian Talmud and that many of them are fictitious, i.e., they are not authentic transmissions of tannaitic opinion but were invented by the Babylonian Amoraim as alleged support for their views. According to Weiss, the only alternatives are that either the Amoraim invented Baraitot to accord with their own views or else they had access to authentic Baraitot but palmed them off as their own sayings! In any event, according to Weiss, something peculiar was going on that succeeds in putting a great question mark against the authenticity of many Baraitot in the Babylonian Talmud. Weiss writes:

> It is extremely hard to believe that both the Amora and the Baraita happened to say the same things in the same style and language word for word by coincidence. Even if the possibility of this kind of coincidence could be accepted in two or three places it is impossible to believe that such agreement should be found in hundreds of instances, as we do indeed find it in the Babylonian Talmud. And it is also no coincidence that Baraitot of this kind are nowhere found in the Jerusalem Talmud. It is true that also in the Jerusalem Talmud we find support adduced for amoraic views from Baraitot ... but complete agreement in style and language between the words of the Amora and the Baraita, as we find in the Babylonian Talmud, is never found there anywhere at all. All this justifies doubts regarding the claim of authenticity and early date of these Baraitot in the Babylonian Talmud.

Abraham Weiss[2] takes strong issue with I. H. Weiss. The earlier Weiss's work, *Dor Dor veDorshav,* he remarks, has become virtually a popular work and since it accuses the talmudic sages of 'forgery and plagiarism' it needs to be vigorously refuted. After a comprehensive survey of the whole field, Abraham Weiss arrives at a very different solution from that of I. H. Weiss. According to Abraham Weiss the solution to our problem is to be found in the fact that the Babylonian amoraim did all their work in a literary atmosphere in which numerous sayings from earlier times had become the common property of the later scholars. It is not surprising, therefore, that a particular saying might be attributed both to a Baraita and to an amora. The amora either quoted consciously from the earlier source without actually mentioning that it was a quote, or he stated that it was a quote but this statement was later omitted. The reason was that the saying had by then become attributed to him rather than to his original source.

Undoubtedly Abraham Weiss is closer to the truth than I. H. Weiss. Abraham Weiss's account is adequate to explain the phenomenon; the process to which he calls attention can be observed generally in world literature. Every dictionary of quotations, for example, knows of famous sayings attributed to more than one author. For all that, Abraham Weiss's explanation is too simplistic. The purpose of this essay is to demonstrate that even if Abraham Weiss is correct in his basic contention this does not rule out the possibility that the redactors of the Babylonian Talmud, at least, occasionally reworked a Baraita so as to fit it into their schematic arrangement of the *sûgyā*. There appears to be sufficient evidence that authentic tannaitic sayings were consciously given a fictitious wording in the form of a Baraita for the purpose of providing a contrived argument which leads by stages towards its climax.[3]

We begin with the *sûgyā* in tractate Rosh Hashanah 24a–b (paralleled by the *sûgyā* in tractate 'Avodah Zarah 43a–b).

The *sûgyā* begins with the report in the Mishnah that Rabban Gamaliel had diagrams of the moon's phases on a tablet on the wall of his upper chamber for the purpose of demonstrating to the unlearned the various phases of the moon. This shows that there is no objection to making representations of the heavenly bodies, but the Gemara asks: 'Is it not written: "Ye shall not make with Me" (Exod. 20:20), which means: 'Ye shall not make the likeness of My attendants?"'[4] To this Abaye replies that the Torah forbids only those attendants of which it is possible to make copies, i.e., the buildings and vessels of the Temple but not the making of a likeness of the moon. A Baraita is quoted in support in which it is stated that it is forbidden to make copies of the Temple or its vessels. The Gemara then objects, 'but is it permitted to make the likeness of attendants of which it is not possible to make copies? Have we not been taught in a Baraita: "Ye shall not make with me" – Ye shall not make the likeness of My attendants which minister before Me on high?' To this Abaye replies that the Torah forbids only the making together of the four faces in the heavenly chariot, i.e., the Gemara now goes back to the original reply that the verse refers to copying the Temple and its vessels.[5] There follows a short digression in the Gemara which we omit as irrelevant to our particular analysis. The Gemara then objects, 'but is it permitted to make the likeness of other attendants? Have we not been taught in a Baraita: "Ye shall not make with Me" – Ye shall not make the likeness of My attendants which minister before Me on high, for example, the Ofanim, the Serafim, the Holy Beasts and the ministering angels?' To this the answer is given that the Torah forbids only the making of the likeness of attendants in the upper sphere but not those in the lower sphere (such as the moon). There follows a digression in which an attempt is made to distinguish between making the likeness of the moon for purposes of worship and for other purposes. The Gemara then asks, 'but is it permitted simply to make (i.e., not for the purpose of worship) the likeness of the moon? Have we not been taught in a Baraita: "Ye shall not make with Me" – Ye shall not make the likeness of My attendants which minister before Me,[6] for example, the sun, the moon, the stars and the planets?' To this the answer is given that the prohibition is only against making them, not against having them, and Rabban Gamaliel had them made for him by gentiles.

A casual glance at this *sûgyā* shows that four successive interpretations of 'Ye shall not make with Me' are quoted, the last three in name of a Baraita. These are:

I. Ye shall not make the likeness of My attendants.
2. Ye shall not make the likeness of My attendants *which minister before Me on high.*
3. Ye shall not make the likeness of My attendants which minister before Me on high, *for example, the Ofanim, the Serafim, the Holy Beasts and the ministering angels.*
4. Ye shall not make the likeness of My attendants which minister before Me, *for example, the sun, the moon, the stars and the planets.*[7]

Now it is surely stretching our definition of coincidence too far to suggest that there were four Baraitot (or three, if the first quotation is not a Baraita,[8]) each of which conveys only part of the full meaning of the text and this so fortuitously that the Baraitot could have been used in the *sugya* so as to work up to a climax the argument that is presented. The only convincing explanation is that originally there was only one Baraita which was divided up by the redactors (or elaborated on by them) in order to serve as bricks in the erection of their literary edifice. The most probable reading of the original Baraita was: 'Ye shall not make the likeness of My attendants which minister before Me on high.'[9] In stage 1) only the first part of this original Baraita is quoted (leaving out *ba-marom,* 'on high'); in stage 2) the full Baraita; in stage 3) the addition of the gloss beginning 'for example'; and, finally, in stage 4) the different gloss which serves to clinch the argument. At each stage a little more is revealed until the full force of the objection is conveyed![10]

Further evidence that the whole truth does not lie with Abraham Weiss's solution to our problem is provided by the following considerations.

Very frequently in the Babylonian Talmud a Mishnah is emended in order to avoid a difficulty presented by the unemended text. The standard formula for this is: *ḥesore meḥasra vehakhi katana* – 'the Mishnah is incomplete and should read as follows'.[11] Now, historically considered, it is clear that this kind of emendation is artificial and is a device adopted by the amoraim. If, therefore, the Gemara quotes a Baraita which accords in every detail with this kind of amoraic emendation this must be an anachronism and the inescapable conclusion is that the Baraita quoted is fictitious, at least in the form quoted. In tractate Bava Qamma 16a, for instance, Rabina makes such an emendation and this is supported by a Baraita which uses the very same words as Rabina! It is impossible to explain this phenomenon on the lines of Abraham Weiss's solution, i.e., that in a literary atmosphere sayings can easily be attributed to teachers of different generations. This can only be applied to sayings which could have originated in the tannaitic period but it obviously cannot apply to the use of a device unknown until the amoraic period.[12]

Berakhoth 39b

In this *sûgyā* there is a debate between R. Huna and R. Joḥanan whether the benediction over bread should be recited over a whole loaf or over a broken piece (i.e., where the broken piece has some other advantage such as size or quality.[13]) R. Naḥman b. Isaac said that the God-fearing man satisfies both requirements. The 'God-fearing man' is said to be Mar son of Rabina[14] who used to place the broken piece underneath the whole loaf and break bread over both of them. We are then told that a tanna taught in the presence of R. Naḥman b. Isaac: 'He should place the broken piece underneath the whole loaf and break bread and recite the benediction over both of them.' R. Naḥman b. Isaac then asks the tanna what his name is and he replies: 'Salmon.' Whereupon R. Naḥman says: 'Thy name is peace and thy teaching is perfect for thou hast made peace among the disciples.' Now if the Baraita quoted is an authentic tannaitic statement we would have the astonishing coincidence that the tannaitic procedure should have anticipated the practice which was only adopted generations later in order to satisfy the requirements of both amoraim, R. Huna and R. Joḥanan. Even if it be argued that already in tannaitic times the matter was debated and the compromise adopted (although this is extremely unlikely) it is surely stretching our definition of coincidence too far to say that after the compromise had been suggested by R. Naḥman b. Isaac the tanna Salmon should fortuitously have produced a Baraita with exactly the same compromise. The most probable explanation is that the Baraita is fictitious and was invented by Salmon. It is not impossible that the meaning of R. Naḥman's pun on the tanna's name is itself a hint that the master had seen through his pupil's subterfuge but approved of it none the less!

Of course, the type of Baraita we are considering here quoted by a tanna of the amoraic school is in a case of its own. Baraitot of this kind are frequently quoted in the Babylonian Talmud itself as inauthentic.[15] But here R. Naḥman b. Isaac does appear to accept the Baraita and does not resort to the usual formula of rejection. Hence, if we are correct, we have here a fictitious Baraita given none the less the semblance of authenticity in order 'to make peace among the disciples'.[16]

Megillah 24b

'R. Huna said: "A man with running eyes (*zebalgan*) should not lift up his hands (to deliver the priestly benediction)."' The Gemara asks: 'But was there not such a one in the neighbourhood of R. Huna who used to lift up his hands?' The Gemara replies: 'That one was familiar to the townspeople (*dash be-iro*)' i.e., the objection is because the people might be distracted by his unusual appearance but this would not apply to one with whom the townspeople were familiar. The Gemara then says: 'We have also been taught so in a Baraita: "A *zebalgan* should not lift up his hands but if he was familiar to the townspeople it is permitted."' The Gemara then remarks: 'R. Joḥanan said: "A person blind in one eye should not lift up his hands."' The Gemara asks: 'But was there not such a one in the neighbourhood of R. Joḥanan who used to lift up his hands?' To this the Gemara replies: 'That one was familiar to his townspeople.' The Gemara continues: 'We have been taught so in a Baraita: "A person blind in one eye should not lift up his hands but if he was familiar to the townspeople it is permitted."'

Now first we note the curious coincidence that both R. Huna and R. Joḥanan should have given a ruling having to do with the priestly benediction that was contradicted in their own neighbourhood. The most probable explanation is that there was doubt in the time of R. Huna and R. Joḥanan whether a *zebalgan* or a person blind in one eye may lift up his hands but these teachers did not object to such persons doing so in their vicinity. In all probability these teachers pointed out that they only permitted it because the persons concerned were familiar to their townspeople but that otherwise it would have been forbidden. The Gemara simply restates this in the form of question and answer. Or it is possible that R. Huna and R. Joḥanan simply tolerated these persons lifting up their hands because they saw no objection at any time to this and it is the Gemara which makes the distinction (between one familiar to the townspeople and one unfamiliar) and places this in the mouths of R. Huna and R. Joḥanan. In any event it seems certain that the distinction in these two cases arose out of actual incidents which occurred in the amoraic period. In that case it is surely stretching our definition of coincidence too far to suggest that quite fortuitously there happened to be two Baraitot which made this distinction, one with regard to the *zebalgan*, the other with regard to the man blind in one eye. The most plausible explanation is that the Baraitot are, in fact, fictitious, and *postdate* the amoraic distinction.

Of particular relevance to our discussion are the very frequent quotations of Baraitot in the form: 'In one Baraita it was taught… but in another it was taught…' and then an attempt is made to reconcile the Baraitot. Higger[17] gives a complete list of instances of this phenomenon. Higger notes that most of these Baraitot are not found elsewhere in the tannaitic literature! It is plausible to suggest that this is, in fact, an amoraic device, i.e., that the Baraitot, at least in the form in which they are quoted, are fictitious, and are introduced as a pedagogical aid, i.e., in order to qualify the statement or law under consideration. As a bare statement this may sound unlikely but the following examples make it more convincing.

Berakhoth 34b

One Baraita is quoted in which it is said that it is praiseworthy to bow during the thanksgiving benediction but in another Baraita it is said to be blameworthy. The Gemara declares that there is no contradiction: the one Baraita refers to the beginning of the benediction (when it is praiseworthy to bow) the other to the end. The Gemara goes on to say that Raba used to bow at both the beginning and the end of the thanksgiving benediction. When the Rabbis asked him why he did this he replied that he had witnessed R. Naḥman and R. Sheshet doing this. The Gemara objects: 'But have we not been taught in a Baraita that one who bows during the thanksgiving is blameworthy?' i.e., one of the previously quoted Baraitot says this and the proposed resolution of the contradiction by distinguishing between the beginning and the end is evidently not accepted by Raba and his teachers. To this the reply is given that the Baraita does not refer at all to the thanksgiving benediction (in the Amidah) but to the thanksgiving in Hallel: 'Give thanks unto the Lord for He is good' (Ps. 118:1). The Gemara objects: "But have we not been taught in another Baraita that one who bows during the thanksgiving *and* during the thanksgiving of Hallel is blameworthy?' i.e., this demonstrates that the first reference cannot be to the thanksgiving in Hallel. To this the reply is given that the reference is to the thanksgiving in the grace after meals.

We have in the *sûgyā* the following Baraitot:

1. One who bows in the thanksgiving is praiseworthy.
2. One who bows in the thanksgiving is blameworthy.
3. One who bows in the thanksgiving and in the thanksgiving of Hallel is blameworthy.

In the Tosefta[18] it is said that one should bow during the thanksgiving (*modim*)[19] at the beginning and the end, i.e., as Raba and his teachers did. This passage from the Tosefta is quoted in the Jerusalem Talmud[20] but more significantly it is quoted at the beginning of this very *sûgyā* in the Babylonian Talmud.[21]

If the Baraitot in the *sûgyā* are all authentic tannaitic productions we have the strange phenomena that they use a different term than the Tosefta for 'thanksgiving'; that they appear to contradict the Tosefta; that this contradiction is not noted, only the contradiction with Raba's practice; that one Baraita simply refers to the thanksgiving while the other refers to the thanksgiving *and* the thanksgiving of Hallel; and that it all fits so conveniently into the argument as developed in the *sûgyā*. But if it is accepted that the pedagogical device of the fictitious Baraita is common to all such instances in the Babylonian Talmud all the difficulties are removed. The whole *sûgyā* can then be seen as a comment in the form of a sustained argument on the original ruling of the Tosefta. It is as if the *sûgyā* is saying that while the Tosefta rules that one should bow at the beginning and the end of *modim,* one should not conclude from this that it is similarly praiseworthy to bow at other forms of thanksgiving. On the contrary, one must not bow at the thanksgiving of Hallel and grace after meals.

Makkoth 7b

The Mishnah[22] rules that if accidental homicide is caused by a downward movement (e.g., by someone coming down a ladder) the one guilty of it must go into banishment but if it is the result of an upward movement (e.g., by someone going up a ladder) he does not go into banishment. In the course of the discussion the

Gemara suggests that both these rulings embrace, too, the case of a butcher cutting meat, i.e., if he kills in a downward movement he goes into banishment but not if he kills in an upward movement. Four Baraitot are then quoted. They all begin with the words: 'If a butcher (killed) while cutting (the meat)' but they then give different rulings, namely: 1) In front he is liable, behind he is exempt, 2) Behind he is liable, in front he is exempt, 3) Whether in front or behind he is liable, 4) Whether in front or behind he is exempt. There is no contradiction, observes the Gemara. Ruling 1) deals with a downward stroke in front and an upward stroke behind; ruling 2) deals with a downward stroke behind and an upward stroke in front; ruling 3) deals with a downward stroke both in front and behind; and ruling 4) with an upward stroke both in front and behind. The Tosefta[23] states simply that if a butcher killed someone behind him he goes into banishment. But further on in the Tosefta[24] it is stated that if the butcher killed while cutting meat he does not go into banishment. It is clear from the Tosefta that the distinction between normal cutting (in front) and killing behind him while swinging his chopper is this, that in the first case so little care has been taken that it comes near to intentional homicide (*karov lemezid*) and banishment is only for unintentional homicide. That this is so can be seen from the Tosefta's comparison of the one case to that of a man who sits on a couch knowing full well that an infant is lying on it (and he smothers the infant) and the other to that of a man who sits on a couch without knowing that an infant is there.

Thus the distinction between a downward movement in front and a downward movement behind, etc., is not based at all on the Tosefta and would appear to be purely academic and amoraic. This only serves to increase the unlikelihood that there should be four actual Baraitot, each with a different ending, which can be fitted so neatly and conveniently into the amoraic scheme. But if the Baraitot are considered to be fictitious – in the nature of an amoraic pedagogical device to which we have called attention – everything falls quite naturally into place.

Qiddushin 48b

A Baraita is quoted beginning with the words: 'Be betrothed to me with this cup ... '[25] It is said that there are three Baraitot (i.e., three different versions of the original). In one it is said: 'With it (the cup itself) and with its contents,' i.e., the marriage is valid if the cup together with its contents amounts to the value of a *peruṭa* (the minimum amount for *qiddushin* to be effective) even if either is worth less than a *peruṭa*. In another Baraita it is said: 'With it and not with its contents', i.e., the contents are disregarded and the cup on its own must be worth a *peruṭa* for the marriage to be valid. In the third Baraita it is said: 'With its contents and not with it', i.e., the cup is disregarded and the contents on their own must be worth a *peruṭa* for the marriage to be valid. There is no contradiction, observes the Gemara. One Baraita refers to a cup containing water, one to a cup containing wine, and one to a cup containing oil.[26] Now it is not beyond the realm of possibility that there really were three actual Baraitot from the tannaitic period which the Gemara seeks to reconcile. But is it not more plausible by far to suggest that the concern of the Gemara is to state that there is no uniform rule in this matter since it all depends on the contents of the cup and that this is expressed by postulating three fictitious Baraitot? Abraham Weiss would evidently call this suggestion an accusation of 'forgery' but if, in fact, as we have suggested earlier, this was an established and acknowledged pedagogical device in such circumstance, there is no need to put forward anything at all resembling an accusation of forgery on the part of the editors but simply to call attention to a well-known means of pointing out distinctions in the form of question and answer.[27]

To sum up. While I. H. Weiss goes too far in postulating that so many of the Baraitot in the Babylonian Talmud are fictitious, Abraham Weiss is similarly in error in going to the opposite extreme. The evidence we have adduced goes to show that occasionally the redactors did use fictitious Baraitot for the purpose of literary device and as a pedagogical means. The talmudic *pilpul* seems to have demanded at times the working up of rules and subtle distinctions into the question and answer form for the sake of greater effectiveness. There is more than a little truth in the old gibe about the yeshiva student who said that he had a marvellous answer and was now looking for a suitable question.

NOTES

1. *Dor Dor veDorshav*, ii, 242–4.
2. Le-ḥeqer ha-Talmud (New York, 1954), pp. 35–63.
3. On the general question of the use of literary device in the Babylonian Talmud see my: *Studies in Talmudic Logic and Methodology* (London, 1961).

4. The version in 'Avodah Zarah adds here: 'which minister before me'.
5. Maimonides, *Yad HaHazaqah, Bet haBeḥirah* 7:10, in fact concludes that, according to the final argument of the Gemara, the Baraita regarding the copying of the Temple and its vessels has nothing to do with: 'Ye shall not make with Me' but is because of the different principle of "fearing the Temple" – *mora miqdash,* see the commentary of Meiri to this passage in Rosh Hashanah.
6. The version in 'Avodah Zarah adds here 'on high'.
7. In Mekhilta to Exod. 20:20, ed. Horowitz, p. 239, the reading is: 'Ye shall not make the likeness of My attendants which minister before Me on high – neither the likeness of the angels nor the likeness of the Ofanim nor the likeness of the Cherubim.'
8. Unless the original reading was *de-tanya* the quote here is best understood on the lines of Abraham Weiss's analysis that this interpretation of the verse was so well-known in the Babylonian schools that it was always automatically associated with the verse itself.
9. As in the first part of the Mekhilta quoted in note 7.
10. The procedure would be that of the novelist today who works out his plot first and then develops it gradually in order to keep the interest of his readers. It has been said that the detective story, for example, 'is written backwards'.
11. The standard methodologies differ as to whether the intention in such instances is really to emend the Mishnah or that this is simply a way of explaining the Mishnah, i.e., the Mishnah does not have to be read differently but this is what it means. For the first view: Rashi to Berakhoth 1b, s.v. *af ligemara;* Rashi to Megillah 28b, s.v. *he tzana* and the other sources quoted by Higger, *Otzar ha-Baraitot,* Vol. X (1948), 130–1. (Some of these are by no means conclusive.) For the opposite view see *Shelah, Torah she-be-al Peh,* s.v. *be-khamah mekomot.*
12. Note the use of the Aramaic *verabbanan* for the Sages instead of *veḥakhamim.* Cf. the emendation and the Baraita quoted in its support in Berakhoth 13b–14a. There, however, the solution is far less forced and artificial.
13. See the standard commentaries to this passage.
14. Cf. Shabbath 61a where Mar son of Rabina is similarly said to have satisfied both requirements when an issue was in doubt. The chronology of our passage is difficult. The meaning can only be that the later redactors applied R. Naḥman's saying to Mar son of Rabina.
15. Both I. H. Weiss, *Dor Dor veDorshav* ii, 242 and Abraham Weiss, *Le-ḥieqer ha-Talmud, loc. cit.,* discuss these Baraitot, see especially the complete list in Higger, *Otzar haBaraitot,* Vol. I (1938), Chapter 8, pp. 74–108.
16. The use of Aramaic in many Baraitot is not really germane to our problem. Even when it seems clear that these are amoraic additions in Aramaic to Baraitot worded in Hebrew these are in all probability *conscious* elaborations by the Amoraim and hence have nothing to do with our problem of the fictitious Baraita, i.e., these additions were not presented in the first instance as part of the Baraita but as amoraic elaborations. Higger, *Otzar haBaraitot,* Vol. I (1938), Chapter 9, pp. 109–24, quotes a number of such Baraitot, e.g., Berakhoth 27b–28a; Berakhoth 54a; Berakhoth 62b; Pesabim 50b; Pesahim 112b. Higger in these instances (we omit Aramaic popular sayings, incantations and the like which, as Higger observes, may well have been recorded originally in Aramaic) expresses doubts whether these were originally part of the Baraita or whether they are amoraic elaborations. It seems, in fact, certain from the style of these passages that they are amoraic elaborations and were never intended to be read as part of the Baraita quoted, but see note 12.
17. *Otzar haBaraitot*, Vol. IX (1946), pp. 113–24.
18. Berakhoth 1:2.
19. In the quote from the Tosefta given in the Gemara at the beginning of the *sûgyā* (Berakhoth 34a) the term used is *hoda'ah.*
20. Berakhoth 1 :5.
21. Berakhoth 34a.
22. Makkoth 2:1.
23. Makkoth 2:4.
24. Makkoth 2:6.
25. The source is Tosefta Qiddushin 2:3.
26. See the standard commentaries in order to determine which is which.
27. Relevant to our theme is the question of the comparison of Baraitot in the Babylonian

Talmud with versions in the Jerusalem Talmud. Further investigation is required but see, for example, the story of R. Eliezer and the Sages in Bava Meẓi'a' 59b compared with the version in Mo'ed Qaṭan 3:1. In the Jerusalem Talmud the story is told quite differently, is not quoted as a Baraita, and contains none of the little asides found in the Babylonian Talmud and typical of it. It might also be noted that there is less of the miraculous in the Jerusalem Talmud version and this fits in with our knowledge of the style and approach of the Jerusalem Talmud. But if this is so the only conclusion to be drawn is that the Baraita in the Babylonian Talmud in the form we have it is fictitious.

— 7 —

The Numbered Sequence as a Literary Device

Robert Gordis (1971, pp. 95–103) has demonstrated the use of the heptad as a literary device by the Biblical and Rabbinic authors. He avoids the risks in this kind of exercise by adducing evidence to show that these authors really had the numbered sequence in mind when they composed their works.

Without supplementary evidence it would be precarious in the extreme to conclude that the occurrence of a given number of instances in a literary unit is anything but coincidental. In any given case the number of examples listed, be it three, seven, or ten, may happen to be the actual number involved, and not a matter of literary style.

U. Cassuto (1959) has brilliantly suggested, for instance, that sequences of seven can be detected in the Pentateuchal narratives. He is often correct in seeing this pattern as a conscious striving for a literary usage based on this number. Yet in some instances, at least, coincidence cannot be ruled out. In general, there is little difficulty in discovering seven words or ideas recurring in any literary work. It is an amusing exercise to discover the number 'seven' in Cassuto's own writings.

If one should be on guard against finding the number seven when it is not really present, it is all the more necessary when the search is for a smaller number like three. The author may have adopted this number 'unconsciously', because of the natural tendency of the human mind to think of things in threes. Consequently, when the claim is advanced that the appearance of a given number in a text is an intentional literary form, one must adduce sufficient evidence to rule out sheer fortuitousness.

In his splendid pioneering essay on the theme of this article (1977), Shamma J. Friedman quotes, in the name of Jacob of Izbica (1910, p. 8), the following illustration of a numbered sequence as a conscious literary device in the Babylonian Talmud. The opening *sûgyā* in tractate *Pesaḥim* considers whether the term *'ôr* means 'day' or 'night'. There are fourteen proposed proofs: the first seven from Scripture, the second seven from early Rabbinic sources. In the first set of proofs, all the instances are advanced to demonstrate that *'ôr* means 'day', except for the fourth, the middle one, which argues that *'ôr* means 'night'. In the second set of proofs, all indicate that *'ôr* means 'night', except, again, for the fourth, the middle one, which is that *'ôr* means 'day'.

This example provides an excellent key to the proper methodology to be pursued in an inquiry of this kind. Two sets of seven proofs certainly suggest contrivance but it still remains somewhat conjectural. It becomes entirely convincing when it is seen that there is not only the seven sequence but the arrangement in a pattern of 3a-1b-3a; 3b-1a-3b. To attribute not only the numbered sequence itself but also the particular neat arrangement to coincidence is to be blind to the obvious.

I cannot pretend that all the following examples of numbered sequence in the Babylonian Talmud meet the same rigorous test as the above illustration (this is not always possible and much remains speculative) but I have tried to exercise as high a degree of caution as I can.

THREE

The use of this number as especially significant is widespread in the Rabbinic literature. We may begin with the series of sayings in sets of three in *Abot*[1] and proceed to the three patriarchs,[2] the three leaders (Moses, Aaron and Miriam)[3] and the three-fold division of Priests, Levites and Israelites.[4]

Friedman has provided important evidence for the use of the number three in the structure of the *sûgyā* in the Babylonian Talmud. What has not hitherto been noted, so far as I am aware, is the remarkable recurring expression in the Babylonian Talmud:[5] 'Hear from this three things' (*šemā' minnah telāt*) i.e. when inferences are drawn from a Tannaitic or other Rabbinic source it is always three, never more or less, that are drawn. The only explanation of this phenomenon is that it was the accepted procedure to draw three and only three conclusions from any given source; that is to say, it is a wholly contrived formulation in no way suggesting any real 'objective' examination of the source for the purpose of discovering the conclusions to be drawn from it.

Another three-formulation is found when a statement is made regarding which authority is to be followed in practice. Unless there is a strong element of pure formality and contrivance, it is difficult to see why three and only three exceptions are generally stated: 'In all cases our master followed the view of Rab except in three where he followed the view of Samuel';[6] 'The ruling is in accordance with Rabbah against R. Joseph except for three cases'[7] 'The ruling is in accordance with R. Joḥanan against Resh Lakish except for three cases';[8] 'Wherever the views of Rabban Simeon b. Gamaliel occur in our Mishnah they are followed except in three cases';[9] 'The ruling is in accordance with Raba aginst Abbaye except in the cases of *ya'al qegam*'[10] (i.e., two sets of three, although this in all probablility Saboraic). Unless there is a formal pattern to all this (i.e. the rules of the game demand that there must always be an exception of three or a multiple of three) it is hard to see why an authority whose opinion is valued should not be followed in three and only three cases. It is, however, possible that the formalism in these instances is not due to the use of a literary device by the editors. There may have been a tacit understanding in the Babylonian schools that it is unfair to his opponents to give the total victory to one teacher. For his protagonist to be protected from complete humiliation, deference must be paid to the protagonist's opinion in three cases. In any event the use of three is not arbitrary but intentional.

The number three is pervasive in the realm of Aggadah, as the following examples show. 'A certain Gallilean preached: 'Blessed is the All-merciful who gave a three-fold Torah to a three-fold people through three persons on the third day of the third month.'[11] 'Scholars are wont to depart from the strict truth in three matters.'[12] All a man's expenses are fixed at the beginning of the year except for the amount he spends on Sabbaths, Festivals and the education of his children.'[13] 'One who loves scholars … One who respects scholars … One who fears scholars … '[14] 'There are three who go down to Hell … '[15] 'Three persons made an improper request …'[16] Many further examples can be easily be adduced.

Far greater caution must be exercised before a three-fold

division can be detected in the structure of the *sûgyā* since here the three sequence is not stated explicitly.[17] There are, however, so many instances of a three-fold pattern that its very ubiquitousness does suggest that the pattern was consciously adopted. It is obviously impossible within the limits of an article to examine all the *sûgyôt* in the Babylonian Talmud. Pending further investigation, the following examples may serve as pointers. These are illustrations of what appears to be an intentional striving for a three-fold pattern in the opening *sûgyôt* of tractate *Qiddušin.* In 4a, a Baraita is quoted and a difficulty raised to which *three* replies are given: by Rabbah, Abbaye and Mar bar R. Aahi. In 5b a Baraita is quoted where the implications of the first clause seem to be in contradiction to those of the second clause and *three* possible solutions are advanced. In 6a a Baraita states six different formulae for betrothal, all of which are valid, but these are not presented as a list of six but of two lists, each containing three items. The reason is given: 'The Tanna heard them in threes and thus he recorded them.' 6b–7a discusses *three* cases in which indirect giving of the betrothal money by the man to the woman is valid. In 7b *three* betrothal problems, all of the same type, are presented: by Raba, R. Pappa and R. Ashi. In 8b a Baraita is quoted containing three betrothal laws, all of the same nature. To each of these an Amoraic comment is added, again, all of the same nature. In 8b–9a *three* cases are recorded of a man asking a woman if she will agree to be his betrothed to which she gave an ambiguous reply. In each case the same ruling is given: twice by R. Hama and once by R. Zabid. This latter illustration would, in itself, prove nothing. It may be that, although each ruling is identical with the others, the editors saw fit to record all three simply because there happened to be three rulings. But since the pattern can be detected in so many instances, does it not become more plausible to suggest that in the Talmudic *sûgyā* we have a literary work, the structure of which requires this particular pattern?

The following examples, taken at random from various *sûgyôt,* would seem to strengthen our case. In *Pesaḥim* 7b *three* proofs are presented on the question whether the benediction to be recited over the search for leaven is *lebāʿēr* or *'al biʿûr* and then *three* proof-texts are quoted to show that the term *'ober* means 'before'. In *Berak̲ot* 3b–4a *three* solutions are provided to deal with an apparent contradiction about David rising at midnight: by R. Oshea, R. Zera and R. Ashi. The further question is then raised: since Moses did not know when it was midnight how could David have known? To this *three* replies are given: by the anonymous Gemara, by R. Zera and by R. Ashi. Later on in the same passage, *three* examples are given of those who feared that a divine promise given to them may not be realized because they had sinned: David, the patriarch Jacob (given, incidentally, by R. *Jacob* bar Iddi)[18] and the people as a whole. In *Pesaḥim* 42b three *Bāraitôt* are quoted, each beginning with: 'Let a man sell all he possesses in order to marry the daughter of a scholar.' In Bêcāh 25b *three* plants serve to rebuke three different types of sinners and there are *three* creatures who are brazen. *Pesaḥim* 3b questions the propriety of Abigail 'riding' (when she should have sat side-saddle as befits a modest woman). To this *three* replies are given: because she was afraid that she would otherwise have fallen off, in fear of the night or in fear of David or in fear of the steepness of the mountain. In *Sotah* 4b *three* replies are given to the question how could Ben Azzai, a bachelor, have known the details of the marital act. In *Ta'anit* 11b and *'Abodah Zarah* 34a it is related that when Mar Ukba came to Ganzaka they put *three* questions to him which he was unable to answer. The point to be noted here is that the three questions have no connection with one another and, it would seem, that they simply follow the demand of the three-fold pattern.[19] In *Pesaḥim* 119a the verses of Psalm 118 are said to have been uttered by David, his brothers, Jesse, Samuel or all them together. The distribution is: DJBS; BDJS; ASDA (Samuel, David, all of them). There are thus *three* sets of four and, moreover, David is the first in the first set, the second in the second set and the third in the third set.

FIVE

The significance of the number five in the Jewish tradition is undoubtedly to be attributed to the Pentateuch.[20] The following examples of its use in what appears to be a contrived manner in the Babylonian Talmud are taken at random. In *Ḥullin* 2a–3b an apparent contradiction is noted in the first Mishnah of the tractate. *Five* solutions are attempted: by Rabbah bar Ulla; Rabina; Abbaye; Raba and R. Ashi. In *Ḥullin* 16b a saying about the *five* acts for which a reed may not be used is attributed either to a Baraita or to R. Hisda. *Ḥullin* 27a–b discusses the Scriptural basis for the requirement that the act of *šeḥiṭāh* takes the form of a cut at the animal's neck. *Five* possible proofs are quoted: by R. Kahana; R. Yemar; the School of R. Ishmael; R. Hiyya and 'another Tanna'. In *Hullin* 29a there arefive attempted proofs on the organ of a fowl to be severed in the act of *šeḥîṭāh.* In *Ḥullin* 29a there are *five* replies to the question, which clause of the Mishnah deals with a sacred animal and which with a non-sacred animal: by R. Kahana; R. Simi bar Ashi; R. Pappa; R. Ashi and R. Simeon b. Lakish. *Ḥullin* 43a records *five* different laws regarding *ṭerêp̄āh* stated by R. Isaac b. Joseph in the name of R. Johanan.

We have noted above the sermon of the Gallilean in *Šabbat* 88a in which there is a series of threes. Here it should be noted that there are five threes: 1) a three-fold Torah; 2) a three-fold people; 3) through three persons; 4) on the third day; 5) of the third month. In *Nedarim* 6b-7a on the question of 'indication' (*yad*) *five* problems are set: 1) betrothal; 2) *Pe'ah;* 3) almsgiving; 4) *hep̄qēr;* 5) a privy. In *Yoma* 6b–7b in the debate between R. Nahman and R. Sheshet regarding a sacrifice when the community is in a state of ritual contamination five proofs are attempted. There are five different interpretations in *Sukkah* 6b of the debate between R. Simeon and the Sages. In *Ḥullin* 8b–9a the *sûgyā* is constructed around *five* sayings of R. Judah in the name of one of his teachers, Rab and Samuel. In *Megillah* 22a there are five attempted proofs on the question of whether it is permitted to sell a Scroll of the Torah in order to buy another.

SEVEN

Seven is the sacred number *par excellence,* appearing in such passages as the creation narrative; in Pentecost at the end of seven weeks; in the Sabbatical and Jubilee years; in the seven days of the Festivals and in many other instances in the Bible and the Rabbinic literature.[21] Apart from the explicit reference to 'seven rulings' (*šeb šema'tātā*)[22] and other passages in which the number seven is stated explicitly, it can be detected as present implicitly in the structure of the *sûgyā* as the following examples suggest.

In *Niddah* 13a there is a curious story about Samuel instructing his disciple, R. Judah, on the roof of a synagogue, to take hold of his genitals when passing water. It is objected, surely this is forbidden because it may awaken lustful thoughts. Abbaye replies that lustful thoughts are banished where there is fear or dread and it is, therefore, permitted. The question is then asked, what fear or dread was there in those circumstances. To this *seven* replies are given. Some of these are very artificial so that it is plausible to suggest that the sole purpose of listing all of them is to make up the number seven. In *Pesaḥim* l0b Raba sets a series of problems regarding the search for leaven before Passover. These are: 1) the mouse; 2) the infant; 3) the mouse enters; 4) 'If you will say'; 5) 'If you will say'; 6) 'If you will say'; 7) a further problem set by Raba in three parts. There are thus six items which together with the final unit of three make a total of *seven*. In *Sotah* 17b–18a we find an almost identical pattern. Here there are six statements regarding the scroll of a wife suspected of infidelity (*megillat Sotah*): 1) at night: 2) backwards; 3) before the abjuration; 4) as a letter; 5) two sheets; 6) one letter written, one erased; 7) then a further problem set by Raba in three parts. It is hard to believe that two quite separate Talmudic passages, dealing with totally different questions, should have had their material arranged in precisely the same way unless it is by contrivance and in obedience to the seven-fold pattern. In *Roš haššanah* 7a the question is discussed, how do we know that Nisan is the first month. *Seven* suggestions are advanced: 1) by anonymous Gemara; 2) by R. Hisda; 3) by Rabina; 4) by Rabbah bar Ulla; 5) by R. Kahana; 6) by R. Aha bar Jacob; 7) by R. Ashi. In *Berakot* 6b there is a list of *seven* items each beginning with the words: 'The reward of ...': 1) R. Zera; 2) Abbaye; 3) Raba; 4) R. Pappa; 5) Mar Zutra; 6) R. Sheshet; 7) R. Ashi. *Berakot* 7b records *seven* sayings of R. Johanan in the name of R. Simeon b. Yohai. The lengthy *sûgyā* in *Baba Qamma* 56b–76b records the discussion between Rabbah and R. Joseph on the legal status of one who looks after a lost article he has found and *seven* attempted proofs are given. Similarly, in the debate between Abbaye and Raba in *Qiddušin* 51a–52b *seven* attempted proofs are recorded. Again, in the discussion around the debate between R. Haninah b. Rabban Gamaliel and R. Meir, on whether the statement of a positive implies an automatic rejection of the negative, in *Qiddušin* 61b–62a, there are *seven* attempted proofs from Scripture. Yet again, in *Pesaḥim* 46a–48b there is a lengthy debate between R. Huna and R. Hisda regarding 'potentiality' and there are seven attempted proofs. *Pesaḥim* 102b–103a discusses the order of the benedictions when a Festival falls at the termination of the Sabbath. The four benedictions to be recited are: *Yayîn* ('wine'); *Nēr* ('light'); *Haḥadālāh* ('distinguishing') and *Qiddûš* ('sanctification'). *Seven* opinions are recorded in the Amoriac debate as to the correct order of these benedictions: 1) YQNH; 2) YNHQ; 3) YHNQ; 4) QNYH; 5) QYNH; 6) NQYH; 7) NYHQ. In *Pesaḥim* 108a there are *seven* discussions regarding reclining at the Passover Seder: 1) *maccāh;* 2) *mārôr;* 3) wine; 4) lying down; 5) right hand; 6) women; 7) son. In *Šabbat* 18b–119a *seven* Amoraim boast of their special virtues, each beginning with the same words: 'May I be rewarded'. A similar list of Amoraim in *Šabbat* 119a, each of whom did something special as a personal preparation for the Sabbath, contains fourteen names, twice *seven.* Again, in *Megillah* 27b–28a *seven* Amoraim explain the virtues to which they attribute their long life. The majority of these are in threes and in the *seventh* one there are *seven* items. In the lengthy *sûgyā* in *Baba Qamma* 2b–3b the discussion centres the statement of R. Pappa that one of the derivatives of the main categories of damage is unlike the category from which it is derived. The Gemara, seeking to discover to which main category R. Pappa refers, examines each in turn in the following order: 1) *qeren* ('horn'); 2) *šēn* ('tooth'); 3) *regel* ('foot'); 4) *bôr* ('pit'); *5) mab'eh* ('spoilator'); 6) *'eš* ('fire'). Unsuccessful in applying R. Pappa's statement to any of these, the Gemara reverts to a more detailed examination of *regel,* which then becomes the seventh in the list examined. In *Baba Qamma* 11a–b there are *seven* rulings of Ulla in the name of R. Eleazar and these have no connection with one another apart from the fact that they belong in a list of *seven.*

TEN

The number ten is significant in Scripture in the Decalogue and the tithing system; in the Rabbinic literature, in the quorum for prayer, the *minyān.*[23] Obviously only the lengthier *sûgyôt* lend themselves to a sequence of ten but there are some apparent instances of this structure. In the complicated *sûgyā* in *Yoma* 13a–b concerning the question of how the High Priest can have a wife in reserve, without having two wives at the same time, there is involved argument and counter-argument. A suggestion is put forward only to be refuted immediately. A careful examination reveals a series of *ten* suggestions and refutations. In *Ḥullin* 11a–b ten Amoraim give their suggestion as to how the principle of reliance on probability is derived from Scripture. *Berakot* 16b–17a contains a list of the private prayers which various Amoraim recited after their formal prayers. There are *ten* Amoraim in the list. *Pesaḥim* 9b–10b presents a number of problematical cases regarding the search for leaven before Passover, each of which is found to have a parallel in a Tannaitic source. The cases are: 1) nine heaps; 2) where one was separated; 3) two heaps; 4) one heap; 5) doubt of entry; 6) entered and searched; 7) entered and found; 8) he left nine; 9) he left ten; 10) he left one in a corner; making a total of *ten* problems. In the debate between Hezekiah and R. Abbahu in *Pesaḥim* 21b–23b *ten* attempted proofs are offered, all in favour of Hezekiah, after which it is suggested that their debate has been anticipated by Tannaim.

THIRTEEN

The number thirteen has special significance in Rabbinic thought in the thirteen attributes of divine mercy[24] and in thirteen hermeneutical principles of the School of R. Ishmael.[25] Naturally, with regard to such a large number as thirteen, even more than with regard to ten, it would be too much to expect to find many *sûgyôt* lengthy enough to adapt themselves to this sequence. The following, however, should be noted.

There are *thirteen* items in the list in *Qiddušin* 49a with the formula: 'Ten measures of . . . nine were taken by . . . '[26] In *Baba Qama* 4b R. Oshea teaches that there are *thirteen* main categories of damage. A particularly interesting example of *thirteen* is found in *Ḥagigah* 4b–5a. Here there is a list of *thirteen* Amoraim each of whom wept when he came upon a particular Scriptural verse speaking of God's judgements. The names are: 1) R. Huna; 2) R. Huna; 3) R. Eleazar; 4) R. Eleazar; 5) R. Ammi; 6) R. Ammi; 7) R. Assi; 8) R. Joseph; 9) R. Joḥanan; 10) R. Joḥanan; 11) R. Joḥanan; 12) R. Joḥanan; 13) R. Joḥanan. A pattern can be perceived in the list itself. There are five 'weepings' of R. Joḥanan and two each of R. Huna, R. Eleazar and R. Ammi. The odd ones out are: 7) and 8), one each of R. Assi and R. Joseph. But if we read 7) as R. Joseph (and there is, indeed such a reading)[27] we have four sets of two each and then the set of five of R. Joḥanan. It is easy to see how the incorrect reading came about – Assi is similar in sound to Ammi in 6) and to Yosef in 8). If this is correct we have an example of a highly artificial, carefully constructed list – four sets of teachers with two 'weepings' each and five of R. Joḥanan, totalling *thirteen.* It is going beyond the evidence but is it possible that there is a hint in the structure of the *thirteen* qualities of divine mercy? This would be appropriate enough in connection with the teachers weeping when they came across Scriptural passages which speak of the divine sternness!

The implications of the above passage in *Ḥagigah,* and the other examples of a numbered sequence in which the names of Amoraim occur, are startling. That the editors of an anonymous passage structured their material occasions no surprise. But when they use the names of Amoraim it can only mean that they have reworked the original sayings so as to fit them into their structure. It is extremely unlikely that by pure coincidence the saying happened to fit the pattern. It can only mean that they were made to fit the pattern either by a selective process or by attributing sayings to certain teachers for the purpose of literary effect.[28] The detection of literary patterns thus not only assists in the task of textual criticism (as in the above illustration from R. Assi and R. Joseph) but is important in determining how the Babylonian Talmud came to assume its present form and how the final editors shaped their material.

We have produced some evidence for the existence of numbered structures as a literary device in the Babylonian Talmud. But, of course, this is not the only structure used by the editors and it would be unreasonable to expect to discover a consistent use of this type of structure. In the presentation of the Talmudic arguments other considerations (such as a contrived development of the course of the debate) may have demanded that an otherwise desirable sequence be abandoned. All we can claim is that the numbered sequence is one of the literary devices used by the editors. There does seem to be a preference for the 'sacred' numbers of three, five, seven, ten and thirteen and an avoidance, where possible, of the even numbers, two, four, six and eight, perhaps because of the belief in the baneful power of even numbers – *zûggôt.*[29] It must also be added that, in any event, this kind of inquiry is frequently hindered because of the uncertain state of the text. At this late date it is often quite impossible to recover the original text so that in some instances an original pattern may be obscured by a faulty text. There is also the problem of editorial revisions of the original text, to say nothing of editorial additions. A strong element of tentativeness must, therefore, remain. But if this article has succeeded in providing a stimulus for further investigation into an important but largely neglected field of Talmudic study it will have fulfilled its purpose.

NOTES

1. E.g. 'they said three things' (*Abot* 1:1); 'The world exists on three things'(1:2) and the sets of three sayings further in *Abot*. For the numbered sequence in the Mishna, see Neusner (1977).
2. See e.g. 'one only calls three by the name patriarch', *Berakot* 16b.
3. See Mic 6:3; *Šabbat* 88a; *Ta'anît* 9a.
4. See, e.g., Mishnah *Ta'ani* 4:1; *Baba Qamma* 38a.
5. *Berakot* 27a; *Šabbat* 40b; *'Erubin* 10a; *Pesaḥim* 4a; 5b; 97a; 107a; *Becah 35b; Mo'ed* Qatan 16a; 20b; *Yebamot* 46b; *Ketubot* 21 b; 90b; *Nedarim* 7b; 8b; *Qiddušin* 7a; 46a; *Baba Meci'a* 63a; *Baba Batra* 24a; *Sanhedrin* 19a; *'Abodah Zarah* 43a; *Zebaḥim* 78a; *Menaḥot* 42b; *Ḥullin* 106a; *Niddah* 30a. Cf. the note of R. Akiba Eger *(Gîlyon haššas)* to *Nedarim* 7b that a fourth rule could have been derived. Also see *Qiddušin* 52a: four things could be derived from the Mishnah but Rab seized hold of three! The sole exception is *Pesaḥim* 105b, where eight matters are derived. However, this is in a category of its own, since it is more in the nature of a mere list of items than an actual series of derivations.
6. *Šabbat* 22a; 40a; *Pesaḥim* 10la; *Menaḥot* 41b. Cf. 'The ruling is in accordance with Rab in these three, whether he takes the stricter or the more lenient view,' *Becah* 4b.
7. *Baba Batra* 11 4b.
8. *Yebamot* 36a.
9. *Ketubot* 77a.
10. *Qiddušin* 52a; *Baba Meci'a* 22b; *Sanhedrin* 27a. Cf. 'all instances except three', *Šabbat* 3a; the three rules of Šamuel's father, *Šabbat* 65a; the three offences for which martyrdom is demanded, *Pesaḥim* 25a–b; the three venerable sages whom people follow, *Berakot* 22a; the three rules given to Moses at Sinai, *Te'anit* 3a.
11. *Šabbat* 88a.
12. *Baba Meci'a* 23b.
13. *Becah* 17a see note of B. Ransburg (Vilna edition) that in the parallel passage in the Midrash *Rôš Ḥodeš* is also included. But if *three* is intentional in the Babylonian Talmud it would explain why *Ros Ḥodes* is not counted since to include it would result in one time too many.
14. *Šabbat* 23b.
15. *Baba Meci'a* 58b.
16. *Ta'anit* 4a and see 2a for the three keys. The following are instances of the use of three in the Tannaitic literature: *Berakot* 3a: 'I learned from him three things . . . three times a day … I destroyed My house … (three items)'; ibid. 'Three reasons why one must not enter a ruin'; Mishnah *Pesaḥim* 3:4 'Three women … '; *Becah* 32b 'Three have no life …'; *Ḥagigah* 3b three conditions for determining whether a man is an imbecile; *Ḥagigah* 16a six chacteristics of demons, three resembling those of angels, three those of humans; *Pesaḥim* 42b the six of Hezekiah, three disapproved of by the Sages; *Šabbat* 88b three characteristics of the *ne'elābîm;* Mishnah *Baba Meci'a* 4:10 three illustrations of 'wronging with words' (in the Baraita *Baba Mecia* 58b there are five); Mishnah *Šabbat* 2:6–7; Mishnah *Gittin* 9:4. Some further illustrations from the Amoraim in the Babylonian Talmud are: *Berakot* 31 a three examples of a fixed law; *Qiddusîn* 11a three cases where the distinction applies; *Ketubot* 111a the three oaths; *Pesaḥim* 62b 'If Beruriah … who learnt *three* hundred … from *three* hundred … and yet in *three* years …and you … in *three* months'; *Pesaḥim* 85b 'the *three* who are haughty and the three-fold reply: Not your cup …your wine … and my stomach'.
17. See examples given by Friedman, op. cit., pp. 392–3. Some further examples are: *Mo'ed Qatan* 18b, three proofs regarding *hot ha-moed; Qiddûšîn* 43a; three different reasons for Shammai's opinion; *Qiddušin* 35a, three proofs that negative precepts are binding upon women; *Quiddušin* 43a–b, a set of three cases; *Qiddušin* 50b–51a, a set of three proofs. Also relevant to our theme is the whole idea of presumptive state *(ḥazākāh)* being established by a three-fold occurence, see *'Encîqlopidîyah Talmûdît* (1970, pp. 453 ff.).
18. On the phenomenon of a teacher making a statement on a theme bearing his own name see Jacobs (1977, pp. 56–57, n. 30).
19. Even if the correct reading is not Mar Ukba but R. Akiba (see Rashi and Malter, 1928, p. 79) this text is obviously Amoraic, not Tannaitic.
20. For the Tannaitic literature see, e.g., Mishnah *Baba Qamma* 1:4, a set of five; Mishnah *Baba*

Meci'a 4:1, five instances; 4:7, five *perûtôt;* 4:8, five fifths; Mishnah *Megillah* 3:3, five matters in connection with a disused synagogue. In the Amoraic literature see e.g. *Šabbat* 60b, five and five are beautiful.

21. Gordis (1971) gives the following illustrations from the Mishnah where the number seven, though not stated explicitly, is clearly implied: seven who are beyond redemption, *Sanhedrîn* 10: 3–6; seven punished by strangulation, *Sanhedrîn* 11:1; seven types of idolatrous worship, *Sanhedrîn* 7:6; fourteen (twice seven) who are punished by stoning, *Sanhedrîn* 7:4; the fourteen ages of man, *'Abot* 5:21. Some further examples in the Tannaitic literature are: Mishnah *Pesaḥim* 3:1, seven items mentioned (see *Pesaḥim* 42b for how these are divided); *Qiddušin* 49a, list of 'on the condition that ...' (seven items if *caddîq* and *rāšā'* are counted as one, as logically they should be); *Pesaḥim* 117a, 'Who said this Hallel?' (seven opinions); *Pesaḥim* 54a, 'seven things created ... seven things hidden ...'; *Baba Qamma* I 7a, seven creatures who change after seven years; *Sanhedrîn* 56b, the seven Noahide laws. It is worth noting that the Mishnah *Makkot* 3:9 gives an example of one who carries out a single act of ploughing and yet transgresses in the process no fewer than eight negative precepts. The Gemara (*Makkot* 21b–22a) is hard put to find eight when there would appear to be only seven. Is it possible that seven is avoided intentionally by the Mishnah so as not to associate this 'sacred' number with transgression?
22. *'Erubin* 43a; *Ḥullin* 42a. Some further illustrations from the Amoraic literature are: *Šabbat* 31a, Resh Lakish and Raba, seven items; *Šabbat* 60b, seven and seven are beautiful. Friedman (pp. 89b–90b) gives: *Baba Batra* 127b–128b, seven cases; *Yebamot* 37b–38a, seven cases; *Yebamot* 97b, seven cases. It is perhaps worth noting in passing that Strauss (1974, pp. xi–xiii) claims to have detected the use of the heptad by Maimonides for his arrangement of his guide. The work consists of seven sections, each divided into seven sub-sections, and the only section which does not permit this arrangement is divided into seven chapters. And of course, Maimonoides' *Mišneh Tôrah* consists of fourteen books.
23. Mishnah *Megillah* 4:3; *Berakot* 21b. Cf. *Sanhedrîn* 74b. There is a series of ten in the Mishnah *'Abot* 5:1–6 and ten *yohasîn* in *Mishnah Qiddušin* 4:1.
24. *Roš haššanāh* 17b. A famous instance of thirteen is the age for *micvot, 'Abot* 5:21.
25. *Sifra,* Introduction. That there is a connection between the thirteen qualities (*middot*) of mercy and the thirteen hermeneutical principles is noted in the Zohar *(Ra'yā Mehēmānā)* III, 228a. Cf. note of R. Margaliot (1973, pp. 217–19). Historically considered, it would appear that the whole notion of thirteen qualities of mercy is an Aggadic association with the thirteen hermeneutical principles. The latter are Tannaitic and hence the earlier of the two sets of *middôt.* (See the standard commentaries to *Roš haššanāh* 17b for the difficulty of finding thirteen qualities in the verse except by an artificial division of words.) On the question of thirteen as a specially significant number see the unhistorical but useful summary by Waldinberg (1978, pp. 13–15), where the following are noted: R. Simeon b. Yohai and his son spent thirteen years in the cave hiding from the Romans, *Šabbat* 33b; the thirteen siftings of the *'omēr, Menaḥot* 76b; and, in post-Talmudic literature, the association by Horowitz (1963, *ša'ar ha'otiyyôt,* p. 42c) of the thirteen hermeneutical principles with Maimonides' thirteen principles of the faith. It is, indeed, plausible to suggest that this is the reason why Maimonides chose the number thirteen.
26. Cf. *Baba Qamma* 27b on the fines for assault, *three, five* and *thirteen.* In Mishnah *Ta'anit* 1:4 there are three fasts; in 1:5 a further three; in 1:6 a further three and then seven, making a total of thirteen. A brief note on some other numbers in the Rabbinic literature is here in order. For the number one thousand see Sevin (1978, pp. 276–80). In *Ta'anit* 8a Resh Lakish states the significance of the number forty, because it corresponds to the forty days during which God taught Moses the Torah, and R. Ada bar Ahaba states the significance of the number twenty-four, because it corresponds to the twenty-four books of the Bible. These two numbers are used in the Rabbinic literature in contexts dealing with the study of the Torah, e.g., 'He repeated the teaching forty times' in *Berakot* 28a and freq.; the twenty-four questions and answers in the story of R. Johanan and Resh Lakish in *Baba Meci'a* 84a and the twenty-four rows of disciples in *Megillah* 28b. The significance of the number forty-eight in *'Abot* 6:5 (the forty-eight ways by means of which the Torah is acquired) is probably because this number is twice twenty-four, i.e., a double effort is required if the study of the Torah is to be effective. In *Baba Qamma* 92a–93a there is a lengthy list of sayings by Raba to Rabbah bar Mari but it is impossible

to tell whether the number of these (seventeen) is intentional (seven and ten) or purely fortuitous.

27. Dimitrovsky (1979, Vol. II, p. 263).
28. On the pseudepigraphic nature of a good deal of the Babylonian Talmud see Jacobs (1977, pp. 46–59).
29. On *zûggôt* the *locus classicus* is *Pesaḥim* 109b–110b. See especially I I0a on ten as immune from the baneful effect of even numbers and the discussion regarding four, six and eight. Cf. *'Encîqlopidîyah Talmûdît* (1967, pp. 16–19). Of some relevance may be the statement in 110b that in Palestine they took no notice of *zûggôt,* the fear of them being only entertained in Babylon.

BIBLIOGRAPHY

Cassuto, U. 1959. *Me'ādam c'ad No'ah.* Jerusalem.

Dimitrovsky, H. Z. (ed.). 1979. *Serîdê baḇlî.* New York.

Eger, A. *Gilyôn haššas.*

Friedman, S. 1977. *'Miḇnē sifrûtî besûgyôt habbāḇlî' Proceedings of Sixth World Conference for Jewish Studies.* pp. 387–402, Jerusalem.

Gordis, R. 1971. 'The Heptad as an Element of Biblical and Rabbinic Style'. *Poets, Prophets and Sages,* pp. 75–103. Bloomington and London.

Horowitz, I. 1963. *Šenê lûḥôt habberît.* Jerusalem.

Jãcob o Izbica. 1910. *Šeder haggādāh šel pesaḥ 'im sefer hazzemannîm.* Lublin.

Jacobs, L. 1977. 'How Much of the Babylonian Talmud is Pseudepigraphic?' *Journal of Jewish Studies,* pp. 46–59.

Malter, H. 1928. *The Tractate Tacanît of the Babylonian Talmud.* Philadelphia.

Margaliot, R. (ed.) 1973. *Sêfer Ḥas îdîm.* Jerusalem.

Neusner, J. 1977. *A History of the Mishnaic Law of Purities,* Vol. 21. Leiden.

Ransberg, B. Marginal Notes in Vilna, Romm, edition of the Babylonian Talmud.

Sevin, S. (ed.) 1967 and 1970. *'Ensiqlopidia talmudît.* Jerusalem.

Sevin, S. 1978. *le'ôr hahalāḵā.* Jerusalem.

Strauss, L. 1974. *The Guide of the Perpkxed,* trans. S. Pines. Chicago and London.

Waldinberg, E. 1978. *Šiš 'El'îezer.* Jerusalem.

— 8 —

The *Sûgyā* on Sufferings in B. Berakhot 5a, b

The *sûgyā* we examine here opens with a homily by the third-century Palestinian Amora, R. Simeon b. Lakish, who is reported as saying: 'Whoever occupies himself with the Torah, sufferings depart from him', for which the proof-text is provided: 'And the sons of Reshef fly upwards (*'uf*)' (Job 5:7; English version: 'as the sparks fly upwards'). R. Simeon b. Lakish quotes the verse: 'Wilt thou set (*hata'uf*) thine eyes upon it? it is gone' (Prov. 23:5) which, traditionally. refers to the Torah.[1] Consequently, by analogy with *hata'uf*, the word *'uf* is made to refer to the Torah. He quotes further the verse: 'The wasting of hunger, and the devouring of the fiery bolt (*reshef*) and bitter destruction' (Deut. 32:24) to yield the thought that 'the sons of Reshef' are sufferings. Thus the verse is interpreted homiletically as: 'The sons of Reshef (sufferings) fly (away) (because of) *'uf* (the Torah).' R. Joḥanan objects that every schoolboy knows of the idea conveyed by R. Simeon b. Lakish since it is implied in a verse in the Torah (i.e. and no complicated homily is required for this purpose). The verse is: 'And he said: If thou wilt diligently hearken to the voice of the Lord thy God, and wilt do that which is right in His eyes, and wilt give ear to His commandments, and keep all his statutes, I will put none of the diseases upon thee, which I have put upon the Egyptians; for I am the Lord that healeth thee' (Ex. 15:26). Thus, argues R. Joḥanan, there is no need for R. Simeon b. Lakish's exegesis since the lesson in stated explicitly in the Torah. R. Joḥanan continues that if a lesson is to be derived, on the lines of R. Simeon b. Lakish's exegesis, regarding the connection between the study of the Torah and sufferings, it is that whoever does not occupy himself with the Torah, when he is able to do so, God brings sufferings upon him. R. Joḥanan's proof-text is: 'I was dumb with silence, I held my peace, had no good (*tov*), and my pain was stirred' (Ps. 39:3). From the verse: 'For I give you good (*tov*) doctrine; forsake ye not My Torah' (Prov. 4:2) we observe that 'good' (*tov)* refers to the Torah. Thus, according to R. Joḥanan, the verse in Psalms can be understood to mean: 'When I was silent and had no *good* (i.e. no engagement in Torah study) my pain was stirred.' R. Simeon b. Lakish's teaching is that when a man occupies himself with the Torah God causes sufferings to depart from him, whereas R. Joḥanan's teaching is that when a man does not occupy himself with the Torah, God brings sufferings upon him. According to R. Simeon b. Lakish's teaching it does not follow that because sufferings depart when man studies the Torah that they come upon him when he does not study the Torah. But according to R. Joḥanan both propositions are true. When a man studies the Torah, sufferings depart from him, as taught in the Exodus verse known to every schoolboy, and when he does not study the Torah, sufferings come upon him, as is implied by the homily on the verse in Psalms.

There now follows a saying of R. Zera, 'or, in another version, R. Ḥanina bar Pappa': 'Come and see that the attribute of the Holy One, blessed be He, differs from that of a human being. The attribute of a human being is that when a man sells something to his fellow, the seller is sad (because, in his need for ready cash, he has been obliged to part with a cherished article) but the buyer is glad. But it is not so with regard to the Holy One, blessed be He. He gave the Torah to Israel and was glad, as it is said: "For I give you good doctrine: forsake ye not My Torah"' i.e., the human seller would be only too happy for the buyer to return the article to him, but God, having given the Torah to Israel, does not want it back and pleads with Israel to hold on to it. This saying has no connection at all with the theme of sufferings. It has been inserted here solely because it is a further comment on the verse quoted by R. Joḥanan. There are numerous examples in the Talmud of this phenomenon, of a saying or comment added merely because of an association of ideas.

The *sûgyā* now reverts to the sufferings theme. Rava, 'in another version, R. Ḥisda', is reported as saying: 'If a man sees that sufferings have come upon him, let him scrutinize his deeds, as it is said: "Let us search and try our ways, and return unto the Lord" (Lam. 3:40). If he did scrutinizse his deeds without finding (i.e. any sin for which he would deserve to suffer), let him attribute it (the suffering) to the sin of neglect of the Torah (i.e., there may be no sin of commission for which he deserves to be punished, but there may be, nevertheless, this serious sin of omission), as it is said: "Happy is the man whom Thou chastenest, and teachest out of Thy Torah" (Ps. 94:12; i.e., God chastises a man so that he should return to the study of the Torah). If he did attribute his sufferings to his neglect of the Torah without finding (that he had been guilty of indolence in Torah study), it then becomes known that they are sufferings of love, as it is said: "For whom the Lord loveth He correcteth"' (Prov. 3:12). Thus 'sufferings of love' (*yissurin shel ahavah*) are neither for sins of commission nor of omission, but are due solely to God's love and are not penal.[2]

A saying of Rava in the name of Seḥorah in the name of R. Huna (early-third-century Babylonian Amora) is now quoted: 'Him in whom the Holy One, blessed be He, takes delight, He crushes with sufferings, as it is said: "Yet it pleased the Lord to crush him by disease" (Isa. 53:10); interpreting the verse homiletically as: "The one with whom God is pleased He crushes…". One might have imagined that this applies even if the sufferer does not accept his sufferings with love, therefore we are taught (in the continuation of the verse): "To see if his soul would offer itself in restitution (*asham*)." Just as an asham ("guilt-offering") can only be offered willingly so, too, the sufferings must be accepted willingly. If he does so accept them, what is his reward? "He will see his seed, prolong his days" (continuation of the verse). Moreover, his studies will endure, as it is said (continuation of the verse): "The purpose of the Lord (interpreted as: 'the one with whom God is pleased', ḥafetz, as above) will prosper in his hand" (or, possibly, the interpretation is: "The purpose of the Lord, i.e., the Torah, will prosper in his hand," i.e., his studies will remain "in his hand", they will endure).'

There now follows a debate between R. Jacob bar Iddi and R. Aḥa bar Ḥanina on how 'sufferings of love' are to be identified. It is not known which, but one of these teachers said that sufferings of love are those which do not involve neglect of Torah study (i.e., they are not sufficiently disturbing to prevent the sufferer from study of the Torah). In support the verse is quoted: 'Happy is the man whom Thou chastenest, O Lord, and teachest him out of Thy Torah' (Ps. 94:12). The other teacher said, sufferings of love are those which do not involve neglect of prayer (i.e., they are not so severe that they prevent the sufferer from concentrating in prayer). In support the verse is quoted: 'Blessed be God, who hath not turned away my prayer, nor His mercy from me' (Ps. 66:20). But

R. Abba the son of R. Ḥiyya bar Abba said to these two teachers: R. Ḥiyya bar Abba said in the name of R. Joḥanan: Both of these (whether there is neglect of study or of prayer) are still considered to be sufferings of love, as it is said: 'For whom the Lord loveth He correcteth' (Prov. 3:12). In that case what are we to make of the verse: 'and teachest him out of Thy Torah', quoted above to demonstrate that sufferings are only of love if they do not involve neglect of the Torah? To this the reply is given: Do not read *telammedennu,* 'and teachest *him'* but *telammedenu,* 'and teachest *us',* i.e., the verse is read to mean: 'Happy is the man whom Thou chastenest, O Lord, and Thou hast taught us this (that the man upon whom God brings sufferings is 'happy') out of Thy Torah'; i.e., we can derive this idea from a law recorded in the Torah. The law referred to is that of the slave who has been the victim of an attack by his master. If, as a result of the attack, the slave loses an eye or a tooth he goes free (Ex. 21:26–27). Now if a slave gains his freedom through losing only a single organ of his body, his eye or his tooth, then how much more so will a man be purged of his sins through sufferings which affect the whole of his body. And, the *sûgyā* continues, this conforms with the teaching of R. Simeon b. Lakish, who taught: The word *berit* ('covenant') is mentioned in connection with 'salt': 'Thou shalt not suffer the salt of the covenant of thy God to be lacking' (Lev. 2:13) and is also mentioned in connection with 'sufferings' at the end of the lengthy 'rebuke': 'These are the words of the covenant' (Deut. 28: 69). Just as with regard to the covenant of 'salt' it is the salt that makes the meat tasty, so, too, with regard to the covenant of 'sufferings', they purge man of all his iniquities.

A Baraita is now introduced, in which R. Simeon b. Yoḥai states that three precious gifts were given by God to Israel and only given through sufferings. These are: the Torah, the Land of Israel, and the World to Come. For each a proof-text is quoted. For the Torah the proof-text is: 'Happy is the man whom Thou chastenest, O Lord, and teachest him out of thy Torah' (Ps. 94:12). This is the verse quoted and discussed in the previous section of the *sûgyā,* which provides the link with this Baraita. For the Land of Israel, the proof-text is: 'As a man chasteneth his son, so the Lord thy God bringeth thee into a good land' (Deut. 8:7). The proof-text for the World to Come is: 'For the commandment is a lamp, and the Torah is light, and reproofs of instruction (understood as "sufferings") are the way of (eternal) life' (Prov. 6:23).[3]

The *sugya* continues that a Tanna (the functionary whose duty it was to rehearse Baraitot) repeated the following Baraita in the presence of R. Joḥanan: 'Whoever occupies himself with the Torah or with acts of benevolence or who buries his children, all his sins are forgiven.' R. Joḥanan observed that he knew of Scriptural support for the first two but not for the third. That the study of the Torah and the practice of benevolence bring pardon can be derived from the verse: 'By mercy and truth iniquity is expiated' (Proy. 16:6). 'Mercy' refers to acts of benevolence, as in the verse: 'He that followeth after righteousness (*tzedakah,* in Rabbinic parlance "charity"') and mercy findeth life, prosperity and honour' (Prov. 21:21). 'Truth' refers to the Torah, as in the verse: 'Buy truth and sell it not' (Prov. 23:23). R. Joḥanan objects, however, that there seems to be no proof from Scripture that there is total expiation of sin for the man who buries his children. In reply, a 'certain old man' produces a *gezerah shavah* in the name of R. Simeon b. Yoḥai.[4] The word *'avon,* 'iniquity' is mentioned in two passages: 'By mercy and truth iniquity is expiated' (Prov. 16:6) and: 'Who recompensest the iniquity of the fathers into the bosom of their children' (Jer. 32:18). Just as 'mercy' and 'truth' bring about expiation for 'iniquity' so, too, the death of children.

A saying of R. Joḥanan is now introduced. R. Joḥanan said: 'Plagues and children are not sufferings of love', i.e., if a man is afflicted with 'plagues' (Lev. 13), or is childless, these sufferings of his do not qualify as 'sufferings of love'. To this it is objected that we have been taught in a Baraita, commenting on the four types of plague-symptoms recorded in the Mishnah (*Nega'im* 1:1): 'Whoever has one of these plague-symptoms, they are nothing but an altar of atonement for him.' Thus we see from the Baraita that plague-symptoms are an 'altar of atonement', presumably implying that they are 'sufferings of love', which contradicts R. Joḥanan. Three replies are given (the second two introduced by the usual formula: 'If you want I can say'). The first reply simply denies that 'altar of atonement' is to be equated with 'sufferings of love'. The two concepts are different, so there is no contradiction. The second and third replies do equate the two concepts and yet observe that there is no contradiction. In the second reply the contradiction is to be resolved on the grounds: 'This is for us and that is for them,' i.e., the Baraita, which states that plague-symptoms are an 'altar of atonement' and, therefore, 'sufferings of love', refers to 'us' (the Babylonians) while R. Joḥanan's statement, that they are not 'sufferings of love', refers to 'them' (the Palestinians). The Palestinian authorities treated these laws very strictly, the Babylonians less so.[5] Consequently, in Palestine, where R. Joḥanan lived, 'Plagues' were treated too severely for them to be considered 'sufferings of love', whereas in the more lenient climate of Babylonia they do qualify as 'sufferings of love'. The third reply is that the Baraita speaks of plague-symptoms on parts of the body that are concealed by garments. These cause the sufferer no acute embarrassment, and so are an 'altar of atonement' and hence 'sufferings of love'. R. Joḥanan, on the other hand, speaks of plague-symptoms on parts of the body that can be seen by others, and these are too much a source of embarrassment to qualify as 'sufferings of love'.

The other part of R. Joḥanan's statement, that 'children' are not 'sufferings of love', is now examined. This cannot mean that, where a man had children but later they died, his sufferings are not those of love, since R. Joḥanan himself used to carry around with him a bone of the tenth son he had buried and would show it people (who had suffered bereavements, in order to console them) saying: 'This is the bone of my tenth son.' This shows that the loss of children is 'sufferings of love', since a teacher like R. Joḥanan would not have been visited with sufferings that were not of love (Rashi), or (Tosafists) R. Joḥanan would not have resorted to this method of consoling others if it were not 'sufferings of love'. Consequently, it is concluded, by 'children' R. Joḥanan must have meant: where a man had never been blessed with children at all. Such a man's sufferings are not those of love.

Three narratives are now related. In the first, R. Ḥiyya bar Abba is taken ill and is visited by R. Joḥanan. R. Joḥanan asks him: 'Are your sufferings dear to you?' To which he replies: 'I want neither them nor their reward.' Upon which R. Joḥanan says: 'Give me your hand,' and he raises the sick man from his bed of sickness (i.e. R. Joḥanan effects a cure by the miraculous power that is in him).

In the second narrative, R. Joḥanan is taken ill and is visited by R. Ḥanina, who asks: 'Are your sufferings dear to you?' to which R. Joḥanan replies: 'I want neither them nor their reward.' 'Give me your hand,' says R. Ḥanina, and he raises R. Joḥanan from his bed of sickness. The Gemara queries why R. Joḥanan did not raise himself from his bed of sickness, since, as is evident from the first narrative, he possessed those healing powers. The reply is given: 'A prisoner cannot release himself from his dungeon' (i.e., R. Jolianan was incapable of exerting his healing powers on his own behalf, only on behalf of others).

The third narrative tells of R. Eleazar being taken ill and visited by R. Joḥanan who notices that R. Eleazar is lying in a dark room, whereupon R. Joḥanan bares his arm, and the room is filled with (numinous) light. Seeing that R. Eleazar is weeping, R. Joḥanan asks him why he weeps. If it is because R. Eleazar had not studied as much of the Torah as he would have liked, we have learnt in a Mishnah (*Menaḥot* 13:11): 'It matters not whether one does much or little, provided one's heart is directed Heavenwards.' And if it is because of R. Eleazar's poverty, not every man has the merit of enjoying two tables (i.e. to prosper in both this world and the next). And if R. Eleazar weeps because of 'children', R. Joḥanan observes: 'This is the bone of my tenth son.' R. Eleazar replies that he is weeping because of none of these, but over R. Joḥanan' s beauty (seen when R. Joḥanan bared his arm to illumine the room) that will eventually come to dust. 'For this, you do well to weep,' declares R. Joḥanan, and they both of them weep. R. Joḥanan then asks R. Eleazar: 'Are your sufferings dear to you?'. 'I want neither them nor their reward,' replies R. Eleazar, whereupon R. Joḥanan says: 'Give me your hand' and raises R. Eleazar from his bed of sickness.

Finally, a narrative is related of which the hero is R. Huna. R. Huna had 400 flasks of wine which turned sour, and so suffered a very heavy financial loss. R. Judah, the brother of R. Sala Ḥasida and the other scholars visited R. Huna 'or, in another version, R. Adda bar Ahavah and the other scholars', and they suggested to R. Huna that he looks into his deeds (i.e., he should see whether he had been guilty of some offence, in connection with wine, for which he deserved to be punished in this way); as above, when sufferings come upon a man he should scrutinise his deeds. R. Huna protested: 'Do you suspect me of sin?' to which the scholars reply: 'Can we suspect God of punishing a man without cause?' R. Huna, thereupon, asked the scholars to tell him exactly what they had in mind. They told him that they had heard he had not given the portion due to his tenant-farmer of the vine-tendrils. R. Huna admitted that this was so, but protested that the man was a thief and had already taken more than his share. The scholars, however, persisted in their rebuke, declaring that there is a popular proverb: 'Steal from a thief and have a taste thereof,' i.e., it is forbidden to steal even from a thief. Thereupon R. Huna acknowledged his guilt and resolved to give the man his share of the vine-tendrils. The Gemara concludes: 'Some say that thereupon the vinegar turned back to wine, while others say that the vinegar remained such, but the price of vinegar shot up, so that it was worth as much as wine.'

For the purpose of literary analysis we must now present the whole *sugya* in diagrammatic form.

1. R. Simeon b. Lakish: sufferings depart
2. R. Joḥanan: sufferings come upon him (interpolation: R. Zera)
3. Rava or R. Ḥisda: when sufferings come:
   a. scrutinize deeds
   b. neglect of Torah
   c. 'sufferings of love'
4. R. Huna: God takes delight in man who suffers
5. Debate on what are 'sufferings of love':
   a. where no neglect of Torah
   b. where no neglect of prayer
   c. both 'sufferings of love' derived from law of slave
6. In accord with R. Simeon b. Lakish: covenant of 'salt' and 'sufferings'
7. Baraita inserted: R. Simeon b. Yoḥai: three gifts
8. The Tanna and R. Joḥanan:
   a. study of Torah
   b. practice of benevolence
   c. burial of children
9. R. Joḥanan objects: what proof-text is there for c?
10. Reply: old man in name of R. Simeon b. Yoḥai: 'iniquity' – 'iniquity'
11. R. Joḥanan: 'plagues' and 'children' are not 'sufferings of love'
12. Objection from Baraita: 'plagues' are 'altar of atonement'
13. Three replies:
   a. 'altar of atonement' but not 'sufferings of love'
   b. Baraita refers to 'us', R. Joḥanan to 'them'
   c. Baraita refers to 'hidden', R. Joḥanan to 'open'
14. 'Children': R. Joḥanan and the 'bone': hence only when 'childless'
15. R. Joḥanan raises R. Ḥiyya bar Abba from his sickbed
16. R. Ḥanina raises R. Joḥanan from his sickbed
17. Let R. Joḥanan raise himself: a prisoner cannot effect his own release

18. Why did R. Eleazar weep? Cannot have been because of:
    a. his inadequate learning
    b. his poverty
    c. 'children'
19. Must have been because of R. Joḥanan's beauty
20. R. Joḥanan raises R. Eleazar from his sickbed
21. R. Huna's wine turns sour
    a. Am I suspect?: Is God suspect?
    b. He is a thief : Forbidden to steal from a thief
    c. I shall give him his portion: either vinegar turns back to wine or price increases

The first thing to be noted is that our *sugya* is a complete unit (apart from the R. Zera interpolation), and is quite independent of the theme of the first Mishnah in *Berakhot* to which it is appended. It has clearly been inserted here by the editors because R. Simeon b. Lakish's proof-text in 1. is from 'the sons of Reshef', which, in the passage immediately preceding it in *Berakhot* 5a, is quoted in connection with 'the *Shema'* on retiring' and that is germane to the theme of the *Shema'* treated of in the first Mishnah of *Berakhot*. By a unit, it is to be understood that we do not have here a simple anthology of teachings on sufferings, but a carefully thought-out pattern. No doubt, the particular sayings were first uttered by the various teachers without any necessary connection between them, but, as they are presented in our *sûgyā*, there is a neat, ordered sequence in which one saying leads to another. Thus in the debate between R. Simeon b. Lakish and R. Joḥanan our attention is called to the connection between the study of the Torah and sufferings which leads naturally on to the discussion of whether neglect of Torah is a cause of suffering. This introduces the theme of 'sufferings of love' (3c), and this leads to R. Huna in 4. This saying of R. Huna fits in with the final narrative of the *sûgyā* of which R. Huna is the hero, and the narrative is an illustration of how God delights in the man who suffers, as R. Huna did. But the editors have left this narrative to the end; it is not too implausible to suggest, because they wished to have a 'happy ending'. In the three narratives of which the hero is R. Joḥanan, the reason for the sequence in which these are presented is fairly clear. First there is the narrative which demonstrates R. Joḥanan's powers. The second narrative is then presented so as to demonstrate that he could not use these powers on his own behalf. The third and most elaborate narrative then follows. All three narratives use the same formal terms: 'Are your sufferings dear to you?'; 'I want neither them nor their reward'; 'Give me your hand.'

Especially deserving of note as evidence of the formal, literary style of the *sûgyā* is the remarkable series of threes throughout the whole.[6] As can be seen from the diagrammatic formulation above, there are sets of three in 3.; 5.; 7.; 8.; 13.; the three narratives 15–20.; in 18.; and, probably, in 21.[7]

Although the *sûgyā* is aggadic, it consistently utilizes Halakhic-type argumentation. Not only are there used the *Kal va-ḥomer* [8] and *gezerah shavah*,[9] but practically the whole construction follows the normal pattern in halakhic debate of question and answer; of fine distinctions between concepts; of thrust and parry: of a kind of discussion for its own sake, quite irrespective of the subject matter. I would maintain that a careful examination of other aggadic passages in the Babylonian Talmud demonstrates that they exhibit similar forms, so that the style of presentation of Aggadah, as distinct from its content, differs little from that which is to be seen in the purely halakhic *sûgyôt*.

If our contention is correct, it has far-reaching consequences for the use of the material in the Babylonian Talmud in attempting to reconstruct a Rabbinic theology. If our analysis is correct, we have in our *sûgyā*, for example, not at all a series of theological propositions intended primarily as such but rather theological material used to build up a literary, contrived piece of argumentation, in which the main interest is not in the content, but in the form. When, for instance, arguments are presented in neat sequences of three, or when the formal attempt is made to reconcile the statement of R. Joḥanan with that of the Baraita, we are far removed from anything like a systematic treatment by the Rabbis of the theological problem of suffering.[10]

In noting the editors' striving for literary effect and the element of contrivance in their work, we cannot rule out even the possibility that they introduced conscious humour in order to appeal to the reader. What else but humour can be the meaning of R. Johanan's declaration that he agrees with R. Eleazar when the latter states that he weeps for R. Joḥanan's beauty eventually coming to dust. 'Now that is something to cry about,' R. Joḥanan says. And what else but pure humour is the second version in which R. Huna's vinegar does not turn back to wine, but R. Huna does not lose because the price of vinegar suddenly goes up?

Joseph Heinemann's work will endure. One of his main fields of activity was that of the Rabbinic Aggadah. This note of caution, that, when the Aggadah in the Babylonian Talmud is studied, the purely academic and literary nature of a good deal of the material should be seen for what it is, is offered as a tribute to his memory.

NOTES

1. Cf. b. *Sotah* 35a.
2. Rashi *s.v. yissurin shel ahavah* explains 'sufferings of love' as: 'The Holy One, blessed be He, chastises him in this world, though he is guiltless of any sin, for the purpose of increasing his reward in the World to Come to a degree greater than his merits would otherwise have deserved.' Maimonides, *Guide*, III, 17, states that in the discourse of our Sages (i.e. in our *sûgyā*) there is found the dictum regarding 'sufferings of love'. According to this opinion, says Maimonides, 'sometimes misfortunes befall an individual not because of his having sinned before, but in order for his reward to be the greater'. Maimonides considers this to be a minority opinion, one, in his view, hard to reconcile with God's justice. Maimonides constrasts it with the other Rabbinic sayings: 'There is no death without sin, and no sufferings without transgression' (b. *Shabbat* 55a) and: 'A man is measured with the measure he himself uses' (*Sotah* 1:7). The latter saying, continues Maimonides, occurring as it does in the Mishnah, enjoys special authority. Cf. S. Schechter's *Studies in Judaism*, First Series (Philadelphia 1945) pp. 225–6.
3. Cf. *Mekhilta, Yitro,* 10, ed. Horovitz, p. 240 and parallel in *Sifre, Va-Ethanan,* 32, ed. Friedmann, p. 73b: 'R. Simeon b. Yohai says: Beloved are sufferings, for three precious gifts were given to Israel which the nations of the world desire and they were only given through sufferings, viz.: the Torah, the Land of Israel and the World to Come.' In the *Mekhilta* and *Sifre* the series of proof-texts differ somewhat from those in our Baraita.
4. For the 'old man' and R. Simeon b. Yoḥai see b. *Shabbat* 34a and Tosafists to m. Ḥullin 6a, top.
5. Following the Tosafists to b. *Berakhot* 5b, top.
6 On the use of special 'mystical' numbers like three and seven in the Talmud see the illuminating article by Shamma Freidman: 'Mivneh Sifruti be-Sugyot ha-Bavli' – *Proceedings of the World Congress of Jewish Studies,* Vol. 3, Jerusalem 1977, pp. 389–402. Cf. the use of three in tractate Avot and the fact that the Talmud always observes *shema' minah telat,* 'three things can be derived from this, never two, four or other numbers!
7. See Tosafists to the R. Huna narrative, *Berakhot* 5b, *s.v. dina be-lo dina,* who are puzzled by the theological implications of the question addressed to R. Huna since, surely, many good people do suffer without being guilty of any serious crime. The Tosafists suggest that the scholars knew all along of R. Huna's offence, and were simply bent on having him acknowledge it. But it is highly probable that, in any event, the narrative is told in this way for the purpose of providing the reader with the recurring three.
8. In law of the slave, 5.
9. In 1.; 6.; 10. Both *Kal va-ḥomer* and *gezerah shavah* are mentioned as hermeneutical principles to be applied in the Aggadah as well as in the Halakhah in the so-called Baraita of R. Eliezer son of R. Jose ha-Gelili, which modern scholarship has established to be a post-Talmudic work, see H. Strack, *Introduction to the Talmud and Midrash* (Philadelphia 1945), pp. 95–8. The Baraita is quoted in full at the beginning of the Vilna edition of the *Midrash Rabbah* and in Samson of Chinin's *Sefer Keritut,* Part III, ed. Y. Z. Rotha, New York, 1961.
10. On our *sugya* see E. E. Urbach: Ḥafal (Jerusalem 1969), pp. 394–5. It is puzzling to find Urbach understanding R. Joḥanan in 5c as stating that both are *not* sufferings of love, since the meaning is surely that, according to R. Joḥanan, both *are* sufferings of love.

— 9 —

'Woe to me if I say it. Woe to me if I do not say it.'

In tractate *Bava Batra* of the Babylonian Talmud (89b) three Baraitot are quoted, dealing with fraudulent practices when buying and selling. The third *Baraita* reads:

> Our Rabbi taught: The strike may not be made thick on one side and thin on the other. One may not strike with a single quick movement, for striking in this manner causes loss to the seller and benefits the buyer. Nor may one strike very slowly because it is disadvantageous to the buyer and beneficial to the seller. Concerning all these Rabban Johanan ben Zakkai said: Woe to me if I say it. Woe to me if I do not say it. If I say it the knaves might learn (to engage in these sharp practices). If I do not say it the knaves might say that the disciples of the wise (*talmidey ḥakhamim*) are unfamiliar with our practices.

Thus far the *Baraita*. The *sûgyā* in the Babylonian Talmud continues:

> They raised the question (*ibbaye le-hu*): Did he say it or did he not say it? R. Samuel ben R. Isaac said: He did say it and it is on the basis of the following verse that he said it: For the ways of the Lord are right, and the just do walk in them; but transgressors do stumble therein (Hosea 14:10).

The difficulty which faces every student is the expression, in the *Baraita,* 'Concerning all these'. The Baraita speaks of only one form of fraudulent practice, the use of the strike. Even if it be argued that there are three different practices – having a strike thick at one end, thin at the other, striking too quickly and striking too slowly – it is surely forced to refer to these as 'all these'. It is just possible that the word 'all' refers to the practices mentioned in this and in the other two *Baraitot* but, as we shall see as our investigation proceeds, a far better solution to the difficulty is to hand.

A further difficulty is the use of the term *talmidey ḥakhamim*, 'disciples of the wise', by Rabban Johanan ben Zakkai. In the Tannaitic period the Sages are called *ḥakhamim* ('sages') not '*disciples* of the sages'.[1] The placing of this term in the mouth of Rabban Johanan ben Zakkai, it is hoped, will also become clear through our analysis.

First a statement in the Mishnah (Kelim 17: 16) must be quoted. This reads:

> A beam of a balance or a strike that contains a (secret) receptacle in which to load it with metal, or a carrying-yoke wherein is a (secret) receptacle for money, or a begger's cane that has a receptacle for water, or a stick that has a receptacle for a *mezuzah* and for pearls – these are susceptible to contamination. Concerning all these Rabban Joḥanan ben Zakkai said: Woe to me if I say it. Woe to me if I do not say it.

Without going into too much detail[2] the principle stated in the Mishnah is clear. Wooden vessels which do not have a receptacle (*peshutey keli etz*) are not susceptible to contamination. But what *is* the law if they have a secret receptacle? Does this count as a receptacle so that the vessels are susceptible to contamination or, since the receptacle is concealed, it does not count and the vessels are not susceptible to contamination. The Mishnah rules that the receptacle, though secret, does count as such. Now, in the nature of the case, such recret receptacles are used by tricksters and robbers of various kinds, i.e. the receptacle in the stick used to smuggle pearls. Rabban Johanan ben Zakkai is concerned with the need to state the law that these objects are susceptible to contamination but his statement might bring to the notice of tricksters that these methods are open to him. Hence Rabban Joḥanan's uncertainty whether or not to speak out.

Turning now to the *Tosefta* (*Kelim*, *Bava Metzia* 7, ed. Zuckermandel, p. 586) we find this elaboration of the Mishnah:

> A beam of a balance or a strike that contains a (secret) receptacle in which to load it with metal, or a carrying-yoke wherein is a (secret) receptacle for money, or a begger's cane that has a receptacle for water, or a stick that has a receptacle for a *mezuzah* and for pearls – these are only susceptible to contamination when they are used for that purpose. Concerning all these Rabban Johanan ben Zakkai said: Woe to me if I say it. Woe to me if I do not say it. If I say it I shall then teach the tricksters how to defraud. If I do not say it I shall then be withholding the teaching[3] and I will contaminate uncontaminated things. Another reason

> (why he was reluctant not to say it): that the tricksters should not say that the sages (hakhamim) are unfamiliar with our practices.

It can be seen that the *Tosefta* spells out why Rabban Johanan ben Zakkai was uncertain whether or not to speak out. This is not stated in the Mishnah. The reason for his reluctance to speak out is obvious. He may put ideas into people's heads. The first reason for speaking out is closely connected with the subject of the Mishnah. Rabban Johanan ben Zakkai feels obliged to state the law, otherwise people will not know that these objects are susceptible to contamination and this might lead to the unintentional contamination of purities. The second reason given in the *Tosefta* would apply to other fraudulent practices, even where the question of the contamination of vessels does not arise e.g. the practice of striking with a strike that is thick on one side and thin on the other. The fact that this is given in the *Tosefta* as a second reason or another reason (*davar aher*) might suggest that the original reason was the first, that it might lead to the contamination of purities. Only at a later date was the reason given that it is to avoid the tricksters saying that the sages are unfamiliar with our ways and this reason extends Rabban Johanan's reason for speaking out to cases where the question of contamination does not arise. According to the first reason given in the *Tosefta*, Rabban Johanan's dilemma is how to weigh his obligation to teach the laws of contamination against the need not to acquaint the tricksters with practices of which they might have been unaware. Even if he eventually came down on the side of teaching, disregarding the consequences, it does not follow that he would have come down on the side of speaking out where the dilemma was whether to expose the fraudulent practices or whether to keep the prospective tricksters innocent of the practices. Here he might well have come down on the side of silence and prudence. At all events by the time of the *Tosefta* the whole matter was taken beyond the confines of the laws of contamination and extended to cover all manner of fraudulent practices by the implications of the second reason.

There are two further elaborations germane to our inquiry, both in Midrash Ecclesiastes Rabbah. The first of these (Ecclesiastes Rabbah 6:1) reads:

> *There is an evil which I have seen under the sun* (Eccl. 6:1). R. Samuel b. Ammi said: This refers to the devices of cheats; e.g. one who adulterates wine with water, oil with the juice of glaucion, honey with the juice of

> the wild strawberry, balsam with ass's milk, myrrh with gum, aromatic leaves with vine-leaves, brine with red colouring matter, pepper with vetch, or uses a weight beam which is longer on one side than the other. Concerning all these Rabban Johanan ben Zakkai said: Woe to me if I say it. Woe to me if I do not say it. If I say it the tricksters will learn what to do. If I do not say it, the tricksters will say, the disciples of the wise (*talmidey ḥakhamim*) are unfamiliar with our ways. Finally he did say it, *For the ways of the Lord are right* (Hosea 14:10).

The Midrash here refers only to the practices which are fraudulent and does not mention the instances in the Mishnah and Tosefta regarding the question of susceptibility to contamination. The emphasis has shifted from secret reptacles to more general instances of secret fraud i.e. where the buyer is unaware that he has been tricked. That is why the passage is in the form of a comment to *There is an evil which I have seen under the sun*, taking 'under the sun' as meaning where it is indiscernible, where it does not 'see the light'. And by the time when this Midrash was compiled[4] the hakhamim of the *Tosefta* has been changed to talmidey hakhamim!

The second passage is that of Ecclesiastes Rabbah 9:13 and is more elaborate than the first. This reads:

> *This also have I seen as wisdom under the sun* (Eccl. 9:13). R. Samuel b. Ammi said: This refers to the devices of cheats in their guile (taking 'wisdom' in the sense of guile) e.g. one who adulterates wine with water, oil with the juice of glaucion, honey with the juice of the wild strawberry, balsam with ass's milk, myrrh with gum, pepper with vine-leaves. One should not use a weight-beam which is longer on one side than the other, nor a strike which is thick on one side and narrow on the other. A weight beam or a strike that contains a (secret) receptacle in which metal can be inserted, or a carrying-yoke in which is a (secret) receptacle for money, or a beggar's cane which has a receptacle for water, or a stick which has a receptacle for a *mezuzah* and for pearls-these are susceptible to contamination. Concerning all these Rabban Johanan ben Zakkai said: Woe to me if I say it. Woe to me if I do not say it. If I say it I may teach cheats what to do. If I do not say it there is the danger that I may hamper a disciple (*talmid*)[5] and he[6] will declare what is clean to be unclean. Another reason is that cheats should not say that the disciples of the wise are not familar with our actions. R. Samuel said: For all that. *The ways of the Lord are right; and the just do walk in them; but transgressors do stumble therein* (Hosea 14:10).

In this passage the practices mentioned in the earlier Midrash *are* first recorded and then the *Tosefta* is recorded *verbatim*.

We can now return to our passage in *Bava Batra*. The section

'Concerning all these ...' is a direct quote from the *Tosefta* or, at least, from the same source as the *Tosefta*. It did not originally refer to fraudulent practices in general but to those which have implications for the laws of contamination. The editors of the *Bavli*, however, like the editors of Ecclesiastes Rabbah, have extended it to general fraudulent practices such as the case of the faulty strike. Moreover, instead of R. Samuel[7] simply quoting the verse from Hosea to show that Rabban Johanan ben Zakkai did say it, the whole matter is put, after the usual style of the *Bavli*,[8] in the form of a *baya – ibbaya le-hu*, which R. Samuel then solves by quoting the verse from Hosea.

Thus the history of our text is as follows. First the Mishnah leaves it an open question whether or not Rabbah Johanan ben Zakkai said it or did not say it. And here the question concerns only the question of practices with implications for contamination. The *Tosefta* elaborates on the pros and cons of speaking out and gives an additional reason for speaking out that would extend speaking out even to instances where contamination is not involved. In the first Midrashic passage the whole matter is applied only to general fraud but in the second both types of fraud, general and those with implication for contemination, are recorded, with the second type only as a simple quote. The editors of the *Bavli* similarly extend the matter by the quote and apply it (or perhaps the Baraita so extends it) to the case of the strike. The whole is an excellent illustration of how the editors of the *Bavli* use earlier material and transform it or adapt it to construct a typical *sugya*.

NOTES

1. See Tosefta, *Kiddushin* 3:10, ed. Zuckermandel p. 339 and *Bavli Kiddushin* 49b for the distinction between the mature sage *ḥakham)* and the disciple (*talmid ḥakham*) in Tannaitic times.
2. For the meaning of the items mentioned in the Mishnah see the standard commentaries. The translation is based on Danby but I have rendered *maḥok* as 'strike' as in the *Bavli*.
3. In our texts *talmud*. The meaning is that if Rabban Johanan ben Zakkai will refrain from speaking he will be guilty of withholding 'teaching'. People will then believe that these objects are not susceptible to contamination and when they do become contaminated they will allow them to come into contact with purities and Rabban Johanan ben Zakkai will then have been indirectly responsible for contaminating purities.
4. My translation of the two Midrashim passages are those of the Soncino Midrash translation with one or two variants. For the date of Midrash Ecclesiastes Rabbah see the Introduction to the work in the Soncino translation, new ed. London, 1977, pp. vii–viii. All scholars favour a late date i.e. well into the Amoraic period at the earliest. R. Samuel b. Ammi is a Palestinian Amora.
5. The 'Talmud' of the *Tosefta* has here become *talmid*.

6. In the *Tosefta* 'I will contaminate' see note 3. It is probable that we have here in any event a corrupt text and the original reading was as in the *Tosefta* from which it is a quote.
7. In the *Bavli* Samuel b. R. Isaac. It is impossible to ascertain which of the two readings – Samuel b. Ammi or Samuel b. Isaac – is the correct one but clearly one of the texts is inaccurate.
8. The Munich Codex does not, in fact, have *ibbaye le-hu* in our passage, see *Dikdukkey Soferim,* but this may well be under the influence of the Midrashic passages. It seems more plausible to suggest that the editors of the *Bayli* have consciously put it in this way so as to fit it in with the usual style of the *Bayli.*

—10—

R. Phinehas ben Jair and His Pious Donkey

In the previous passages in Ḥullin, there are references to the maxim: 'If the Holy One, blessed be He, allows no mishap to result through the animals of the righteous, *a fortiori* He does not allow it to happen to the righteous themselves.'[1] In illustration of the maxim the Talmud tells the story of R. Phinehas and his donkey.

> R. Phinehas b. Yair was on the way to redeem captives. When he came to the river Ginai[2] he said: 'O Ginai, divide thy waters on my behalf that I may cross over.' Said the river: 'Thou art going to do the will of thy Maker and I am going to do the will of my Maker. For thee it is doubtful whether thou wilt carry it out whereas I certainly carry it out.'[3] Said he to the river: 'If thou wilt not divide I shall decree that no water will ever pass through thee', so it divided for him. There was another man there carrying wheat for Passover. Said he to the river: 'Divide also for that man who is engaged in the performance of a *mitzvah*!' It divided for him. There was an Arab accompanying them. He said to the river: 'Divide also for that man so that people should not protest: "Is that how one treats companions on a journey?"' The river divided for him as well. Said R. Joseph: 'How much greater was the power of this man than that of Moses and the six hundred thousand! For there was only a single division of the sea and here it happened three times.' But perhaps here, too, there was only a single parting?[4] Say, rather: 'like Moses and the six hundred thousand'.[5] When he arrived at an inn they cast some barley before his donkey but it refused to eat. They winnowed the barley but it still refused to eat. They cleansed it but it still refused to eat. Said he to them: 'Perhaps they have not been tithed,' whereupon they gave the tithes and the donkey ate the barley. Said he: 'This poor creature is going to do the will of its Maker[6] and you dare to make it eat untithed produce.' But is there any obligation for produce to be tithed in such circumstances? Have we not learned:[7] 'If one buys produce for sowing or for an animal or flour for skins or oil for lighting or oil to polish utensils there is no obligation to give the tithes for produce of uncertain status'?[8] But there we have the observation of R. Joḥanan who said:

'This only applies where he bought the produce for an animal in the first instance. Where he bought it for human consumption and then changed his mind to give it to the animal he does have an obligation to tithe it.' And so we have been taught: 'If one buys produce in the market place in order to eat it himself and then changes his mind and decides to give it to his animal he must not give it to his animal or to his neighbour's animal until he has given the tithes.'

Rabbi (Judah the Prince) heard that he was coming and went out to meet him. Said he: 'Wilt thou dine with me?' 'Yes,' he replied, whereupon Rabbi's face shone with delight. Said he: 'Dost thou imagine that I have given a vow never to enjoy any benefit from Israelites? Israelites are holy.[9] But there is one who desireth (to invite guests) but he hath no means and there is one who hath means but no desire, and it is written: 'Eat thou not the bread of him that hath an evil eye, neither desire thou his dainties. For as one that hath reckoned within himself, so is he: "Eat and drink," saith he to thee; but his heart is not with thee' (Proverbs 23.6–7). Thou, however, hast the means and the desire. Yet now I must make haste for I am busily occupied in carrying out a *mitzvah*. I shall come to thee on my return? On his return he happened to enter by a door where he saw standing some white-legged mules. Said he: 'The angel of death is in this one's house and shall I dine with him?'[10] Rabbi heard of his coming and he went out to meet him, saying: 'I shall sell them.' Said he: '"Thou shalt not place a stumbling block before a blind man"' (Leviticus 19.14).[11] Said he: 'I shall abandon them.'[12] Said he: 'There will then be an increase of harm.'[13] Said he: 'I shall hamstring them.' Said he: 'That will offend against the prohibition of cruelty to animals.'[14] Said he: 'I shall kill them.' Said he: 'That would offend against the prohibition: "Thou shalt not destroy"' (Deuteronomy 20.19).[15] He was very insistent but a mountain rose between them.[16] Rabbi wept saying:[17] 'If this is how it is with them during their lifetime how much more when they are dead.' For R. Hama b. Hanina said: 'Greater are the righteous in their death than in their lifetime, as it is said: "And it came to pass, as they were burying a man, that, behold, they spied a band; and they cast the man into the sepulchre of Elisha; and as soon as the man touched the bones of Elisha, he revived and stood upon his feet"' (2 Kings 13.21).[18] Said R. Pappa to Abbaye: 'Perhaps it was in order for Elijah's blessing to be fulfilled[19] as it is written: "Let a double portion of thy spirit be upon me"?' (2 Kings 2.9). Said he: 'In that case why have we been taught,"He stood on his feet but did not return to his home"?' But then how was Elijah's blessing fulfilled?[20] As R. Joḥanan said, in that he healed the leprosy of Naaman, a leper being considered as one dead, as it is written: 'Let her not, I pray, be as one dead'... (Numbers 12.12).[21] They said regarding R. Phinehas b. Yair that in all his days he never broke bread over a loaf that did not belong to him and from the day he reached independence[22] he did not enjoy a repast of his father.[23]

Thus far the story and its elaboration in the Babylonian Talmud. It is fruitful to compare this version with that in the Jerusalem

Talmud,[24] appended to the Mishnah in *Demai*, quoted in BT as part of the discussion and evidently quoted in *JT* for the same purpose. First, however, in *JT* a series of stories about the miraculous powers of R. Phinehas b. Yair occurs. For the purpose of comparison three of these stories (there are others in the list) must be examined. In the first of these, the donkey of R. Phinehas is stolen by robbers during the night. For three days the robbers tried unsuccessfl.illy to feed the donkey but it refused to eat. Fearful that it would die and cause a stench in their hideout the robbers decided to return the donkey to its owner, R. Phinehas. The donkey began to bray as it reached the gateway of R. Phinehas's house. R. Phinehas urged the members of his household to open the gate since, he said, this poor animal[25] has not eaten for three days.[26] They let it in and R. Phinehas ordered them to give it food. They placed barley before it but it refused to eat. 'Rabbi,' they declared, 'it refuses to eat.' 'Did you separate the tithes from the *demai*[27] produce?', asked R. Phinehas. They replied: 'But our Master has taught us that if one buys Demai produce for an animal there is no need to tithe it' (quoting the Mishnah to which the story is appended, as in *BT*). R. Phinehas replied: 'What can we do if this poor beast wishes to be strict beyond the letter of the law?' They thereupon gave the tithes and the donkey ate.

The second story in *JT* relevant to our purpose tells how R. Phinehas b. Yair went to the House of Learning.[28] The river Ginai, being in full flood, was a barrier. R. Phinehas said: 'O Ginai, why dost thou prevent me from going to the House of Learning?' So the river parted for him to cross. His disciples asked him whether the river would part for them. He replied: 'Whoever knows that in all his days he had never put a fellow Israelite to shame may cross and it will not be deducted from his merits.'[29]

The third story tells of R. Phinehas b. Yair visiting Rabbi (Judah the Prince, *Nasi)* in order to express his disapproval of the latter's attempt to permit work in the fields on the Sabbatical year.[30] Rabbi asked R. Phinehas whether the produce in the fields was doing well. He asked him this twice but each time R. Phinehas replied: 'The endives are doing well,' from which reply Rabbi understood that R. Phinehas was not in agreement with him regarding the Sabbatical year.[31] Rabbi then invited R. Phinehas to dine with him but when R. Phinehas came to Rabbi's house he saw the mules[32] of Rabbi standing there. R. Phinehas expressed his astonishment that Jews[33] should keep such dangerous animals and he expressed the hope that Rabbi would fail to note that he had arrived at the house. When Rabbi was told that R. Phinehas had returned home he sent messengers to apologize to R. Phinehas. R. Phinehas at first requested his townsfolk to surround him so that the messengers of Rabbi would not be able to reach him. The townsfolk, however, left R. Phinehas out of respect for Rabbi, whereupon R. Phinehas asked the members of his household to surround him and eventually fire came down from Heaven to cut R. Phinehas off from Rabbi's messengers. When this was told to Rabbi he exclaimed: 'Since I did not have the privilege of seeing the splendour of his countenance[34] in this world, perchance I will enjoy the privilege in the World to Come.'

In the JT version we have three stories each relating to a separate event in the life of R. Phinehas: the story of the donkey who refused to eat; the story of the river through which R. Phinehas passed; and the story of the meeting between Rabbi and R. Phinehas. In the *BT* version these three separate stories have become three episodes in the same story. It follows that the three story version must be the earlier. One can readily understand how, for the purposes of dramatic effect and in order to produce a coherent and consistent narrative, the three separate stories have been told as a single story. But it is impossible for an original single story to have been separated into three separate ones, each with circumstantial detail on its own, different from the details in the single story. Moreover, the *JT* version records the three stories together with other separate stories about R. Phinehas. It is as clear as can be that the *BT* version consists of a reworking of the earlier material. This is not, of course, to suggest that the BT editors had the actual text of the *JT* version before them,[35] only that in *JT* an earlier version has been preserved. Nor does it necessarily rule out the possibility that the *JT* version is also a reworking of earlier material.

We must now revert to the BT version to compare it with the *JT* version, noting the strong resemblances and the equally strong differences, for which latter some explanation must be sought.

In the *BT* version, as the beginning, corresponding to the second story in the *JT* version, R. Phinehas is on an errand of mercy, to redeem captives. In *JT* he is journeying to the House of Learning. In both versions he meets the resistance of the river Ginai and in both there are others who wish to cross the river; in BT the man with wheat for Passover and the Arab, in *JT* the disciples. In *JT* there is no lengthy dialogue with the river as in *BT*. It is possible that 'redemption of captives' is used in the *BT* version because here the river is made to argue that R. Phinehas can only be in doubt whether he will be successful in his errand; i.e. the captives may have escaped or he will fail to ransom them. Conversely, in the *JT* version the 'house of Learning' may be R. Phinehas's destination because the disciples are going on the same errand for the same purpose. That there are three persons in *BT* may be because of the general fondness of *BT* for sets of three.[36] The comparison of R. Phinehas's powers to those of Moses and the six hundred thousand is possibly due to the tendency of BT generally to ascribe exaggerated miraculous powers to the saints.[37] For the same reason it may well be that in *BT* R. Phinehas threatens the river that unless it parts he will decree that water will never flow through it, *BT* believing strongly in the powers of the saint to issue such decrees.[38] To be noticed, too, is the play on doing God's will in *BT*. R. Phinehas goes to do the will of his Maker, so does the river, and, in the continuation of the story, so does the donkey, which, evidently, goes to do God's will because R. Phinehas is riding on the donkey when he goes to redeem the captives.

In the story of the donkey refusing to eat, the *BT* version places the episode at an inn, whereas in the *JT* version the donkey is first stolen by the robbers and its final refusal to eat is at the home of R. Phinehas where the donkey has been returned. The difficulty from the Mishnah that animal food need not be tithed is raised in both versions (in *JT* of R. Phinehas by his servants, in *BT* by the Talmud) but in *BT* a legalistic distinction is made, whereas in *JT* R. Phinehas states that the animal is strict beyond the letter of the law.[39] The difference is no doubt because in the *BT* version, since the affair happens at an inn, the barley might well have been bought for human consumption. In the *JT* version, on the other hand, it occurs in R. Phinehas's own home and he orders the servants to feed the donkey. In such circumstances they would presumably give the donkey its usual feed of barley, and the reply in BT will not be applicable.

In the continuation of the story in *BT* and in the third story in *JT*, R. Phinehas meets Rabbi but in the *JT* version R. Phinehas journeys especially to Rabbi to express his disagreement with the latter's attempt to abolish the Sabbatical year prohibitions. In *BT* R. Phinehas is in any event reluctant to eat at another's table, using the mules as a valid excuse, whereas in *JT* the sole reason for R. Phinehas's refusal to dine with Rabbi is because of the mules.

Reflected in both stories is the suggested conflict between the House of the *Nasi* and others who resented his authority.[40] In both stories there is a miraculous intervention – the mountain in *BT*, the fire from Heaven in *JT* – to prevent Rabbi inviting R. Phinehas. In both versions the 'punch-line' has to do with this world and the next but there is a vast difference between the two versions. In JT Rabbi expresses the hope that he will meet with R. Phinehas in the next world. In *BT* there is nothing about Rabbi meeting with R. Phinehas in the next world but Rabbi declares that if R. Phinehas has these powers in this world how much more in the next. Indeed, it is possible that the *BT* version means that if Rabbi did not have the merit of inviting R. Phinehas in this world how much less will he have the opportunity in the next.[41] This would explain why Rabbi weeps in the *BT* version. The *BT* story concludes with the statement about R. Phinehas's independent spirit, a motif of the BT version but unknown in the *JT* version.

The whole passage in *BT* is a carefully worked-out story, each feature of which is made to be introduced at just the right time. The third episode, the meeting of Rabbi and R. Phinehas, must come at the end, after the other two, as the climax of the story, Rabbi and R. Phinehas parting for ever. The whole story is presented so as to convey progressively the powers of the saint. First he exercises his power over the river. Then even his donkey is seen to have been imbued with this power. Finally, the power works not only against a natural object, the river, and not only against the ignorant men at the inn, but also against the *Nasi* who is obliged to admit that the power will be even greater after the saint's death. Implied in the whole manner in which the tale is told is the idea that because the saint is determined to do the will of his Maker, his Maker bows, as it were, to his will,[42] so that he can threaten the river and bring about its parting; he can avoid unwittingly have his donkey eat untithed food; and he can pursue without hindrance the way he has chosen of refusing to enjoy any benefit from others. In the story, too, R. Phinehas does not go out intentionally to exercise his powers but does so only when he is obliged to face opposition through unforeseen circumstances. He is no knight in shining armour going out to do battle but a good man doing God's will and only invoking the powers he has when he has no alternative. This explains the verbs used in the narrative. R. Phinehas *meets*[43] the river. He *happens*" upon an inn. The man with the wheat and the Arab just happen to be there. Rabbi happens to *hear*[45] that R. Phinehas has come. When R. Phinehas returns he just *happens*[46] to enter the gate where the mules are waiting to provide him with the excuse he needs. In the Elisha story, too, the dead man is accidentally cast into Elisha's sepulchre.

The story of R. Phinehas and his donkey is also told in *Genesis Rabbah*.[47] This is basically the story as told in *JT* with a few variants. Thus in the Midrash the robbers send the donkey away and it arrives by itself at the house of its master and R. Phinehas replies to the question: 'What can I do if she wishes to be strict?'[48]

In *Aboth deRabbi Nathan*[49] there is yet another parallel to the *JT* story, but here the story is in Hebrew and is not told of R. Phinehas ben Yair but of the other renowned miracle-working saint, R. Hanina ben Dosa. In this version, too, the donkey makes its own way home but it is the saint's son who recognizes from the braying of the donkey that it is their own donkey. More significantly, in this version there is no reference to the donkey refusing to eat the barley because it is untithed. Here the point of the story is rather that the animal refused to eat or drink in the robbers' den.[50]

In both the *Genesis Rabbah* and the *JT* versions, the story of R. Phinehas and the donkey that would not eat untithed produce is told in connection with the story of R. Jeremiah who sent a basket of untithed figs to R. Zera. R. Jeremiah relied on R. Zera not to eat until the figs had been tithed while R. Zera relied on R. Jeremiah to have tithed them. In connection with this it is said that R. Abba bar Zamina said in the name of R. Lezer:[51] 'If the earlier teachers were like angels we are like human beings. But if they were like human beings then we are like donkeys.' To this R. Mana adds: 'We are not even like donkeys. The donkey of R. Phinehas b. Yair was given untithed barley and it did not eat but we have eaten figs that were untithed.'[52]

One further source must now be mentioned. This is in *b. Shabbat* 112b and reads: 'R. Zera said that Rabbah bar Zimona[53] said: If the earlier teachers were the sons of angels we are the sons of human beings. But if the earlier teachers were sons of human beings then we are like donkeys but not like the donkeys of R. Hanina b. Dosa[54] or R. Phinehas b. Yair but like other donkeys.'

In the light of the above analysis the development of the tale can plausibly be traced. Of the sources referred to above we have the following:

A. *The ARN version*

Hero of the tale: R. Hanina b. Dosa. The donkey neither eats nor drinks in the hideout of the robbers. Thus the theme is that of the animal who prevents his master benefiting from stolen property. The passage is in Hebrew.

B. *The Genesis Rabbah version*
Hero of the tale: R. Phinehas b. Yair. The donkey does not eat in the hideout of the robbers, hence the stolen property motif (and it is appended to the account of Abraham's camels who did not enjoy stolen food). But here the additional motif is found of the animal refusing to eat untithed food (appended to the story of R. Jeremiah and R. Zera).

C. *The JT version*
This is a parallel to B but is presented as one in a series of tales about R. Phinehas b. Yair and other miracle-workers (including R. Hanina b. Dosa, but excluding the story of his donkey as in *ARK*). (In both B and C the saying, 'If the earlier ones…', – occurs, but they both end only with the donkey of R. Phinehas b. Yair, no reference being made to R. Hanina b. Dosa).

D. *The BT version*
Hero of the story: R. Phinehas b. Yair. But here the three separate stories of the JT version have been put together to form three episodes in the same story as a coherent tale. The robbery motif is not found here. Further motif found only here: 'If God prevents a mishap through the animal of the righteous…'

E. *The BT Shabbat passage*
'If the earlier ones…' as in B and C but here in Hebrew. And in addition to the donkey of R. Phinehas b. Yair there is the donkey of R. Hanina b. Dosa.

F. *The BT passage Taanit 24a* (a similar story)
Hero of the story: R. Jose of Yokereth. Motif: the donkey who prevents his owner enjoying benefit from stolen property as in A.

It would appear that, in the stories told regarding the donkeys of the saints who refused to eat, the reason for the refusal was either to prevent their owner enjoying benefit from stolen property (R. Hanina b. Dosa in A and R. Jose of Yokereth in F) or from enjoying benefit from untithed property (R. Phinehas b. Yair in B, C and

D). In B and C there are echoes of the robbery motif in the beginning of the story which makes the robbers steal the donkey which refuses to eat in their hideout. The conclusion drawn from the story is: 'If the earlier ones...' In D the robbery motif is omitted, probably because it is necessary to give a coherent tale of the events that befell R. Phinehas on his travels in which the saint presumably rides on his donkey; to have the donkey stolen would interrupt the narrative for no purpose. Here in D the conclusion drawn from the story is: 'If God does not allow a mishap to the animals of the righteous...' E seems to know of both motifs (unless the reference to R. Hanina b. Dosa or R. Jose of Yokereth is a later gloss, in which case the saying is a paraphrase in Hebrew of that in B and C). In any event it is clear that in the D passage, our chief concern in this article, earlier material has been used and reshaped in order to provide a consistent and coherent narrative with a beginning, middle and end.

NOTES

1. B. Ḥullin 5b, 6a and 7a. The maxim is also found in *Yevamot* 99b; *Ketubot* 28b; *Gittin* 7a. I hope that this analysis is a not unfitting contribution to a *Festschrift* for a scholar who has done important work on Talmudic notions of saintliness and saintly powers.
2. There is no other mention in the Talmud of a River Ginai. In the parallel passage in y. *Demai* 3 (22a) R. Phinehas finds *ginai* in flood, not 'River Ginai'. See Jastrow (*s.v.*), for *ginai* as 'a dyke for irrigating gardens' (from *gan*); but it is unlikely that such a dyke is referred to since here the reference is to the River Ginai which could not be crossed except by a miracle. For the redemption of captives as a great mitzvah, see b. Baba Bathra 8a.
3. That the doubtful yields to the certain (*eyn safek motzi meydey vaddai*) is a legal principle, see b. *Pesaḥim* 9a.
4. Rashi: this means R. Phinehas kept the river 'talking' so that the other two could cross, but the river was only parted once.
5. Exodus 14.21–22.
6. I.e. on the errand of mercy; the same expression 'will of the Maker' is used in the narrative previously by R. Phinehas and by the river.
7. *M. Demai* 1.3.
8. The significance of this is that the barley had the status of food brought from an *am ha-aretz, demai* which is only prohibited, when untithed, by Rabbinic law and hence there are certain leniencies.
9. Rashi: 'and it is fitting to enjoy benefit from them'. The expression *yisrael kedoshim hem* is found in *b. Niddah* 17a. The expression *yisrael kedoshim* without *hem* is found in b. Ḥullin 91a, 92b and *b. Pesaḥim* 83b, all three, in fact, the same text.
10. See *b. Nedarim* 49a where the expression 'the angel of death is in this one's house' is used by a physician who sees in a house he visits food injurious to health.
11. Interpreted by the Rabbis to include causing another to sin. Since it is forbidden to keep these dangerous animals it is forbidden to sell them, because then the purchaser would sin and the seller would have placed a 'stumbling block before the blind'.
12. Rashi comments: 'I shall send them away into the forest', i.e. simply to abandon them would still offend against placing a stumbling block before the blind, in that those who acquired the mules after they had been abandoned would be guilty of keeping dangerous animals.

13. Rashi: since in the forest they will run wild without anyone to keep them in check.
14. Rashi: this would not offend against the prohibition of wanton destruction, mentioned after this, since the mules, no longer dangerous, could still be used for ploughing.
15. Interpreted by the Rabbis as referring to any unnecessary waste of natural resources.
16. This expression might be understood figuratively as 'they fell out' or 'they were no longer on speaking terms', and is so used in post-Talmudic literature, but here it seems to have been intended to be taken literally. In the parallel passage in JT it is 'fire from Heaven' that causes the separation of one from the other.
17. For Rabbi 'weeping' see *b. Ḥagigah* 15b; b. *'Avodah Zarah* 10b, 17a, 18a–all these in connection with someone's death and his entrance into Paradise.
18. Rashi: but during Elisha's lifetime great effort was required for him to revive the son of the Shunamite (2 Kings 4.32–38).
19. Rashi: and had nothing to do with Elisha's own powers.
20. Rashi: Elisha had to revive two corpses for Elijah's one.
21. Here is inserted some further material by association, but this is not germane to our theme.
22. Lit. 'from the day he stood by his own mind'.
23. In *Seridey Bavli*, ed. Z. Dimitrovsky, New York, 1979, the text has 'even of his father'.
24. *Y. Demai* 1.3 (21d–22a).
25. *ha-da alivta* but here in *BT aniyah zo* in Hebrew. Although the framework of the story is in Aramaic most of the direct speech is in Hebrew.
26. That is, R. Phinehas knows that the animal would not have eaten outside its own house in the hideout of the robbers. There is consequently a double theme: a) the animal refused to eat anything in the den of the robbers; b) the animal refused to eat untithed food even in its own home.
27. Here in *JT* it is stated explicitly that it was *demai* produce that was given to the donkey.
28. *Bet Vaad* usual in *JT* for *Bet ha-Midrash.*
29. See *b. Shabbat* 32a for the idea that if a miracle is performed on a man's behalf there is a deduction from the reward due to him because of his merits. Possibly, the idea here is that if the disciples 'give way' to others the river will 'give way' to them; see *b. Yoma* 23a 'whoever gives way (*ma'avir al middotav*) his sins will be forgiven'.
30. Because, in Rabbi's day, the majority of Jews did not live in Palestine and hence the Sabbatical Year was no longer in operation.
31. I.e. because R. Phinehas referred to the endives and so avoided any reply to Rabbi's question about produce. For a similar evasion by referring to something other than the topic of the question, see *b. Pesaḥim* 3b.
32. Here in *JT mulvata*, in *BT kudnaita*.
33. *yehudai* see *Peney Moshe*, possibly a pun on R. Yehudah; or perhaps *yehudai* does not mean 'Jews' but 'of Yehudah', i.e. the servants of R. Judah the Prince.
34. Lit. 'to be sated by him'.
35. On this question see L. Greenwald, *Harau Mesaderey ha-Bavli et haYerushalmi*, New York, 1954 and J. N. Epstein, *Mevuot le-Sifrut ha-Amoraim*, Jerusalem, 1962, pp. 290–2. On the use of Palestinian material in the Babylonian Aggadah, see the important remarks of J. Heinemann, *Aggadot ve-Toledotehen*, Jerusalem, 1974, chapter 11, pp. 163–79.
36. See my article, 'The Numbered Sequence as a Literary Device in the Babylonian Talmud' in *Biblical and Other Studies in honor of Robert Gordis*, ed. Reuben Ahroni, *Hebrew Annual Review* 7 (1983), pp. 137–49. It might also be noted that in the *JT* version only two attempts are made to feed the donkey but in the *BT* version there are three attempts.
37. See e.g. *b. Berakhot* 20a and the miracle tales in the third chapter of *Taanit* (unless R. Joseph is being sarcastic; but this is unlikely).
38. See *b. Shabbat* 59b, where the same root *gazar* is used.
39. Lit. 'she is very strict with herself'; but obviously the meaning is on behalf of R. Phinehas, not that the donkey had to obey the law or be very strict in its observance.
40. See A. Büchler, 'The Conspiracy of R. Nathan and R. Meir against the Patriarch Simon ben Gamaliel', in *Studies in Jewish History* by A. Büchler, ed. I. Brodie and J. Rabbinowitz, Oxford, 1956, chapter 6, pp. 160–79. Rabban Simon b. Gamaliel was, of course, the father of Rabbi Judah the Prince.
41. The meaning then would be: if there was a miraculous intervention to separate the two in this world *a fortiori* they would be kept apart in the next world. Cf. *b. Baba Bathra* 75a

for the righteous occupying separate 'canopies' in Paradise.

42. Cf. *m. Abot* 2.4 'Make His will as thy will so that He will make thy will His will'.
43. *paga'beh.*
44. *'ikliai.*
45. *šama'.*
46. *'itrami.*
47. *Gen. Rabbah* 60.8, ed. Theodor-Albeck, pp. 648–50.
48. In y. Demai R. Phinehas replies: 'What can I do if this poor beast is very strict on herself?' There is no significance to these minor variants. On the relationship between JT and *Genesis Rabbah,* see Epstein, *Mevuot,* pp. 287–90.
49. Ed. Schechter, New York, 1967, A, chapter 8, *p.* 38.
50. In the *Genesis Rabbah* passage the story of R. Phinehas is appended to the verse, 'and he freed the camels' (Gen. 24.32), upon which there is the comment: 'he undid their muzzles'. Abraham's camels were muzzled (*Gen. R.* 59.11) so that they would not eat of anything that did not belong to their owner. To this the question is asked: why did Abraham's camels require to be muzzled (see Albeck's note 3 on this), since R. Phinehas's donkey did not eat and the beasts of Abraham would surely not be inferior to R. Phinehas's donkey. This 'robbery' motif is the one in *ARN* where R. Hanina b. Dosa's donkey refuses to eat or *drink* in the robber's hideout, i.e. because their food and drink was all stolen property.
51. Thus in *Genesis Rabbah,* adding the name *Zeira* after R. Lezer – R. Lezer Zeira (see Albeck's note for variants). Eleazar Zeira is mentioned in Baba Kamma 59b. Is it possible that he was called Eleazar *Zeira* ('young', 'immature', 'inferior') because he was the author of this saying that the later ones were 'inferior' to the ancients? On the phenomenon of the author of a saying having a name connected with the saying, see my article, 'How much of the Babylonian Talmud is Pseudepigraphic?', *JJS* 28 (1977), p. 56 n. 30.
52. In the parallel passage in *y. Shekalim* 5.1 (48 c–d) R. Mana says, 'At that time they said', i.e. when R. Jeremiah sent the untithed figs to R. Zera, 'they' being R. Jeremiah and R. Zera. Possibly 'R. Mana' is a corruption of the name 'Zamina' or perhaps there is a confusion with R. Zera.
53. Here the order is reversed. It is certainly puzzling that 'Zamina' resembles 'R. Mana' and 'Eleazar Zeira' resembles 'R. Zera'. The texts are in any event confused.
54. Thus the reading in the current texts. But see Rashi and the marginal note in the Vilna Romm edition for the reading 'R. Jose of Yokereth' (in *Taanit* 24a), as in F.

—11—

Israel and the Nations

In this article the Talmudic *sûgyā* in tractate *Avodah Zara*h, 2a–3b is examined.* The *sûgyā* is an interesting example of how Halakhic style argumentation is employed in the Aggadah and how this type of argumentation is even ascribed to the gentile nations which appear in it. Although the *sûgyā* contains material found elsewhere, in its entirety it is peculiar to this section of the Babylonian Talmud and is not found in any other early source.[1]

> 'All the nations are gathered together;
> And the peoples are assembled;
> Who among them can declare this,
> And announce to us former things?
> Let them bring their witnesses, that they
> may be justified; And let them hear, and
> say: "It is truth"' (Isaiah 43:9).

*An interesting development in modern Talmudic scholarship is the detection of literary structures in the Babylonian Talmud compiled at the end of the fifth century. The major part of the Talmud is *Halakhic* (the legal exposition) hut a considerable portion is *Aggadic* (legends, history, ethics and so forth). The technical terms used in the paper are *Baraita* (a source from the period of the *Tannaim*, in the first two centuries A.D.); *sûgyā* ('complete section', 'unit'); *Amoraim* (teachers in the post-Tannaitic period, from 200–500); *Avodah Zarah* ('Strange Worship', idolatry, the name of a Talmudic treatise dealing with this suhject); *derashah* ('sermon; 'homily'; 'Aggadic exposition'); and, in addition, *Midrash* (synonymous with *derashah* but also the title of a collection of derashot). The term *Torah*, originally referring to the Five Books of Moses, means 'teaching' and came to include the whole of Jewish religious doctrine. The language of the Talmud is Aramaic with a strong element of Hebrew.

Obviously, the *genre* to which the homily belongs is that of consolation. It consists of a message of hope for Israel that, despite their lowly situation, God still cares for them and that, no matter how inferior the Jews feel themselves to be, they are still far superior to 'the nations of the world'. The original homily is attributed either to the Palestinian Amora R.* Hanina bar Papa (end of the third and beginning of the fourth century) or to the third century Palestinian Amora R. Simlai. The *sûgyā* begins with the words: 'R. Hanina bar Papa – others say, R. Simlai – expounded' (*darash*). Although the *sûgyā* as we now have it is a complete unit, it is clear that some, at least, of the arguments and references are not those of the Palestinian Amora at all but are later additions by the final editors of the Babylonian Talmud.

The *derashah* of R. Hanina bar Papa or R. Simlai begins by stating that in the future (i.e. in the Messianic Age) the Holy One, blessed be He, will take a Scroll of the Torah in His bosom and declare: 'Whoever has occupied himself with this let him come and receive his reward.' Thereupon all the nations come in confusion, as it is said: *All the nations are gathered together* (i.e. 'together' in the sense of unseparated from one another, without their specific identity, hence 'in confusion'). The Holy One, blessed be He, will say to them: 'Do not come before Me in confusion but let each nation come separately together with its scribes', as it is said: *And the peoples are assembled* and the term 'people' refers to a kingdom, as it is said: *and one kingdom shall be stronger than the other kingdom* (Genesis 25:23). (The term *leom,* 'kingdom', is used in both verses, hence first they come as 'nations' in 'confusion', and then as 'kingdoms', each with its own separate identity and with its own 'scribes' who have recorded its specific history).[2]

On this the Talmud interjects: 'But is there any confusion before the Holy One, blessed be He?' i.e. He can identify them as separate kingdoms even if they do come in 'confusion'. To this the reply is given that it is not for His benefit that the nations should not come together but in order each present its own case, as in the continuation of the passage.

The kingdom of Rome is the first to enter. The Talmud adds: What is the reason? Because it is the most important. And how do we know that Rome is the most important? Because it is written: *And he shall devour the whole earth and shall tread it down and break it in pieces* (Daniel 7:23) and R. Johanan said that this refers to Rome whose dominion has gone out to the whole world. And, the

* R. – an abbreviation for Rabbi; in Hebrew 'ר stands for רבי.

Talmud continues, how do we know that the most important comes in first? The reply is, because R. Hisda has said: When a king and a community appear before God to be judged, the king enters first, as it is said: *That He maintain the cause of His servant and the cause of His people Israel* (I Kings 8:59), i.e. first 'His servant', King Solomon, and then 'His people Israel'. On this the Talmud asks: And what is the reason for it? i.e. why does the king enter first? The reply is: You can either say that it is because it is unfitting to keep the king waiting outside or you can say that it is so that the king should enter before the divine wrath is increased, i.e. if the community were to enter first, God's anger at their sins would rebound on the head of the king who comes in later, he being, in some measure, responsible, and this would prevent the king being given a 'fair hearing'.

Now, the *sugya* continues and tells us that the Holy One, blessed be He, will then say to the Romans: With what did you occupy yourselves? i.e. what contribution did you make to the Torah that you should deserve to be given the reward due to those who occupy themselves with the Torah? Romans reply: Sovereign of the Universe! We have set up many market-places, we have erected many bath-houses, we have amassed much gold and silver, and all this we did only that Israel should occupy themselves with the Torah, and, therefore, we, too, are entitled to the reward. The Holy One, blessed be He, replies: Foolish ones of the world! Whatever you did was for yourselves. You set up market-places so that harlots could be placed therein; bath-houses so as to delight yourselves therein; and as for the gold and silver, that is Mine, as it is said: *Mine is the silver and Mine is the gold saith the Lord of Hosts* (Haggai 2:8). Is there anyone among you who can declare this? (Continuing the exposition of the Isaiah verse: 'Who among them can declare this?') *This* refers to the Torah, as it is said: 'And *this* is the Torah which Moses set before the children of Israel' (Deuteronomy 4:44).[3] On hearing this, Rome will depart crushed in spirit.

Rome makes its exit and then Persia enters. The Talmud interjects: What is the reason? Because Persia is second in importance after Rome. How do we know this? Because it is written: *And behold another beast, a second like to a bear* (Daniel 7:5) – upon which R. Joseph commented, the verse refers to the Persians who eat and drink like a bear, are muffled with flesh like a bear, grow their hair long like a bear's and are as restless as a bear. The Holy One,

ט כָּל־הַגּוֹיִם נִקְבְּצוּ יַחְדָּו, וְיֵאָסְפוּ לְאֻמִּים;
מִי בָהֶם יַגִּיד זֹאת, וְרִאשֹׁנוֹת יַשְׁמִיעֻנוּ?
יִתְּנוּ עֵדֵיהֶם וְיִצְדָּקוּ, וְיִשְׁמְעוּ וְיֹאמְרוּ: אֱמֶת.
י אַתֶּם עֵדַי, נְאֻם־יְהוָה, וְעַבְדִּי, אֲשֶׁר בָּחָרְתִּי;
לְמַעַן תֵּדְעוּ וְתַאֲמִינוּ לִי, וְתָבִינוּ, כִּי; אֲנִי הוּא,
לְפָנַי לֹא־נוֹצַר אֵל, וְאַחֲרַי לֹא־יִהְיֶה.
יא אָנֹכִי, אָנֹכִי יְהוָה, וְאֵין מִבַּלְעָדַי מוֹשִׁיעַ.
יב אָנֹכִי הִגַּדְתִּי וְהוֹשַׁעְתִּי וְהִשְׁמַעְתִּי, וְאֵין בָּכֶם זָר;
וְאַתֶּם עֵדַי, נְאֻם־יְהוָה, וַאֲנִי־אֵל!

(Isaiah 43:9–12)

דרש ר׳ חנינא בר פפא, ואיתימא ר׳ שמלאי: לעתיד לבא מביא הקדוש ברוך הוא ס״ת [ומניחו] בחיקו, ואומר: *למי שעסק בה יבוא ויטול שכרו. מיד מתקבצין ובאין עובדי כוכבים בערבוביא, שנאמר: ׳כל הגוים נקבצו יחדו [וגו׳ ׳], אמר להם הקדוש ברוך הוא: אל תכנסו לפני בערבוביא, אלא תכנס כל אומה ואומה וסופריה, שנאמר: ׳ויאספו לאומים׳, ואין ׳לאום׳ אלא מלכות, שנאמר: ׳ולאום מלאום יאמץ׳. ומי איכא ערבוביא קמי הקב״ה?! אלא, כי היכי דלא ליערבבו אינהו [בהדי הדדי] דלישמעו מאי דאמר להו. [מיד] נכנסה לפניו מלכות רומי תחלה. מ״ט? משום דחשיבא. ומנלן דהשיבא? דכתי׳: ׳ותאכל כל ארעא ותדושינה ותדוקינה׳, אמר רבי יוחנן: זו רומי חייבת, שטבעה יצא בכל העולם. ומנא לן דמאן דחשיב עייל ברישא? כדרב חסדא, דאמר רב חסדא: מלך וצבור — מלך נכנס תחלה לדין, שנאמר: ׳לעשות משפט עבדו ומשפט עמו ישראל [וגו׳ ׳]. וטעמא מאי? איבעית אימא: לאו אורח ארעא למיתב מלכא מאבראי, ואיבעית אימא: מקמי דליפוש חרון אף. אמר להם הקב״ה: במאי עסקתם? אומרים לפניו: רבש״ע, הרבה שווקים תקנינו, הרבה מרחצאות עשינו, הרבה כסף וזהב הרבינו, וכולם לא עשינו אלא בשביל ישראל כדי שיתעסקו בתורה. אמר להם הקב״ה: שוטים שבעולם, כל מה שעשיתם - לצורך עצמכם עשיתם, תקנתם שווקים להושיב בהן זונות, מרחצאות - לעדן בהן עצמכם, כסף וזהב שלי הוא, שנאמר: ׳לי הכסף ולי הזהב נאם ה׳ צבאות׳, כלום יש בכם מגיד זאת? [שנאמר: ׳מי בכם יגיד זאת׳], ואין ׳זאת׳ אלא תורה, שנאמר: ׳וזאת התורה אשר שם משה׳! מיד יצאו בפחי נפש. יצאת מלכות רומי, ונכנסה מלכות פרס אחריה. מ״ט? דהא חשיבא בתרה. ומנלן? דכתיב: ׳וארו חיוא אחרי תנינא דמיא לדוב׳, *ותני רב יוסף: אלו פרסיים, שאוכלין ושותין כדוב, ומסורבלין [בשר] כדוב, ומגדלין שער כדוב, ואין להם מנוחה כדוב. אמר להם הקב״ה: במאי עסקתם?

(The opening lines of the Talmudic *sugya Avoda Zarah*)

blessed be He, will say to them: With what did you occupy yourselves? They will reply: Sovereign of the Universe! We built many bridges; we conquered many cities; we fought many battles; and all this we did so that Israel could occupy itself with the Torah. The

Holy One, blessed be He, will reply: Whatever you have done was for yourselves. You have built bridges so as to exact the toll. You have conquered cities so as to impose forced labour on their inhabitants. And as for the battles, it is I who does battle, as it is said: *The Lord is a man of war* (Exodus 15:3). *Is there anyone who has declared this?* and *this* refers to the Torah (as above). Thereupon Persia, too, makes its exit with its spirit crushed.

At this stage, the Talmud asks: since Persia has observed that Rome's plea was to no avail why should it enter at all? Why should Persia imagine that it will fare better than Rome? To this the reply is given: The Persians imagine they will fare better because while Rome destroyed the Temple they, the Persians, rebuilt the Temple (by the edict of Cyrus the Jews were allowed to return and rebuild the Temple: *Ezra,* 1).

The Talmud continues with the tale. After Rome and Persia have departed, crushed in spirit, the other nations enter in turn and each is similarly refuted. But why should they imagine that they will fare better than mighty Rome and Persia? The reply is that they will seek to plead, Rome and Persia subjected Israel to servitude but we did not. The Talmud goes on to ask another question. If the verse implies that all the other nations also present their case, why refer specifically to Rome and Persia? The answer is that the reign of Rome and Persia will endure until the days of the Messiah, i.e. the nations will be replaced by others so that no specification is possible, whereas Rome and Persia will still be there in the Messianic Age.

Continuing with the tale, the Talmud now observes that the nations, seeing that their plea of helping Israel has proved to be ineffective, will present a different plea: Was the Torah offered to them that they refused it? That is to say, had they have been offered the Torah they would have kept it, and are, consequently, entitled to the reward in their own right even if they did not help Israel to keep the Torah. But, objects the Talmud, how can they offer such a plea since it is written: *The Lord came from Sinai and rose from Seir unto them, He shined forth from Mount Paran* (Deuteronomy 33:2) and it is written: *God cometh from Teman* (Habakkuk 3:3), and it was asked, what was God doing in Seir and Mount Paran? To this R. Joḥanan has said in reply, these verses teach us that the Holy One, blessed be He, offered the Torah to every nation and tongue but none accepted it until he came to Israel who did accept it. How, then, can the nations plead that they were not offered the Torah?

The reply is that the nations will plead that *if* they had accepted the Torah they would have kept it. But that is no reply, claims the Talmud, since God will say: Why did you not accept it? The plea of the nations will rather be: Did God invert the mountain over them to force them to accept the Torah, as He did for Israel? Israel was compelled by God to accept the Torah. Why did He not compel us so to do? the nations will plead. That God coerced Israel into accepting the Torah is adduced by R. Dimi bar Hama. Scripture states: *And they stood at the nether part of the mountain* (Exodus 19:17). R. Dimi bar Hama observed, this teaches us that God suspended the mountain over them like a cask, saying: 'If you will accept the Torah well and good but if not here you will be buried.'

Our homily now turns to the exposition of *And announce to us former things* in the verse from Isaiah. So far the nations of the world have been getting the better of the argument by their plea that if God would have compelled them to accept the Torah, as He did for Israel, they would have kept it. God replies by referring to the 'former things'. He will say to the nations: 'What of the "former things", of the seven Noahide laws which you did accept and yet you have not kept them?'

How do we know, Talmud continues, that the nations did not keep the seven Noahide laws? Because it was taught in a *Baraita,* quoted by R. Joseph, as a comment on the verse: *He standeth and shaketh the earth, he seeth and maketh the nations to tremble* (Habakkuk 3:6). The *Baraita* takes the word *va-yatter,* translated as 'to tremble', to mean rather 'and He permitted'. And the interpretation is: What did He see? He saw that the nations had not kept the Noahide laws so He permitted them to abandon these laws, i.e. He released the nations from their obligations to keep the Noahide laws. But, objects the Talmud, in that case the nations gained from their sinful conduct, i.e. if the nations have been released from keeping these laws they gain from their non-observance. To this the reply is given, Mar son of Ravina has said: God only released them from their obligation so that if they do keep the Noahide laws they receive no reward for so doing since the obligation to keep them has been cancelled. But is that really so, asks the Talmud. Is it not taught that R. Meir said: How do we know that even a Gentile who studies the Torah is equal to the High Priest? Because the verse says: *Ye shall keep My statutes and My ordinances which, if a man do, he shall live by them* (Leviticus 18:5). The verse does not say: 'If a priest, Levite or Israelite do' but 'a man'. From this you can learn that even if a

Gentile studies the Torah he is equal to the High Priest, and Gentiles who keep their laws, the Noahide laws, are rewarded for so doing. To this the Talmud replies: When it is said that God released the nations from the Noahide laws it means that He released them from their obligation so that they do receive reward if they keep the laws but only the reward of one who keeps laws he has no *obligation* to keep. And R. Hanina's dictum is quoted: 'Greater is one who does what he is commanded to do than one who does a good deed without being commanded to do it.'

It should here be noted that the whole of this section on God releasing the nations from the obligation and the application to this of R. Hanina's dictum is found in tractate *Bava Kama* 38a and is obviously independent of our *sûgyā*. It seems certain that in the original homily all that appeared was the suggestion that God replies to the nations: 'Have you kept the Noahide laws?' which is, after all, all that is required as a comment on *And announce former things*. It is the later editors who have introduced the section as it appears in *Bava Kama*.[4]

At this stage God is getting the better of the argument. The nations cannot protest that if God had coerced them to accept the Torah they would have kept its laws since they have not kept the Noahide laws they had been given. The homily continues with a comment on: *let them bring their witnesses, that they may be justified* in the Isaiah verse. The nations now admit that they would not have kept the Torah just as they did not keep the Noahide laws. But, the nations argue, what proof is there that Israel has kept the Torah? God replies: I Myself will testify that Israel has kept the Torah.But, the nations will object, Can a father be believed to testify in his son's favour and of Israel it is said: *Israel is My son, My firstborn* (Exodus 4:22). God will agree but will call Heaven and Earth to witness that Israel has kept the Torah. The nations will then object that Heaven and Earth are biased witnesses since if Israel does not keep the Torah the very existence of Heaven and Earth is in danger. This idea is derived from the verse: *If not for My covenant with day and night, I should not have appointed the ordinances of Heaven and Earth* (Jeremiah 33:25), i.e. if not for My covenant, the Torah, I would not have appointed the ordinances of Heaven and Earth. And R. Simeon b. Lakish said: What is the meaning of the verse: *And there was evening and there was morning the sixth day* (Genesis 1:31)? It means that God made a condition with the works of creation, saying to them: If Israel will accept My Torah well and good but if not I shall reduce you once again to utter chaos, i.e. 'evening and morning' only endure because of the 'sixth day', the sixth day of Sivan upon which the Torah was given at Sinai. And Hezekiah commented on the verse: *Thou didst cause sentence to be heard from Heaven, the earth trembled and was still* (Psalm 76:9). If the earth trembled how could it be still, and if still how could it tremble? But at first (until Israel accepted the Torah) it trembled (being uncertain of its fate), and then (when Israel did accept the Torah) it was still. Thus Heaven and Earth are biased witnesses.

Here it should be noted that the interpretations of R. Simeon b. Lakish and Hezekiah are given in tractate *Shabbat* 88a where the theme is that of the giving of the Torah. That would appear to be their proper place from which they have been adapted here. Especially to be noted is that the Jeremiah verse: *If not for My covenant* is relevant here in support of the plea by the nations that Heaven and Earth are biased, but the verse is not quoted in the *Shabbat* passage.

At this stage the nations of the world are once again getting the better of the argument. There are no witnesses that Israel has kept the Torah since neither the testimony by God nor that by Heaven and Earth is admissible.[5] But God now says: You yourselves will testify that Israel has kept the Torah. Let Nimrod come and testify that Abraham did not worship idols; let Laban come and testify that Jacob was not a thief (Genesis 33:37); let Potiphar's wife testify that Joseph was not to be suspected of sin; let Nebuchadnezzar testify that Hananiah, Mishael and Azariah did not bow down to the image; let Darius come and testify that Daniel did not neglect his prayers (Daniel 6:11); let Bildad the Shuhite, and Zophar the Naamathite, and Eliphaz the Temanite come and testify that Israel kept the whole of the Torah, as it is said: *let them bring their witnesses, that they may bejustified* (continuation of the Isaiah verse, i.e. let *them,* the nations testify themselves as to Israel's loyalty).

The nations, having been forced to acknowledge defeat, now present a new plea. Let God give them the Torah now and they will show that they will keep it. God replies: Foolish ones of the world! Only one who takes trouble to prepare food on the eve of the Sabbath can eat on the Sabbath. One who has made no preparations beforehand cannot eat on the Sabbath, i.e. it is now too late. Nevertheless, says God, I have a light precept called *sukkah* (the command to dwell in booths on the festival of Tabernacles). Go, now, and carry it out. Here the Talmud interjects: How can God give them a new precept to perform in the Messianic Age? Did not R. Joshuas b. Levi say: What means the verse: *The ordinances which I command this day to do them* (Deuteronomy 7:11)? *This day* can they be done and not *tomorrow* (in the World to Come); *this day* to do them, *tomorrow* to receive the reward. How, then, can God, in the Messianic Age, offer the nations a precept to perform? The reply to this is: God does not behave imperiously with His creatures, and He must, therefore, give the nations another chance even though, strictly speaking, this is not the time when the precepts can be carried out. And why, the Talmud asks, is the precept of *sukkah* called 'a light precept'? The answer is, because it involves no loss of money, i.e. all that one has to do is to cover a booth with easily obtainable covering. Everyone, the tale continues, will go on to his roof and erect here a *sukkah.* But God will make the sun blaze down on them as at the time of the Tammuz cycle (the Summer Solstice) and each one will kick over his *sukkah* and get out, as it is said: *Let us break their bands asunder, and cast away their cords from us* (Psalm 2:3). But the Talmud objects, you have just said that God does not deal imperiously with His creatures, so, having given them a second chance, why does He spoil it by making it too hot for them to remain in the *sukkah*? The reply is that for Israel, too, it sometimes happens that the heat of the Summer Solstice is still hard to bear at the time of Tabernacles, so the test is a fair one.

Here we must note that for the *sukkah* test no part of the Isaiah verse is quoted. The verse has, in fact, been exhausted before this stage of the debate. The verse quoted is from Psalms. This may suggest that the original homily finished with the final plea of the nations, that Israel, too, did not keep the Torah, and God's reply that they themselves can testify. This is the end of the homily woven around the Isaiah text. The section on the *sukkah* should then be seen as a later addition to the homily, appended by the final editors of the whole passage. In fact, in Midrash on *Psalms* to the verse quoted in our passage there is a similar reference to *sukkah* and the nations of the world. (And see also Zechariah 14:19).

The Talmud now asks: Since it is so hot there is, in fact, no obligation to dwell in the *sukkah.* Rava has ruled that one who experiences extreme discomfort in the *sukkah* is exempt from the obligation to stay there and he may leave. Why, then, should the nations be blamed for leaving the *sukkah*? The reply to this is: Granted that Israel would also be exempt in these circumstances they would not kick the *sukkah* over, as the nations will do, but would leave quietly and respectfully. At that time, states the Talmud, God will laugh at them, as it is said: *He that sitteth in Heaven laugheth* (Psalm 2:4), upon which R. Isaac said: Only on that day is there laughter for the Holy One, blessed be He.[6]

With a modicum of conjecture and leaving out the various interjections, obviously of a later date and referring to the teachings of later Babylonian Amoraim, it is not too difficult to reconstruct the pattern of the original Palestinian homily in which the verse in Isaiah is laid under tribute to provide the main features of the debate between God and the nations of the world. The following is a possible reconstruction of the arguments in the debate as they are made to emerge from the Isaiah verse.

1. God takes the Scroll and states that He wishes to reward those who have kept the Torah.
2. The nations enter 'in confusion'.
3. God tells them to present themselves in proper order.
4. Rome enters first and presents its case.
5. God rejects Rome's plea – exit Rome, enter Persia.
6. Persia presents its case.
7. God rejects Persia's plea – exit Persia, enter the other nations.
8. God rejects these as well.
9. All nations appear again with a new plea: Who will testify that Israel had kept the Torah?
10. God says that He will testify.
11. Nations object: God is a Father and His testimony inadmissible.
12. God says that Heaven and Earth will testify.
13. Nations object: these are biased.
14. God says: You yourselves will testify.
15. (Addition) the *sukkah* episode.

On (2) and (3) the Talmud, in Aramaic, raises the question about 'confusion' and supplies the answer. After (4) the Talmud again interjects, in Aramaic, asking why Rome enters first, and supplies the answer. This is followed by the material about why the most important must enter first. This, too, is in Aramaic. After (5) the Talmud explains why Persia enters next. After (6) there is the Talmud's question and answer on why Persia bothers to enter since Rome has been rejected. After (8) there is the Talmud's question and answer on why the other nations bother to enter since both Rome and Persia have been rejected. And this is followed by the further question and the reply on why only Rome and Persia are mentioned explicitly. This is followed by the lengthy discussion, in which, as above, there is material from elsewhere, in regard to what was then said. It would seem that the material on the Noahide laws does belong to the original Palestinian homily since the clause from the Isaiah verse is quoted, but surely not in the form in which it is here presented with the debate proceeding backwards and forwards. After (13) there is the interpolation, as we have suggested, of the material regarding the statements of R. Simeon b. Lakish and Hezekiah.[7]

Thus our *sûgyā* can be seen as a kind of Midrash on an earlier Midrash. The original Palestinian homily is the text for a sustained Babylonian Midrash in which there is a point-by-point comment in the typical style of the Babylonian Talmud.

NOTES:

1. The appearance of this *sugya* in *Pesikta de-Rav Kahana,* ed. Buber, *Piska* 29, to *Sukkot,* pp. 185–6, is a later addition, and, as the editor notes, has been taken from our *sûgyā,* see Buber's note. Cf. PRK, ed. B. Mandelbaum, New York, 1962, Vol. I, pp.452–3, and PRK, translated W. G. Braude and I. J. Kapstein, London, 1975, pp. 461–2. The passsage is, in fact, in a Supplement to PRK and was added later.
2. The point is obscure in English. The meaning is that the word *goyim,* translated as 'nations', is a generic term, best translated here as 'peoples', whereas *leom* is best translated as 'nations' i.e. each with its own separate identity.
3. The use of this method of taking a word in a given context and then applying it in other contexts for homiletical purposes is, of course, found throughout the Talmudic and Midrashic literature.
4. It would, however, go beyond the evidence to suggest that the editors of our passage had before them the actual passage in *Bava Kama.*
5. It is noteworthy that God obeys the judicial processes as laid down in His Torah. This *motif* of God keeping the Torah is frequent in the Rabbinic literature.
6. The verse quoted on God's 'laughter' is also from Psalm 2 which lends support to our contention that this *motif* was originally part of an independent Midrash on Psalms and was added to our *sûgyā* at a later date by the editors.
7. It is possible that the original homily only contained the material about 'confusion' and 'order' without specifying either Rome or Persia, and the more specific reference was added by the editors of our *sûgyā.* It is also possible that the original homily did have the reference to Rome but not to Persia, since Persia was less relevant in a Palestinian context.

Part Three
General

—12—

The *Qal Va-Ḥomer* Argument in the Old Testamrent

Every student of Rabbinic literature is aware of the formal argument known as *qal va-ḥomer* 'the argument from the minor to the major'.[1] There are numerous instances of the argument in Rabbinic literature, dating from pre-Tannaitic times down to the close of the Talmud. The argument runs: if A is so then B must surely be so; if the 'minor' has this or that property then the 'major' must undoubtedly have it. It is of interest to Old Testament scholars that the Rabbis purported to detect many examples of the use of this argument in Scripture. The Rabbis use the argument as one of their hermeneutical principles by means of which they expand and elaborate on the Biblical teachings. However, they rightly contend that they did not invent the argument but that it is found in the Bible itself. The purpose of this paper is to examine this contention more fully and to note possible implications for Old Testament studies.

We begin with the statement in the Midrash[2] attributed to the second-century Palestinian teacher R. Ishmael. R. Ishmael comments on: 'Behold, the money, which we found in our sacks' mouth, we brought back unto thee out of the land of Canaan; how then should we steal out of thy lord's house silver or gold?' (Gen. xliv, 8). R. Ishmael remarks: 'This is one of the ten instances of *qal va-ḥomer* in the Torah.' (In this context the term 'Torah' refers to the whole Bible, not to the Pentateuch alone.) In what is in all probability an editorial, or even later, gloss, the Midrash gives the other nine as follows.

(1) 'And Moses spoke before the Lord, saying: "Behold, the children of Israel have not hearkened unto me; how then shall Pharaoh hear me, who am of uncircumcised lips?"' (Exod. vi, 12).

(2) 'And the Lord said unto Moses: "If her father had but spit in her face, should she not hide in shame seven days? let her be shut up without the camp seven days, and after that she shall be brought in again"' (Num. xii, 14). (The argument here is: if when her human father showed his disapproval of her actions she would hide herself in shame for seven days then when the Lord shows His disapproval all the more should she be shut away for seven days.)

(3) 'For I know thy rebellion, and thy stiff neck; behold, while I am yet alive with you this day, ye have been rebellious against the Lord; and how much more so after my death?' (Deut. xxxi, 27).

(4) 'And David's men said unto him: "Behold, we are afraid here in Judah; how much more then if we go to Keilah against the armies of the Philistines"' (1 Sam. xxiii, 3).

(5) 'If thou hast run with the footmen, and they have wearied thee, then how canst thou contend with horses?' (Jer. xii, 5).

(6) 'And if in a land of peace where thou art secure (they have wearied thee), then how wilt thou do in the thickets of the Jordan?' (Jer. xii, 5).

(7) 'Behold, when it was whole, it was meet for no work; how much less, when the fire hath devoured it, and it is singed; is it profitable for any work?' (Ezek. xv, 5).

(8) 'Behold, the righteous shall be requited in the earth; how much more the wicked and the sinner!' (Prov. xi, 31).

(9) 'And the king said unto Esther the queen: "The Jews have slain and destroyed five hundred men in Shushan the castle, and the ten sons of Haman; what then have they done in the rest of the king's provinces?"' (Esther ix, 12).

In another Rabbinic passage[3] it is said that there are five instances of *qal va-ḥomer* in the Torah (and here 'Torah' means the Pentateuch). In addition to the four Pentateuchal instances recorded above, this source gives: 'If Cain shall be avenged sevenfold, truly Lamech seventy and sevenfold' (Gen. iv, 24) i.e. if Cain who killed Abel was not to be 'avenged' until seven generations had passed then Lamech who had not killed would surely not be 'avenged' until seventy-seven generations had passed. In yet another passage[4] a *qal va-ḥomer* is found in the verses: 'And as for Ishmael, I have heard thee; behold, I have blessed him, and will make him fruitful, and will multiply him exceedingly; twelve princes shall he beget, and I will make him a great nation. And My covenant will I establish with Isaac, whom Sarah shall bear unto thee at this set time next year' (Gen. xvii, 20–1) i.e. if Ishmael, the son of the handmaiden, will be blessed in this way then all the more will Isaac, the son of Sarah, be blessed.

To complete the picture of how this idea features in Rabbinic literature we must refer to the so-called *Baraita* of R. Eliezer b. R. Jose the Galilean in which[5] a distinction is drawn between an explicit and implicit *qal va-ḥhomer,* both of which, it is said, are found in the Bible. The examples quoted of an explicit *qal va-ḥomer* are those in Jeremiah and Esther, as above. As examples of the implicit *qal va-homer* the following are quoted.

(1) 'He sweareth to his own hurt and changeth not' (Ps. xv, 4). If he 'changeth not' (i.e. does not go back on his word) where it is to his own hurt how much more *(qal va-ḥomer)* will he not change where it is to his own good.

(2) 'Nor taketh a bribe to side with the innocent' (Ps. xv, 5). The *Baraita* understands the verse to mean this (*'al* being rendered not 'against' but 'on behalf of'). Hence the *qal va-ḥomer:* if he refuses to take a bribe to support the innocent how much more will he refuse to take a bribe to support the guilty!

It is here suggested that there are instances in which the verse does not state the *qal va-ḥomer* argument explicitly but invites us to draw the *qal va-ḥomer* from the premiss that is stated in the verse. At least one of these two examples is homiletical but it is still possible that there is something in the idea of an implicit as well as an explicit *qal va-ḥomer* in Scripture.

So far we have surveyed the relevant material on the subject in Rabbinic literature. But the commentators to the Midrash and other scholars are puzzled by R. Ishmael's reference to only ten Scriptural cases.[6] In fact, they point out, there are many more instances of an explicit *qal va-ḥomer* in the Bible. Wolf Einhorn of Grodno[7] observes that his researches have yielded no fewer than forty instances and other commentators come up with similar results. Some of these must be rejected as far-fetched and dubious but the following list contains all the definite references.

(1) 'And he said unto her: "Behold, I have not told it my father nor my mother, and shall I tell thee?"' (Judges xiv, 16).

(2) 'Then said Jonathan: "My father hath troubled the land; see, I pray you, how mine eyes are brightened, because I tasted a little of this honey. How much more, if haply the people had eaten freely to-day of the spoil of their enemies which they found? had there not been a much greater slaughter among the Philistines?"' (1 Sam. xiv, 29–30).

(3) 'And it came to pass on the seventh day that the child died. And the servants of David feared to tell him that the child was dead; for they said: "Behold, while the child was yet alive, we spoke unto him, and he hearkened not unto our voice; how then shall we tell him that the child is dead, so that he do himself some harm?"' (2 Sam. xii, 18).

(4) 'And David said to Abishai, and to all his servants: "Behold, my son, who came forth of my body, seeketh my life; how much more this Benjaminite now?"' (2 Sam. xvi, 11).

(5) 'But will God in very truth dwell on the earth? behold, heaven and the heaven of heavens cannot contain Thee; how much less this house that I have builded!' (1 Kings viii, 27). The same argument is implied in Isa. lxvi, 1: 'Thus saith the Lord: The heaven is My throne, and the earth My footstool; where is the house that ye may build unto Me? And where is the place that may be My resting-place?'. The argument is: if the heaven is only My throne and the earth only My footstool, then where could there be a house worthy of the Lord?

(6) 'But they were exceedingly afraid, and said: "Behold, the two kings stood not before him; how then shall we stand?"' (2 Kings x, 4).

(7) 'For, lo, I begin to bring evil in the city whereupon My name is called, and should ye be utterly unpunished?' (Jer. xxv, 29).

(8) 'Thou shalt say unto him: "Thus saith the Lord: 'Behold, that which I have built will I break down, and that which I have planted I will pluck up; and this in the whole land. And seekest thou great things for thyself?"' (Jer. xlv, 4–5).

(9) 'For thus saith the Lord: "Behold, they to whom it pertaineth not to drink of the cup shall assuredly drink; and art thou he that shall altogether go unpunished?"' (Jer. xlix, 12).

(10) 'Abraham was one, and he inherited the land; but we are many; the land is given us for inheritance' (Ezek. xxxiii, 24).

(11) 'And the Lord said: "Thou hast had pity on the gourd, for which thou hast not laboured, nor made it grow, which came up in a night and perished in a night; and should not I have pity on Nineveh, that great city, wherein are more than six score thousand persons that cannot discern between their right and their left hand, and also much cattle?"' (Jonah iv, 10–11).

(12) 'The nether-world and Destruction are before the Lord; how much more then the hearts of the children of men!' (Prov. xv, 11).

(13) 'All the brethren of the poor do hate him; how much more do his friends go far from him!' (Prov. xix, 7).

(14) 'Luxury is not seemly for a fool; much less for a servant to have rule over princes' (Prov. xix, 10).

(15) 'The sacrifice of the wicked is an abomination; how much more, when he bringeth it with the proceeds of wickedness!' (Prov. xxi, 27).

(16) 'Behold, He putteth no trust in His servants, and His angels He chargeth with folly; how much more them that dwell in houses of clay whose foundation is in the dust, who are crushed before the moth!' (Job iv, 18–19).

(17) 'God will not withdraw His anger; the helpers of Rahab did stoop under Him. How much less shall I answer Him, and choose my arguments with Him?' (Job ix, 13–14).

(18) 'Behold, He putteth no trust in His holy ones; yea, the heavens are not clean in His sight. How much less one that is abominable and impure, a man who drinketh iniquity like water!' (Job xv, 15–16).

(19) 'Behold, even the moon hath no brightness, and the stars are not pure in His sight; how much less man, that is a worm! and the son of man, that is a maggot!' (Job xxv, 5–6).

(20) 'Did not Solomon king of Israel sin by these things? yet among many nations was there no king like him, and he was beloved of his God, and God made him king over all Israel; nevertheless even him did the foreign women cause him to sin. Shall we then hearken unto you to do this great evil, to break faith with our God in marrying foreign women?' (Neh. xiii, 26–7).

It might be mentioned that in addition to the many hundreds of instances of the use of *qal va-ḥomer* in the Rabbinic literature, a device derived directly from the Old Testament, there are instances of *qal va-ḥomer* in both the New Testament[8] and the Apocrypha. Three examples from the New Testament may be cited.

(1) 'And behold, there was a man which had his hand withered. And they asked him, saying, is it lawful to heal on the sabbath days? that they might accuse him. And he said unto them, What man shall there be among you, that shall have one sheep, and if it fall into a pit on the sabbath day, will he not lay hold on it, and lift it out? How much then is a man better than a sheep? Wherefore it is lawful to do well on the sabbath days' (Matt. xii, 10–12).

(2) '... doth not each one of you on the sabbath loose his ox or his ass from the stall, and lead him away to watering? And ought not this woman, being a daughter of Abraham, whom Satan hath

bound, lo, these eighteen years, be loosed from this bond on the sabbath day?' (Luke xiii, 15–16).

(3) 'For if, when we were enemies, we were reconciled to God by the death of His Son, much more, being reconciled, we shall be saved by his life' (Rom. v, 10).

Three examples from the Apocrypha may be cited.

(1) 'He that is honoured in poverty, how much more in riches? and he that is dishonourable in riches, how much more in poverty?' (Ecclus, x, 31).

(2) 'He that is evil to himself, to whom will he be good?' (Ecclus, xiv, 5).

(3) 'It was through delight in the beauty of these things that men supposed them to be gods. They ought to have understood how much better is the Lord and Master of it all; for it was by the prime author of all beauty that they were created' (Wisdom of Solomon xiii, 3).

It is clear, then, that this type of argument was resorted to even before the Rabbinic period as, it would seem, a heritage from the Old Testament period.

From all that has been said it is surely well established that the argument from the minor to the major is used frequently throughout the Old Testament. Its use is not limited to any single phase in Israel's history but, it would appear, was employed in all periods. Neither is the usage confined to any single book of the Old Testament nor to any particular document, stratum, and trend. The sage uses it as well as the prophet, the narrator as well as the psalmist. Moreover, as in many of the examples quoted, its use is generally of a formal nature, beginning with *hien* or *hinneh* and concluding with *'eykh* or *'aph.*

The ubiquity of this argument and its strictly formal nature raise important questions, hitherto barely considered by Old Testament scholarship, regarding the use of rhetoric in ancient Israel.[9] Eissfeldt, discussing the question of rhetoric and the examples of the 'wise woman' in 2 Sam. xiv, 1–24, and 2 Sam. xx, 14–22, remarks: 'It is self-evident that such men and women, specially skilled in speech, possess a technique which does not depend solely upon a particular gift, but also upon tradition and "training"; there were, in other words, certain fixed forms for speech. The two examples just cited confirm this; for the two women employ what is essentially the same device, that of first obtaining from the person addressed an admission which does not appear to be relevant to the matter in hand, and this admission then compels him to grant the request which is really involved.' In view of the evidence that has been presented for the use of *qal va-ḥomer,* it would certainly seem that Eissfeldt is correct. In the Rabbinic period formal argument was consciously and extensively cultivated. The student was introduced at an early stage to the various methods of argumentation. For all the diversity of arguments in the Rabbinic period, there are certain stereotyped rules which are closely observed and which follow regular patterns. Was there anything like this during the Old Testament period? When we consider the evidence produced by this investigation as well as the numerous instances, in the Old Testament literature of every period, of sustained argumentation with very formal patterns, there seems to be no doubt that the answer should be in the affirmative. Of course, it is hard to find anything like an explicit reference anywhere in the Old Testament to schools in which rhetoric was taught. Perhaps further research will throw new light on this problem.

Attention has been called[10] in this connexion to the references to 'speech' and 'speakers', e.g. David is 'skilled in speech' (1 Sam. xvi, 18); Moses declares that he is not 'a man of speech' (Exod. v, 10); Aaron can 'speak well' (Exod. iv, 14). In these passages the root *dbr* is used. Further investigation is required into the possible connotation of other Old Testament passages in which this root occurs in formal argument rather than mere 'speech'.

A few examples might suggest that this topic is worth pursuing. Judah's sustained argument in Gen. xliv, 18–34, begins with: 'O my lord, let thy servant, I pray thee, speak a word in my lord's ears' (verse 18). Since the expression *yedabber dabhar* is used, should it be translated as 'present an argument'? When *ken* and *dobheroth* are used of the daughters of Zelophehad (Num. xxvii, 7) and of the tribe of the sons of Joseph *ken* and *dobherim* (Num. xxxvi, 5) are we justified in translating, instead of the pallid 'speak rightly', 'argue convincingly'?[11] Can *'elleh ha-debharim* at the beginning of Deuteronomy (i, 1) be rendered: 'These are the arguments which Moses presented' since Moses' discourse is in the form of a sustained argument? Similarly, is it not possible that the words *dibkreykhem, nidhbarnu,* and *nidhberu* in Mal. iii, 13 and 16, refer to 'argument' rather than to mere 'speech'? Should the expression *dobher tamim* in Amos v, 10, be rendered 'one who argues convincingly' rather than 'speaketh uprightly'? If so, the parallelism with 'him that rebuketh in the gate' would be more reasonable.[12] And, finally, may not *dabhar dabhur 'al ophnav* in Prov. xxv, 11 be rendered as 'a well-presented argument' rather than 'a word fitly spoken'? Such an argument would be 'like apples of gold in settings of silver'.

NOTES

1. Adolf Schwarz, *Der hermeneutische Syllogismus in der talmudischen Litteratur: em Beitrag zur Geschichte der Logik im Morgenlande,* Karlsruhe, 1901. Cf. L. Jacobs, *Studies in Talmudic Logic and Methodology,* London, 1961, 3–8. The correct reading is in all probability *qol va-homer, v.* Schwarz, 8–14, and the Theodor–Albeck ed. of Gen. Rabbah, p. 474, n. 3, but the conventional form is *qal,* perhaps in order to avoid any association with *qol* 'a voice'. Schwarz's identification of the *qal va-ḥomer* with the Aristotelian syllogism is untenable. In the syllogism the inference concerns the relationship between genus and species; since e.g. Socrates belongs to the class *man* he must share the characteristics of that class. In the *qal va-ḥomer,* on the other hand, it is not suggested that the 'major' belongs to the class of the 'minor' but that what is true of the 'minor' is true of the 'major'. There does not appear to be, in fact, any real parallel to the *qal va-ḥomer* in Greek thought. But, in an important article, Arnold Kunst ('An overlooked type of inference', *BSOAS,* x, 4, 1942, 976–91) has pointed to a striking parallel in the Indian form of inference known as *kim-punar.* Kunst remarks: 'Whether the similarity of this inferential procedure between the Jews and the Indians was a result of mutual influence, or whether it was only an expression of a common human tendency to eulogize great things by comparing them with smaller, or to raise the value of small things by juxtaposing them with greater – this problem may be left to further historical researches. The author would rather vote for the latter alternative' (p. 991).
2. Gen. Rabbah 92:7, ed. Theodor–Albeck, pp. 1145–6; Yalkut, 1 Sam. 132 (which refers to ten but lists only nine). See Theodor's lengthy note in which it is suggested that the actual list is a gloss.
3. *Avot de-Rabbi Nathan* (version B) 44; Gen. Rabbah 4: 24 (ed. Theodor–Albeck, p. 225) and Jerusalem Talmud *Sank.* 10:1 (27d) mention Gen. iv, 24 as a *qal va-ḥomer.*
4. Gen. Rabbah 17:20–1 (ed. Theodor–Albeck, p. 225).
5. Sections 5 and 6. A number of editions of this *Baraita* have been published e.g. in the introduction of Wolf Einhorn of Grodino at the beginning of the Vilna edition of Midrash Rabbah.
6. Schwarz, op. cit.; H. Hirschensohn, *Berure ha-Middot,* Jerusalem, 1929, 39–60; Samuel Jofe Ashkenazi, *Yephe toar,* comment to Gen. Rabbah 92:7 in the Vilna edition. Cf. H. Strack, *Introduction to the Talmud and Midrash,* Philadelphia, 1945, p. 285, n. 3.
7. Hirschensohn, op. cit., 40–5, adds the following examples (but these are extremely doubtful): Gen. iii, 22; Gen. xi, 6; Gen. xvii, 17.
8. *v.* Daube in *HUCA,* xxii, 1949, 239f.
9. *v.* the literature cited by O. Eissfeldt, *The Old Testament: An Introduction,* Oxford, 1965, 12, and Eissfeldt's general remarks, 12–15.
10. Eissfeldt, op. cit., loc. cit.
11. *NEB* renders Num. xxvii, 7, as 'The claim of the daughters of Zelophehad is good' and Num. xxxvi, 5, as 'The tribe of the sons of Joseph is right'. But this overlooks entirely that the same terms – *ken* and *dbr* – are used in both passages.
12. cf. Targum Pseudo-Jonathan: *demalel keyvanta.*

—13—

The Economic Conditions of the Jews in Babylon in Talmudic Times Compared with Palestine[1]

A Baraitha[2] records that '"ten measures of poverty descended into the world, nine of them were taken by Babylon'. There is the further statement of R. 'Asi[3] that the festivals are celebrated with great joy in Babylon as a compensation for the great poverty of the Babylonians. On the basis of these two statements some modern scholars[4] conclude that the Jews in Babylon were in worse financial circumstances than their Palestinian brethren. Samuel Krauss[5] is at pains to refute this view and he argues convincingly for the thesis that the Babylonians were the wealthier. From the evidence here to be presented there can no longer be any doubt whatsoever of the correctness of Krauss's view. In fact it follows from this evidence that Krauss has failed to underline sufficiently the very real differences, especially in the economic sphere, between the two communities.[6]

Palestine was never a commercial country. Josephus[7] points to this fact with pride. After the destruction of the Temple and the devastations caused by the wars with Rome, the whole economic position rapidly deteriorated and conditions became increasingly worse. Büchler[8] describing these conditions writes:

> Of trade, hardly any evidence is found, though there must have been grocers and bakers. R. Eleazar b. Azaryah dealt in wine and oil (B.B. 91 a); R. Jehudah was a baker, and bakers' shops are mentioned in Yad. II. 16 and Joshua was grit-miller (*sic*) (Erub. 21b). Lydda had vendors who sold their goods dear (B.M. IV. 3), and a synagogue of weavers or metal workers (Naz. 52 a). R. Joshua gave up his studies and took up

> business, for which his colleague R. Mathia blamed him (A.R.N. 1a) and R. Akiba seems to have been connected with shipping (Ned. 50a, b). A R. Johanan was a sandal-maker (Sifre Deut. 80); a Jehudah a perfumer (Hull. 53b), Simeon a cotton dealer (?); R. Ishmael a Torah-writer (Sot. 20a); and Eleazar a writer (Ḥull. 55b); and in connection with the deposition of R. Gamliel, a fuller is mentioned (jer. Ber. IV. 7d).

How different from this is the rich variety of trades and occupations followed by Jews in Babylon and recorded in the Talmud![9]

It is therefore not surprising that, despite the many rabbinic teachings about the importance from the religious aspect of residence in Palestine,[10] and despite the many injunctions against leaving it, there was a constant stream of Jewish emigrants to Babylon where life had more to offer in the economic sphere. This emigration was no doubt behind the teaching (sent we are told from the Palestinian authorities to those of Babylon):[11] 'Take care of the sons of the poor for the Torah proceeds from them.' The 'sons of the poor' were probably the poor emigrants from Palestine who came to Babylon to seek their fortunes.[12] This is borne out by the account of a Palestinian scholar who came to Babylon and, being disappointed by the cold reception given to him by the 'rich men of Babylon', who refused to set him up in business or help him financially, taught that these men were destined for Gehinna.[13]

Samuel ruled in Babylon that a scholar should first marry and then devote himself to the study of the Torah, whereas R. Johanan in Palestine ruled that he should study before marriage:[14] 'A millstone around his neck, shall he be able to study the Torah?' The Gemara explains that the ruling of each authority refers to his own land. This does not mean, as Hirschberg suggests,[15] that because of the greater degree of immorality in Babylon it was obligatory for Jews to marry early. It is clear that it is financial considerations which are the determining factor ('a millstone around his neck'). The correct interpretation of the passage is that in Babylon economic conditions were such that a scholar could afford to live in financial comfort even after his marriage, whereas in Palestine this was most difficult.[16]

It is no mere coincidence that hardly any of the Babylonian Amoraim were poor men. Their comparative freedom from economic cares explains their greater brilliance in the study of Halachah which requires intense concentration. Furthermore the far more highly developed economic life explains the existence of a greater abundance of legal material dealing with civil law in the Babylonian Talmud than in the Palestinian.[17]

The apparent contradictions to the greater wealth of the Babylonians in the two statements with which this article begins can easily be dispensed with. The statement of R. 'Asi is an ironic skit on Babylonian life by its author who had emigrated from Babylon to Palestine, and far from proving the greater poverty of the Babylonians, it proves the exact opposite.[18] The statement ofthe Baraitha, quite apart from the fact that it pre-dates the rise of the Sassanian Empire, and the consolidation of Jewish life in Babylon by Rab and Samuel, does not refer to the Jewish Community at all but to the general population, as is clear from the similar observations made on other lands in the same Baraitha. Krauss[19] makes the interesting suggestion that the general decline in wealth gave the Jews an opportunity to accumulate it and there is, at least, a kernel of truth in this in so far as commerce in Babylon was mainly in the hands of the Jews and other minorities.

The contributory factors to the greater wealth of Babylonian Jewry were as follows. The Sassanians, unlike the Romans, were not a commercial race, preferring, under the influence of Zoroastrianism, agriculture to commerce.[20] This provided far greater commercial opportunities for Jews in the Sassanian Empire. One example of this is the government monopoly in the trade in silks in the Roman Empire[21] which prevented Jews in Palestine from trading in this commodity, and the extensive trade in silks in Babylon.[22] Palestine too was devastated by the Roman wars and by the Roman system of taxation whereas, with the exception of a few outbursts by the Magi and their followers, the Jews in the Sassanian Empire were comparatively safe from persecution and were immune from discriminatory taxes levied against them.[23]

Another important factor, not to be underestimated, was the far greater stringency with which the agricultural laws were applied in Palestine. The observance of these laws in Palestine was so burdensome that for many farmers it became virtually impossible to keep them and pay the heavy taxes demanded by the Romans at the same time. In Babylon, though these laws were observed, there were so many relaxations that their observance was hardly burdensome.[24]

Finally, the famous dictum of Samuel, 'The law of the land is law',[25] must have gone a long way to affecting a proper adjustment between the members of the Jewish community and their Gentile neighbours. In Palestine a ruling of this kind was never contemplated by the Jewish authorities, who never ceased to look upon the Roman invaders as intruders.[26] As a further example of the attempt at adjustment on the part of the Babylonian authorities, we may cite R. 'Asi's recognition of the right to sell arms to the Persians despite the earlier prohibition of the sale of arms to Gentiles.[27]

It is not surprising therefore that on the one hand the wages of a worker in Babylon were generally higher than in Palestine,[28] and that, on the other hand, certain important commodities were cheaper. Livestock, wheat, dates, and possibly clothing, were all cheaper in Babylon.[29] Land too was less expensive than in Palestine.[30]

As a direct result of the far more highly developed economic life in Babylon, greater efforts were made by the Jewish authorities there to exercise controls to stabilize that life. For example, while in Palestine only weights and measures were controlled, prices being allowed to find their own level, in Babylon the Exilarch appointed market-commissioners for the control of prices too.[31] On the other hand, due to the severity of economic conditions, it was forbidden, according to some authorities, for a dealer in Palestine to profit on the sale of life's necessities such as oil, wine and flour.[32] No controls of this kind existed in Babylon.

Hellenistic influences were at work in shaping the administrative and general economic life of the whole of the Near East. Some of the Hellenistic institutions, such as the appointment of the agoranomoi, persisted in their original form in the Parthian and Sassanian Empires,[33] others assumed an Iranian colouring such as the taxation system.[34] Yet there were important differences between the Graeco-Roman and Iranian Empires. The Roman Empire was on a gold standard, after the reforms of Diocletian; the Iranian Empires were on a silver standard of currency.[35] The large fair, so prominent a feature of Roman economic life, was unknown in Babylon.[36] This helps us to understand why an institution such as the money-changer, so widespread in the Hellenistic and Roman worlds, was hardly developed at all in Babylon.[37]

Usury being prohibited, it became vitally necessary for the rabbinic authorities in Babylon to devise ways and means of encouraging people to lend money and of allowing the possibility of various forms of credit buying. Thus we find the possibility of the creditor consuming the profits of a pledge greatly developed in Babylon.[38] Similarly, we find that the institution of the 'arebh ḳablan – the guarantor who could be approached by the creditor directly – was a feature of Babylonian Jewish economic life, though apparently unknown in Palestine despite its Roman parallels.[39] The numerous details concerning credit buying found in the Babylonian Talmud[40] are further evidences of the concern of the Rabbis to allow a full economic life to develop without an infringement of the usury laws.

In view of the indisputable evidence of Babylonian economic superiority we cannot possibly accept Rashi's interpretation of a Talmudic passage[41] according to which a distinction is drawn between Palestine and Babylon in that more slaves were to be found in Jewish houses in the former. If the passage deals with slaves, and this is by no means certain,[42] the opposite interpretation would be nearer the truth, especially after the edict of Constantine forbidding Jews to own non-Jewish converted slaves,[43] which, as Dubnow remarks,[44] had a crippling effect on Palestinian economic life.

We have now to notice some differences in the industries of Babylon and Palestine and certain other differences in the economic life of the two centres.

There was far more vine cultivation and wine manufacture in Palestine.[45] In Babylon only the comparatively wealthy could afford wine daily, its place being taken by beer made from dates, the palm being the most extensively cultivated tree here.[46] In Palestine, too, olives were cultivated and olive-oil was widely used. In Babylon its place was generally taken by sesame-oil. Thus a Baraitha[47] rules according to the interpretation of the Gemara that one who vows not to partake of oil is permitted, in Palestine, to use sesame-oil (because this oil was not used in Palestine and was consequently not usually referred to as 'oil') and forbidden to use olive-oil. In Babylon he may use olive-oil but not sesame-oil. At a later period, after the Persian war with Julian, the olive was cultivated in Babylon too.[48]

There were no stone quarries in Babylon as in Palestine, clay bricks being used for building.[49] Despite the fact that two shops discovered at Dura appear to have been stone-cutters' shops,[50] the craft of stone-cutter is nowhere referred to in the Babylonian Talmud. Only in the wealthy town of Maḥoza were stone floors to be found in the houses.[51]

That characteristic Roman institution, the public bath, was well-known in Palestine, but owing to Sassanian religious objections to them, there were fewer of these in Babylon. 'The poor of Babylon die in anguish without light or baths' is the statement of the Palestinian Talmud.[52] The Magi considered the institution of the public bath after the Roman fashion to be a profanation of the sacred element. King Barlash (484–88) is said to have scandalized the Magi when he introduced this fashion.[53] From which it follows that before Barlash there were few bath-houses in Babylon, which accords with the remark of the Palestinian Talmud mentioned above and with the fact that the majority of The Talmudic references to the bath-house refer to conditions in Palestine.[54]

Further support to the above is given by a report of Babylonian and Palestinian interpretations of the institution known as 'the cup of peace', evidently the drinking of a cup of wine as a form of greeting and an expression of goodwill. In Babylon this was explained as the cup partaken of in the house of mourning. In Palestine, where the bath-house was a regular feature of Jewish life, it was understood as the cup partaken of in the bath-house.[55]

Of the industries connected with clothing, dyeing was one of the most important in Babylon. The famous Babylonian dye was known all over the ancient world.[56] The flax industry too was a most important Babylonian one. The manufacture of linen was so important that Rab, in a homily on 'hope in your latter end' (Jer. xxix. 11) understood this to refer to the dates and flax of Babylon.[57] On the other hand Palestinian laundrymen were more skilful than their Babylonian counterparts.[58]

With regard to the rearing of livestock, there are references to the sale of elephants in Babylon,[59] none in Palestine. It is of interest in this connexion that in the Gospels[60] the expression used in the famous saying is 'a camel through the eye of a needle' whereas in a parallel Babylonian Talmudic saying[61] the expression is 'an elephant through the eye of a needle'. The substitution of elephant in the popular proverb was no doubt due to the fact that this animal was far more frequently found in Babylon.

We learn that in Babylon the ox was used for ploughing; in Palestine, the cow.[62] It seems certain that the reason for this is to be found in the Talmudic report that, in Babylon, friendly non-Jews, who were aware of the Jewish prohibition of the castrating of animals (based on the rabbinic interpretation of Lev. xxii. 24), used to steal bulls from Jews, castrate them and return them to their Jewish owners so that they could be used for ploughing.[63] In Palestine there were few non-Jews prepared to do this service for their Jewish neighbours.

Finally we may note that the followers of trades connected with entertainment such as dancers, singers and actors appear to have flourished in Palestine under the influence of Graeco-Roman civilization,[64] but, apart from a stray reference to a slave dancing in a tavern,[65] there are no references to entertainers of this kind among the members of the Babylonian Community.

There is a Talmudic saying that Adam's body came from Babylon and his head from Palestine.[66] Getzow[67] applies this to primitive man – the cradle of civilization being Mesopotamia; the birthplace of early man's spiritual consciousness, the Holy Land. We can fittingly apply this to the history of the Jews. In the land of the Prophets the Jews acquired their original spiritual and moral approach to life. But it was in Babylon, the second great centre of Jewish life, that the transition took place which transformed the Jewish people from an agricultural to a commercial people. The effects of this transformation are told in many subsequent pages of Jewish history.

NOTES

1. In accordance with the regulations of the London University I have to state that this article is based on part of a thesis for the PhD degree of that university.
2. Ḳidd. 49b.
3. Ṡabb. 145b.
4. See N. Getzow, *'Al Naharoth Babhel* (Warsaw, 1879), *'Ozar Yisrael,* II, 294 nl, fo 5. *Ḳadmonioth Ha-Talmudh* (Berlin and Tel-Aviv, 1914–29), I, 7–22.
6. Cf. J. Juster, *Les Juifs dans l'empire romain, leur condition juridique, économique et sociale* (Paris, 1914), I, 20 and 24–5; II, 39 n. 2.
7. *Contra Apion.* I, 12. Cf. L. Jacobs: 'The Economic Situation of the Jews in Babylon' in *Melilah* (Manchester, 1955), v, 83f.
8. *The Economic Conditions of Judaea after the Destruction of the Second Temple* (Jews' College Publications, London, 1912), Publ. no. 4, pp. 49f., cf. Juster, *loc. cit.* II, 291f. and 297 n. 1.
9. Cf. the remarks of S. W. Baron in his 'The Economic Views of Maimonides' in *Essays on Maimonides* (New York, 1941), pp. 171–2: 'By the Middle Ages commerce was accepted by Jewish thinkers such as Maimonides as a necessary and unobjectionable human institution. The anti-commercial statements of Ḳidd. IV. 14, and so forth, had been so thoroughly disposed of in the Talmudic and Geonic periods that Maimonides had no compunction about leaving the Mishnah without comment.' The facts are that in Babylon we find Jews engaged in all the occupations forbidden or frowned upon by the Tannaim in the Mishnah referred to by Baron and in Ḳidd. 82a. Thus we find Jews in Babylon active as physicians and cuppers (Sanh. 17b, B.Ḳ. 85a, Sabb. 129b, B.B. 22b–23a, Ta'an. 21b); as ass- and camel-drivers (B.K 116a, Hag. 9b); as sailors (Sabb. 100b, 125b, Soṭ. 48a, Pes. 112b, Bekh. 8b); as shopkeepers (B.B. 29b, B.Ḳ 21a, B.M. 69b); as butchers (B.B. 9a, Ḥull. 94–95a, Nidd. 3a, Bekh. 30a, Bez. 28b–29a) and as tanners (Keth. 77a, B.B. 5a, Ned. 56b, Ḥull. 48 a). It should however be noted that it is difficult to believe that in Palestine no Jews followed these callings. From the Palestinian references to

them it appears rather that the Tannaitic expressions of disapproval were academic. Of importance in this connexion is the way the disapproval of the craft of shepherd, never very strongly accepted in Palestine, was virtually disregarded in Babylon, see Rapoport, *'Erekh Millin* (Prague, 1852), p. 214, S. Krauss, 'La Défense d'élever du menu bétail en Palestine et questions connexes' in *R.E.J.* LIII, 14–55, Büchler, *op. cit.* p. 45, J. Newman, *The Agricultural Life of the Jews in Babylonia between the Years 200 C.E. and 500 C.E.* (London, 1932), p. 115 and S. W. Baron, *A Social and Religious History of the Jews* (New York, 1937), I, 279 and III, 69 n. 16.

10. Tos. A.Z. IV. 3, p. 446, Yer. M.K. III. I Keth. 110b.
11. Ned. 81a.
12. Krauss, Ḳad. *ad loc.*
13. Bez. 32b, cf. Juster, *bc. cit.* II, 320 n. 5.
14. Ḳidd. 29b.
15. *He'athid* (Berlin, 1912), p. 14 n. I.
16. See *'Aruch Koh.* VII, 267, *'Erekh Millin,* p. 226, Krauss, *Ḳad.* I, 13 n. 3.
17. Y. H. Tabyob, 'Talmudah shel Babhel vetalmudah shel Ereẓ Yisrael' in *Ha-Teḳuphah* (Moscow, 1918), I, 558, cf. Cant. R. I. 6.
18. See the other statements of R. 'Asi (*ibid.*)מצויינים לפי שאינם מפני מה עופות שבבבל שמנים א״ל בני תורה כלך למדבר עזה ואראך שמנים מהן. מפני מה תלמידי חכמים שבבבל. Even if this is not a skit on Babylonian life it is evident that R. 'Asi is seeking to persuade R. Ḥiyya B. 'Abba of the greater advantages of life in Palestine, hence his disparagement of Babylonian life. Obviously, no conclusions can be drawn from this concerning the actual poverty of the Babylonians.
19. Ḳad. *ad loc.*, cf. Yer. Kil. 9. 4, Pesiḳta, ed. Friedmann, I, p. 2 and Sifre Deut. 116, p. 98.
20. See M. N. Dhalla, *Zoroastrian Civilization from the Earliest Times to the Downfall of the last Zoroastrian Empire 651 A.D.* (New York, 1922), pp. 295 and 356, F. Spiegel, Eranische Altertumskunde (Leipzig, 1871–1902), III, 658, Finlay, quoted by W. Cunningham in *Western Civilization in its Economic Aspects (Ancient Times)* (Cambridge Historical Series, Camb., 1898), I, 203.
21. *Oxford Classical Dictionary*, p. 222, Lev. R. 34. 12, cf. Gen. R. 77. 2.
22. See especially Ḳidd. 7b, 32a, 73a.
23. For special taxes levied against the Jews in the Roman Empire see Juster, *loc. cit.* II, 280 f.; for taxation in Babylon see Newman, *loc. cit.* 161f., F. M. Heichelheim, 'The Influence of Hellenistic Financial Administration in the Near East and India', in Economic History (London, Feb. 1938), pp. 2f. and in Tenny Frank's *Economic Survey of Ancient Rome* (Baltimore, 1938), iv, s.v. Syria; M. I. Rostovtzeff, *The Social and Economic History of the Hellenistic World* (Oxford, 1941), I, 468 and III, 1434 n. 257 and more recently Y. A. Soloducho's comprehensive, though highly tendentious account, in Russian, in *Sovietskoye Vostokovedeniye*, V (1948), 55–72.
24. See Boaz Cohen in *J.Q.R.* New Series, XXVII, 70–5.
25. B.Ḳ. 113b, B.B. 54b, Giṭṭ. 10b, Ned. 28a, Newman, *loc. cit.* pp. 196f., Juster, *loc. cit.* II, 34 n. 2.
26. See L. Ginzberg, *Meḳomah Shel Ha-Halakhah beḤokhmath Yisrael* (Jerusalem, 1931), pp. 11f.
27. A.Z. 16a.
28. According to an anonymous statement of the Babylonian Talmud (B.M. 76 a), mentioned in a casual discussion which lends it great credence, a labourer received 3—4 zuz for one day's work. In Palestine in the early first century the daily wage of a vineyard worker was 1 denarius (= 1 zuz) a day (Matt. xx. 2). Hillel, we are told, earned only half a denarius a day (Yom. 35a). In an edict of Diocletian a land worker was to receive 25 copper dinars a day; 16 of these equalled one silver dinar (L. Herzfeld, *Handelsgeschichte der Juden des Altertums* [Brunswick, 1879], p. 195). Tacitus (*Annals,* 1, 17) refers to the wages of a Roman soldier as being 1 dinar a day. Under Septimius Severus, the Roman soldier's pay was 500 denarii a year, under Caracalla 750 denarii (Tenny Frank, *loc. cit.* v, 86, Bellinger in *The Excavation at Dura-Europos,* Final Report VI [New Haven, 1949], p. 196 n.). (Heichelheim, *Syria,* p. 181, remarks that in the second century in Babylon only 1 zuz was paid for hair cutting 100 times! This is obviously absurd. Heichelheim evidently relies on the interpretation of Tos. *s.v.* to Sabb. 129b but this is clearly unhistorical.)
29. In Palestine a young lamb or goat was worth 2, 3, 4, and 5 dinars (Sheḳ. II. 4, Tos. Ker. V. 2); in Babylon in the time of R. Joseph (d. 333) a young lamb was worth one-sixth of a

zuz (Bekh. 1 1 a). In Palestine, in the Mishnaic period, the normal price of an ox was 1 maneh =100 denarii (B.K. III. 9); in Babylon, at a later period, the hide of an ox cost as little as 1–4 zuz (B.Ḳ. 11 a). Wheat in Egypt was generally cheaper than in Palestine (Heichelheim, *Syria*, p. 181, Tenny Frank, *loc. cit.* II, 36f.). The Babylonian prices compare favourably with the Egyptian. A griva (= I se'ah) of wheat in Babylon was worth 1–4 zuz (Pes. 32a). In the time of Samuel (d. 254) I kor (= 30 se'ah) of wheat was worth 1sela = 4 zuz (B.M. 102b). According to the figures given by Heichelheim and Tenny Frank, *loc. cit.* the price of 1 se'ah (=13.131 lit.) in Egypt, was, on the average, 1 denarius, that of I artaba (= 39.2 lit.) was ½–2 denarii. In the time of Samuel 1 kor of dates was sometimes worth only 1 dinar (Ḳidd. 12a). Allowing for the element of exaggeration in this statement it is clear that dates were very cheap in Babylon. In the time of 'Ulla (early fourth century) three basketfuls of dates could be bought in Babylon for x1 zuz (Pes. 88a). From 'Ulla's expression of amazement at the cheapness of dates in Babylon when he came there on a visit from Palestine, it follows that in Babylon, where the date palm was so extensively cultivated, dates were far cheaper than in Palestine. Heichelheim, *Syria*, pp. 181–2, is of the opinion that the Palestinian prices of clothes in the first to second century C.E. are as a rule higher than those of Babylonia of the third century, but he adduces no convincing evidence of this. In Palestine a ṭalith (robe) cost 18, 20 or 50 denarii, the cost of weaving it was 8 denarii (Me'il. IV. 4, Tos. 'Arak. IV, Tos. Sheḳ. a, Tos. B.M. 7). At a clothier's shop found at Dura robes of various kinds are priced at from 16 to 90 denarii (*Dura*, Preliminary Report IV [New Haven, 1933], pp. 140–3), but this is not very helpful for comparative purposes seeing that there is no evidence as to such matters as the quality of the materials used and the tailoring skill.

30. See B.B. 12a and comment of R. Gershon, S. Funk, *Die Juden in Babybonien* (Berlin, 1902), p. 1 6 and his "Beiträge zur Kulturgeschichte Babyloniens aus der Zeit der Sassaniden" in *J.J.L.G.* VII (1910), 214.
31. B.B. 89a, Tos. B.M. VI. 14, Yer. B.B. V. 2, cf. I. Epstein, *Social Legislation in the Talmud*, Torah Va'abhodah Ideological Series (London, n.d.), p. 9.
32. B.B. 91a.
33. Heichelheim, *Syria*, Rostovtzeff in the *Cambridge Ancient History*, XI, 116, Pauly-Wissowa, *Real-Encyclopädie der Classischen Altertumswissenschaft* (Stuttgart, 1894), I, 883, Tos. B.M. VI. 14, Lev. R. 18.
34. See Heichelheim, 'The Influence of Hellenistic Financial Administration in the Near East and India', in *Economic History* (1938), p. 2, p. 7 n. 12, p. 9 n. 35, and p. 11.
35. Palestine, after the reforms of Diocletian, was on a gold standard, as was the rest of the Roman Empire (see *Chambers's Encyclopaedia* (London, 1950), X, 127). The Sassanian Empire, on the other hand, was on a silver standard. 'The Arsacids do not seem to have struck gold coins; they were content with those of silver and bronze currency. A few years before the accession of Ardeshir I, there had been a sudden influx of Roman gold into Western Asia, in consequence of the treaty concluded between Artabanus and Macrinus (217 C.E.), whereby Rome undertook to pay Parthia a large indemnity. It is probable that the payment was made mostly in aurei. Ardeshir thus found in the countries which he conquered and formed into an Empire, three coinages current, of gold, silver and bronze, coming from three different sources and possessing no common measure. It was simpler and easier to retain what already existed and had sufficiently adjusted itself owing to the working of commercial needs, than to invent a new currency; hence the anomalous character of the Sassanian money system' (D. J. Paruck, *Sassanian Coins* [Bombay, 1924], p. 31). On the other hand E. Herzfeld in his *KushnaSassanian Coins* (Calcutta, 1930), is of the opinion that the Sassanian aurei represent the gold currency of the eastern dominions of the Persian Empire, while in the western dominions there was a silver currency. This is supported by the fact that no gold coins were found at Dura (see Bellinger in Final Report VI, p. 195).

    There appears to be a trace of the different standards of Roman Palestine and Sassanian Babylon, in the Amoraic period, in the different versions of the Palestinian and Babylonian Talmuds of a Mishnah dealing with currency. The general legal principle concerning the transfer of goods is that the act of purchasing becomes complete, not as soon as the price is paid, but when the commodity is delivered. The question discussed in the Mishnah is, in the cases of the sale of gold coins for silver coins, or silver for gold, which of the two is to be considered the commodity and which the purchase

price? There are two versions of the Mishnah's ruling on this question. According to the version of the Babylonian Talmud, the ruling is that the delivery of gold coins affects the transfer, i.e. the gold coins are the commodity and the silver coins the purchase price (B.M. 44a–b to Mish. IV. 1). The Palestinian version is that the silver coins are the commodity, the gold coins the purchase price (Yer. B.M. IV. 19b–c). There can be little doubt that the two Talmuds were influenced by the currency conditions of their respective lands. In Palestine silver coins had long been adulterated and, after the reforms of Diocletian, the standard was gold. Consequently silver was in the nature of a commodity in relation to gold. In Babylon, where silver coins were far more current than gold, the latter would be the commodity (cf. Heichelheim, *Syria*, Krauss, *Talmudische Archäologie* (Leipzig, 1910–12), II 714 n. 649, Marmorstein in R.E.J. XCVIII (1934), 36.
36. A.Z. 13, Gen. R. 67. 7 and 47. 10. Cf. Gen. R. 67. 7 on Gen. XXVII. 40: 'thou hast fairs (*yeridim*-speaking to Esau, with play on the word *tarid*) and he (Jacob) has no fairs".
37. See Gulak in *Tarbiz*, V (1934), 164–5 nl, fo.
38. See Gulak in *Tarbiz*, I (1934), 89f.
39. A. Gulak in *Toledoth Ha-Mishpaṭ Beyisrael Biteḳuphath Ha-Talmudh* (Jerusalem, 1939), ch. VI, and G. Allon in *Ḳiryath Sepher*, XVII, 172f.
40. See especially the fifth chapter of B.M. in the Babylonian Talmud.
41. Beẓ. 14b.
42. Cf. Maimon. Yad Hil.. Yom Tobh, 3. 13 and the stricture of R. Abraham Ibn David *ad loc.*
43. See Juster, *loc. cit.* II, 72f.
44. *History of the Jewish People* (Hebrew ed., Debhir, Tel-Aviv, 1933), III, 179.
45. B.B. 69b, Hastings' *Dictionary of the Bible,* II, 31–5.
46. Pes. 107a, Yeb. 63a, B.B. 69b, B.Ḳ. 91b, Mid. Lam. Proems XXXIV, Funk, 'Beitrage zur Kulturgeschichte Babyloniens', in *J.J.L.G.* VII, 222.
47. Ned. 53a.
48. Funk, *Die Juden in Babybonien,* II, 81.
49. See Mid. Teh. XXIV. 10, Pirḳe D.R.E. ch. 24.
50. *Dura,* Prelim. Report, V p. 86.
51. Sabb. 95a.
52. Yer. Ber. IV. 1, Mid. Lam. Proems XXIV. Cf. Krauss, *Kad.* I, 17.
53. See Warner's note to Firdausi's Shahnama in Trübner's Oriental Series (London, 1905–25). VII and E. Herzfeld, *Zoroaster and his World* (Princeton, 1947), p. 795.
54. Tos. Nidd. 6. 15, Tos. Keth. 7. 6, Giṭṭ. 90b, Yer. Keth. 7. 4. Cf. Hirschberg in *He'athid,* IV (1912), p. 23.
55. Ned. 38b.
56. Gen R. 85. 14, Mid. Tanh. Mishpaṭ. 17, Krauss in *J.E.* II, 405.
57. Ta'an. 29b. I have been unable to discover any authority for Heichelheim's contention *(Syria,* p. 131) that the Talmud absolutely forbids the export of linen products from Babylon to prevent a dearth of this important material, thus demonstrating that the native flax production was not sufficient for the needs of the Babylonian population. Heichelheim's source citation (B.B. 91a) refers to the offering of public prayers when linen garments became too cheap and not to a prohibition against export.
58. Ta'an. 29b, Keth. 10b.
59. See Ḳidd. 25b, Tos. *ibid.* 26a *s.v.*
60. Matt. xix. 24, Mark x. 25, Luke XVIII. 25.
61. Ber. 55b, B.M. 38b, cf. Krauss in J.E. III, 521.
62. See Krauss, *Talmudische Archäologie,* II, 116.
63. B.M. 90b.
64. See Yer. Ta'an. 1. 4. 64a, S. Lieberman, *Greek in Jewish Palestine* (New York, 1942), pp. 31f. For Jewish gladiators, etc., in the Roman Empire, see Juster, *loc. cit.* II, 239 n. 2.
65. B.Ḳ. 86a, B.M. 64b.
66. Sanh. 38a–b.
67. *Loc. cit.* Introd.

—14—

Montefiore and Loewe on the Rabbis

The subject of my address is 'Montefiore and Loewe on the Rabbis'. I am referring of course to the book known as *A Rabbinic Anthology,* which has fortunately been republished in Meridian Books and which is, without doubt, the most remarkable example of collaboration between a great Liberal Jew and a great Orthodox Jew.

I am not here, I hope, either to defend the Rabbis against some of the strictures of Claude Montefiore, nor am I here to pick holes in some of the things that have been said in this book by Montefiore and by Loewe. I doubt if it would be possible for anybody to write a book which goes into about a thousand pages, on a subject so difficult as the interpretation of Rabbinic thought for men and women today, without making, here and there, minor slips. I am not here to pick holes; but on the other hand, although I did not have the privilege of knowing personally either Montefiore or Loewe, one feels on reading their work that they were the kind of people who, above all, prized integrity and honesty. And the Rabbis – I believe this passage is quoted in the Anthology – go so far as to say that even God does not welcome flattery, expecting us even in our prayers to say what we really believe. Surely they were men who would have taken kindly to criticism of the right sort; criticism is not quite the word we ought to use – to honest differences of opinion. What I want to do here is to examine some of the ideas of this book and to differ from the learned authors in certain matters of emphasis. I think this can be done by dealing with four different topics. First of all, the question that concerns most Jews today, what is our attitude to these men we call the Rabbis? Secondly, I hope that we can examine in our discussion the kind of thinking that was typical of the Rabbis. Thirdly, I want to discuss the attitude of the learned authors of the *Rabbinic Anthology* to Halachah, to the legal side of Judaism. Finally, we should consider the question which, more than any other, is discussed so excitingly in the pages of the *Rabbinic Anthology,* the different attitudes towards the Rabbis and towards Rabbinic authority on the part of Liberal Jews and Orthodox Jews. There is certainly no other work where this debate is carried out with such learning, with such charm, with such wit, and in such impeccable English.

To deal first with the question of our attitude to the Rabbis. Since we are trying to be honest, one must confess that there seems to be (I may be reading this wrongly) on the part of Montefiore a rather condescending attitude to the Rabbis. On page 609 for example, in a remarkable note in which he criticizes those Christian theologians who use the adjective 'Jewish' in a pejorative sense, he says, .'It is agreed [nowadays] that in A.D. 28 there were doubtless many black sheep among them [the Rabbis], but it is also allowed that there were many white ones, as well as a large number of mixtures – grey sheep, not wholly white, but by no means completely black. Such a view of these old gentlemen is, I am convinced, much nearer to history and truth.' I have no doubt that Montefiore saw no great harm in referring to the Rabbis as 'these old gentlemen', but, to put it no higher, there are many hundreds of thousands of Jews in the world of today who would find this offensive. Indeed, I suppose it would be true to say that a major problem in Jewish theology is precisely how to assess the contribution of the Rabbis. How do we look upon these men who lived during a period of about 600 years and who laid the foundations of Rabbinic Judaism and who are our teachers, whether we are Orthodox Jews or Liberal Jews? On the whole, there have been two attitudes among Jews. There have been Jews who have looked upon the Rabbis, and there are Jews today who look upon the Rabbis, as infallible supermen – men who somehow (and this is a favourite expression used in the later Rabbinic literature, the literature produced during the past 200 or 300 years) were gifted, it was said, with the holy spirit, who were, in some mysterious way, as much the recipients of a kind of direct revelation as the Biblical authors themselves. You may say that this is not your attitude to the Rabbis, and I am quite sure that hundreds of thousands of Jews do not have this attitude to the Rabbis, but we would fail to understand the problems of Jewish life today if we did not recognise that there are men to whom the

Rabbis are infallible supermen, whose every word is true. How often do you find quoted the passage in Rabbinic literature which goes like this! "If the earlier scholars were like angels, then we are like human beings; but if the earlier scholars were like human beings, then we are like donkeys." No doubt the Rabbi who first said that was expressing natural humility in the face of earlier teachers. But this has become for many Jews a kind of dogma, that you have to believe that the Rabbis were infallible, that who are we – at the worst donkeys and at the best mere human beings, in the face of angelic beings – to criticize anything that they said? Professor Katz has recently pointed out that even an innocent saying like, 'One does not derive principles of faith or practice from the Aggadic literature' is only accepted by the more rationalistic Spanish school. But the German scholars tended to accept *every* statement in the Rabbinic literature, including the contradictory statements, as divine truth. Hence you find people who take this line objecting vehemently to any saying that contradicts even a stray passage in the Rabbinic literature, and they will tell you that this is against *chazal* – *chazal* being *chachamenu zichram livrachah,* our sages of blessed memory. A famous Chasidic saint of the last century said: 'God in His wisdom allowed a spark of the divine fire to proceed from under the throne of glory, it came down to earth where it was called Abbaye' (one of the great Talmudic sages). 'And another spark from under the throne of divine glory came down to earth where it was called Raba.' That is one attitude towards the Rabbis: a very different attitude from that which refers to them as 'old gentlemen'.

But, of course, this is not the whole story, and leaving aside the attitude of modern Jews to the Rabbis, even in the traditional sources, even among the interpreters of Rabbinic literature, there was another point of view, one which challenged this doctrine of the infallibility of the Rabbis. Maimonides was bold enough to say that the Rabbis were mistaken occasionally in matters of science, because they only had the science of their day. It was the same Maimonides who said that man was created with his eyes in the front of his head and not in the back of his head, so that even though many of the Rabbis believed in astrology, he did not believe in astrology. It is well known that, with regard to the Aggadic literature, men like Ibn Ezra could say that while some of the Aggadot of the Rabbis are like beautiful, fine silk, many others are as coarse as sackcloth. Azariah de Rossi, the famous

Renaissance scholar, went further and suggested that the Rabbis might have been mistaken in matters of history or geography, for which he was severely criticizsed and for which his book *Meor Enayim* was banned.

What is our attitude? Well I am sure that it is impossible to speak of a common attitude held by everyone. But many of us feel that it is possible to speak of the Rabbis as our teachers, to speak of them as *chazal,* as our Sages, while recognizing that they were human beings, not uninfluenced by ideas of their own time, children of their own age, as we all are, but without adopting the kind of condescending attitude that does appear from some pages of this book, to put it no higher than that. I make no more of it than this.

Perhaps this also ought to be said, that if the Rabbis were really as childish as some modern theologians suggest, how do you explain the fact that so many of the best Jewish brains have been nourished on the intellectual fare provided by this Rabbinic literature? How do you account for the fact that in the great Yeshivot, for example, of Eastern Europe, men spent laborious years pouring over the works of the Rabbis and finding much intellectual stimulus in those works? You may say, of course, and you will probably be right, that this was partly because they were reading into the literature ideas that were not really there. With those who argue in that way I would be prepared to go a long way. But then, would it not be true to say that, in a sense at least, those ideas that have been drawn out of the Rabbinic literature are not all without value even if they were not contained in that literature from the beginning? If we take seriously the idea that Jewish thought is capable of development, then we must apply this to the interpretations of Rabbinic literature as well as of Biblical literature. This is surely true of every literary work of genius. Ideas are read into the work which may not have been present in the mind of the author, or may only have been present in the mind of the author in germinal form. There used to be an old jingle:

> I dreamt one night that Shakespeare's ghost
> Sat for a civil service post.
> The subject chosen for the year
> Was taken from the play King Lear,
> And Shakespeare failed. He did it badly,
> Because he had not read his Bradley.

No doubt this is true of Rabbinic literature, as it is true of all great literature. No doubt those great minds in Eastern Europe who were so familiar with the Talmud that they knew it by heart found much in it that was not really there. But this we can say, that the germs of the ideas, the kernels, must have been there.

And that leads me to the second point. Montefiore, for all his keen understanding of the nature of Rabbinic thought, does here and there suggest that the Rabbis were philosophers, but not particularly good philosophers. To read just one passage in this vein: he says, 'They' (that is the Rabbis) 'had no training in philosophy. How enormously they might have benefited if, under competent teachers, they had been put through a course of Greek philosophy and literature.' This is to assume that the Rabbis were thinking as philosophers but, unfortunately, were not trained in philosophical thinking, and had they sat at the feet of the great Greek philosophers their work would have been improved. There have been some important studies of Rabbinic thinking published in recent years which remind us that, in fact, it is in many ways a complete misunderstanding of the Rabbis to think of them as philosophers. They were not inferior philosophers, they were not bad philosophers or philosophers without an adequate philosophic training. They were not philosophers at all. The thinking of the Rabbis – to use the expression which has now become current, thanks in particular to the work of two men, Max Kadushin and Isaac Heinemann – was not systematic thinking but organic thinking. It was not a question of trying to construct a complete system that would cover all situations in life, it was not an attempt to construct a Jewish theology or a Jewish philosophy of life. The Rabbis were responding in a direct and elemental way to life's problems, and they realized that life is complex, that life contains contradictions, that you cannot fit life into a system and that there may be responses, valuable in one particular situation, that will be less than valuable in a different situation. So that they were capable of saying that the patriarchs, for example, were men without sin, when it was necessary for them to remind their people that they had a great past, and yet at other times it was possible for them to be more critical of the patriarchs than the Biblical writers are on occasion. It was possible for one Rabbi to say that, in his view, a person should always say that the world was created for my sake, and for the same Rabbi, or for one of his colleagues, without sensing the contradiction, or sensing the contradiction but realizing that life is full of contradictions, to say that man must pursue humility and must never say anything of that sort. And it is doubtful if the Rabbis would have agreed that you can compile a Rabbinic Anthology.

The history of the Rabbis, for example, is not sober history. We can admit to the point made by both Montefiore and Loewe that the Rabbis were not great historians, but they did not try to be great historians. Heinemann uses the interesting expression 'creative historiography' for the history of the Rabbis. *'Creative* historiography' – they were not really interested in what happened in a once-and-for-all sense, but they were interested in what the happenings of the past have to say to the present. It is undoubtedly true that many of the anachronisms in Rabbinic literature are real anachronisms and are due to ignorance, but it is equally true that many of their anachronisms are conscious, and they have as their aim the cultivation of an attitude of mind which makes the past live in the present. For example, when one Rabbi said (it is doubtful if we can speak of 'the Rabbis') that Abraham kept the whole of the Torah before it was given, and he even kept the Rabbinic law long before it was given. Historically that is nonsense, but it is true if what the Rabbis were trying to convey is the meaning of Abraham for the Jew of their day. I understand that most historians would tell you that Luther did not say, 'Here I stand, I can do no other.' But whether he said it or not, it is this that is typical of the man. And if he did not say it, then it was invented by the people in this organic role which is typical of (we ought not to be afraid of using the word) primitive thinking. Not systematic thinking, not sophisticated thinking, not philosophical thinking, but that kind of thinking which is direct response, based on faith, and based on certain concepts and ideas, to the problems of life. Perhaps the nearest analogy would be that of the poet rather than the philosopher. To criticise the Rabbis for not having a good training in philosophy is rather like saying that a poet would have been a better poet had he had a training in philosophy. I doubt very much whether that would be true.

There is a remarkable passage in the Rabbinic literature which illustrates very clearly this aspect of creative historiography. The Rabbis saw that in the Book of Genesis we find that Esau, when he was cheated by Jacob, cried out, and the Hebrew is *va-yitzak tzeakah gedolah,* 'he cried out with a great and bitter cry', and a Rabbi noted that these very words were used of Mordecai when Haman plotted against the people of Israel. He, too, cried out, and Scripture uses in the Book of Esther the very same words *va-yitzak tzeakah gedolah.* The Rabbis say, because the ancestor of the Jewish people was guilty of a degree of treachery, therefore his descendants were obliged to suffer under Haman. Mordecai cried because Esau had cried. What a remarkable thing this is. It is not history, it is not philology, it is not a sober account of the meaning of a Biblical text. It is quite clear that the author of the Book of Esther used this expression either because he was quoting from Genesis because the idea was familiar to him, or it just happens to be a coincidence. But the Rabbis were not concerned with the interpretation of events, they were concerned with the eternal truth of Judaism as they saw it and as they tried to apply it in their own lives and for the benefit of their flock. Although the Romans, who were considered to be the descendants of Esau, were the enemies of the Jewish people, none the less they could have said that the principle of tit-for-tat and measure-for-measure – of which much is made in this Anthology and on which many wise things are said in it – applied even to the Romans, even to the Gentiles, and when the Gentiles are offended, then God acts in his role of judge and punishes even the descendants of the Jews who offended them. Seen against the background of its time, this means more to those of us who wish to understand what Rabbinic thinking is about than the occasional sayings in the Rabbinic literature in which the Rabbis are concerned to interpret the text. In other words, we do not go to the Rabbinic literature for the understanding of the Bible. We do not go primarily for that in any event. We go to these texts rather to try to see how great Jews hundreds of years ago read the Bible in the light of their own day.

Now let me give one or two examples of this kind of thinking and the way it seems to me the Anthology has sometimes been less than just to the Rabbis. On page 341 the Anthology quotes that marvellous story about Rabbi Eliezer and the Sages. Rabbi Eliezer, you may remember, disagreed with the Sages on a matter of ritual (the actual point of discussion need not concern us here). However, Eliezer was convinced that he was right and he said, 'If I am right then let the canal prove it,' and the water of the canal ran backwards, and he said, 'You see, I am right.' The Sages said, 'We take no notice of this.' Then he said, 'If I am right, let the walls of the House of Study prove it,' and the walls began to cave in, and the Sages said, 'We take no notice of this.' Eventually he said, 'If I am right, let the heavens prove it,' and a heavenly voice came forth, and the heavenly voice said, 'The Halachah [ruling] is always with Rabbi Eliezer. He is right.' And Rabbi Joshua got up and said, 'It is not in heaven.' What did he mean by this? Rabbi Jeremiah said, "The Law was given us from Sinai. We pay no attention to a heavenly voice. For already from Sinai the Law said, "By a majority you are to decide."' And then comes what we might term the 'punchline' of this story. 'Rabbi Nathan met Elijah and asked him what God did in that hour. Elijah replied, "He laughed and said, My children have conquered Me."' I am afraid that Montefiore's comment here does less than justice to this idea. Montefiore says, 'The naive, but daring, anthropomorphism at the end of this last extract may seem almost flippant to modern readers. The apparent flippancy is not due to any Rabbinic lack of deep reverence for God or of fervent love; it may rather be said that this very reverence and love produced a certain intimate familiarity, which may be compared to the familiarity of a loving son who is on very intimate terms with his father, and can even make jokes about him to his face.' That is all very well so far as it goes. Loewe comments on Rabbi Joshua's refusal to accept the miracle of the carob tree: 'Abrahams says' (that is Israel Abrahams): '"Liberals have no interest in Rabbi Joshua's point of law, but his assertion of the rights of private judgment interest Liberals very much."'

But surely, far from this last comment being in any way flippant, it is the real point of the story: the point that God is pleased that His children have conquered Him, and the word 'conquered' is used advisedly, and if any other expression were used, the point would be missed. The point being that, for these Rabbis at least, for whoever recorded this story in the Talmud, the Torah was not something that was given once and for all so that we can speak of ultimate truth when applied to the Torah. God alone, they were saying, knows what ultimate truth is. God alone can know what the actual ruling is. Human beings can never know it, but human beings have no need to know it; and even, as the author of this story is saying, if human beings go wrong but they go wrong in the right way through the exercise of their reason, according to the principles of the Torah, then they cannot be wrong. Even if they are offending in some way against ultimate truth they are still right. They are conquering God and God is pleased to be conquered.

I do not think that this is a kind of apology for the Rabbis, I think this is implicit in Rabbinic thinking. It is not a systematic presentation of a theory of revelation, but if we try to give it systematic form then something of the sort emerges. Or to quote another example: on page 286 there is an interesting discussion on a problem that ought to bother those who read the passage to which the discussion is appended. Let me read you the passage first of all. The passage is taken from Tractate *Kiddushin* and it reads as follows: 'One who is "good" towards God and "good" towards men is a good righteous man: and one who is "good" towards God but "bad" towards men is a not good righteous man. Similarly: one who is bad towards God and bad towards men is a bad bad man; one who is bad towards God but not bad towards man is a not bad bad man.' Now Montefiore says, and I am sure he is right, at least on the surface he is right, he says: 'In these strange words the Talmud seeks to distinguish between the commands in the Law which are ordered by God, but which do not relate to our fellowmen. The former set of commands are less weighty than the latter. Thus one might say that, from this point of view, the Jew who violates the Sabbath, does not observe the Day of Atonement, etc., but who honours his parents and is charitable, just and kind towards his fellows is a "not bad bad man", whereas he who does just the reverse, is "a not good righteous man".' And Loewe says, 'The difficulty to which Mr Montefiore refers was a very real one. One might say that the cause of it was the absence of abstract terms, a deficiency which is very remarkable in classical and post-classical Hebrew. Syriac is far better equipped in this respect, often by borrowing from Greek. The fact that abstract adjectives in the Bible have to supply many diverse connotations hardly needs mention. But this paucity of terms may be regarded, perhaps, as a symptom rather than as a cause, for had the Jews had a bent for philosophy, they surely would have created the requisite vocabulary.' Then he concludes by saying: 'The Rabbis tended to express themselves practically rather than philosophically, because their main interest lay with the practical details of life rather than with speculation.'

I take it most of us would agree with that, except that surely on this discussion, today at least, it ought to be said that many people, many distinguished religious thinkers, have given a great deal of thought to the precise relationship between religion and ethics. One thinks in particular of the work of a man like Otto and his school and those who were influenced by him. As the result of his work we can perhaps see, without necessarily agreeing with, what the Rabbis were trying to say. Religion is not ethics, and you can have a religious person who is not a good man in the ethical sense. The Rabbis surely, as teachers of Judaism, would have refused to look upon that man as anything like an ideal, but they were saying here, at least so it seems to me, that, in a sense (and I know this is dangerous doctrine), religion is man's relationship with his God. I know that this is open to discussion; I know that very few of us would take kindly to this thought, and I am quite sure that it cannot be taken as baldly as it is stated here in this particular passage. But surely an idea is hinted at which requires much more discussion than is given in the Anthology. Is it not true that for the Rabbis the concept of *yirat shamayim,* the fear of heaven, had very little to do with ethics? This is not to say, of course, that the Rabbis were not interested in the ethical side of life. Anyone who has read this *Rabbinic Anthology* or who has read anything of the Rabbis will know how untrue that is. But they thought, and many modern thinkers are in agreement with them, that there is a demarcation line between religion and ethics and that you do not use religion for ethics or indeed for anything else. Religion is *sui generis,* it is a relationship between God and man.

Perhaps here one should say just a word or two about the Rabbinic attitude to sex, on which there are some interesting comments in this book. The problem is partly this: one can hardly read even an anthology such as this without realizing that the Rabbis were concerned about sexual matters, and one can certainly not study the Halachah for very long without realizing this concern. What is one to make of it? Montefiore, on page xix, has this to say: 'The evil impulse – the *yetzer hara* – is especially' (that is for the Rabbis) 'and mainly the impulse which leads to sexual impurity. The result was not entirely healthy. The Rabbis were prevailingly chaste; there was probably much less adultery and fornication among the Rabbis than among us. But this chastity was obtained at a certain cost. The lack of healthy, simple companionship and friendship caused a constant dwelling upon sexual relations and details. In the Rabbinic literature sexual allusions are very frequent. Immense are the Halachic discussions about the details of sex life, and sexual phenomena. 'Repel nature, and it recurs.' Repress it, and it grows up again, and not always in a healthy form. Where we should not dream of thinking that any sexual desire could be evoked, the Rabbis were always on the watch for it, dwelling on it, suggesting it. Though they were almost invariably married men, they yet seem to have often been oddly tormented by sexual desires; perhaps, too, the very absence of natural and healthy social intercourse between men and women drove them to dwell theoretically with double frequency upon every sort of sexual details and minutiae. Loewe defends the Rabbis in a note here, and he deals with the subject elsewhere in the Anthology; he says, 'This tendency was characteristic of the age. Patristic literature is similarly marked. On the other hand, the Rabbinic writings do not eulogize virginity and monasticism.' But surely there is more to be said than this. It is difficult indeed for us to put ourselves in the minds of men who lived so many centuries ago, but in some ways the complaint is trivial, particularly when it is applied to the Halachic literature. The Rabbis are nowhere pornographic, all their discussion of sexual details is clinical in the extreme. One might just as well accuse a gynaecologist of a morbid interest in sex as accuse the Rabbis of it.

To turn to the question of Halachah. Although this great book is called *A Rabbinic Anthology,* in fact, as the authors point out, it deals almost entirely with Aggadah, with the non-legal side of Judaism. It does not deal with Halachah. Montefiore explains why this is. He says: 'The total omission of Halachah from my book, though unavoidable, must, I fear, tend to give a false, because one-sided, impression of the Rabbinic religion, and more certainly, of Rabbinic life. For all these legal discussions, all this "study of the Law", all these elaborations and minutiae were to the Rabbis the breath of their nostrils, their greatest joy, and the finest portion of their lives. And yet to most of us, it has almost all become distant and obsolete: to most of us the larger part of it seems a waste of mental energy and of time. If a very big percentage of the Halachic portion of the Rabbinic literature were destroyed, archaeology, comparative jurisprudence, and so on, would be the poorer, but our modern religious life would hardly be affected. A gulf separates us from the Rabbis, and this gulf has to be recognized. Their most absorbing interests were not ours.' Loewe says that while this is partly true, it is not entirely true, and he puts it in this way: he talks about Halachah as 'a necessary discipline for life'. 'In Europe, today,' he says, 'Gentlemen's Agreements are not particularly successful: there is something to be said for the thorough-going precision of the Victorian Foreign Office. Bye-laws are not a burden: they are essential. Yet dull they certainly are. No one would take as his light reading a Memorandum on Public Health, or a report on the administration of Local Option. One cannot make an entertaining anthology out of Blue Books or Local Government Bye-Laws. In his choice of material, Mr Montefiore was clearly right. Yet, in the past, history shows no such clash' (that is, clash between Aggadah and Halachah). 'Legislation and mysticism could go hand in hand: Safed could produce both poetry and law books, Cabbalah and Codes, as Schechter, in his famous essay, has demonstrated. It is scarcely necessary to remind the reader that the author of the *Shulchan Aruk,* Joseph Caro, himself was a profound mystic, for the fact is commonplace, and Caro was far from being exceptional in this respect.'

Perhaps three observations are called for in this connection. First that, as we said before, the sober fact is that generations of students have not found the Halachah dull or boring, or uninteresting; they have found it an absorbing occupation and have spent all their days on it. It used to be said that in the great Yeshivah of Volozhin they would skip the Aggadic passages of the Talmud and study only the Halachah. I doubt if any of us would agree with that, and Professor Heschel was right when he said that the reason why today Orthodox Jews are bothered by problems of Halachah was because in Volozhin they used to skip the Aggadah. True. But Halachah is abstract thinking. Even the apparently stupid, far-fetched discussions have as their aim the attempt to classify and to clarify legal conceptions. The best way of understanding the Rabbinic approach to Halachic problems in the abstract would be to compare it to, shall we say, mathematics. You talk about three men papering a room; one takes two hours, one takes three hours, one takes four hours. In fact no rooms are papered in this way. Zeno's discussion of whether Achilles can overtake the tortoise is another case in point. Questions of this sort are abstract, they will never happen, they are not practical, but they deal with the principles of law or the principles of thinking, the principles of logic, and there is nothing more ludicrous in the Rabbis discussing this kind of question than there is in the pure mathematician discussing this kind of question in exactly the same way.

The second point is that for the Rabbis the Halachah was the word of God, and for them nothing was trivial, because it was all a matter of determining what it was that God would have them do. It had a cosmic significance. And because of that it was all shot through with the kind of meaning that enabled men of deep religious feeling to use their intellect in matters which in themselves had little to do with religion, in the belief that this too was God's will. Rav Kook, a poet himself, and a distinguished Halachist himself, was not far off the mark when he said that, just as there are laws of poetry, there is poetry in laws; and to the Rabbis certainly there was poetry in laws. There is a poem by H. D. C. Peplar, which goes something like this:

> The law the lawyers know about
> Is property and land.
> But why the leaves are on the trees,
> Why horses have such tender knees,
> Why winter comes when rivers freeze,
> And faith is more than what one sees,
> And hope survives the worst disease,
> And charity is more than these,
> They do not understand.

It is not for me to express any opinion on lawyers or to say whether Peplar was right about 'the law which lawyers understand' or do not understand, but the lawyers in the Rabbinic period were people who could produce the kind of material that is found in the *Rabbinic Anthology* together with the Halachic material, and somehow discussions on why hope survives the worst disease, and why faith is more than what one sees, and even why horses have such tender knees, are found side by side with the minutiae and the dull discussions, or the apparently dull discussions, on the details of Halachah.

Further, in this connection, it is in Halachah that you find Rabbinic thinking crystallized, not in Aggadah. I am quite sure that anyone who takes the trouble – and people ought to take the trouble – of going through the *Rabbinic Anthology,* will have a very good idea of what many Rabbis have said. But if you wish to arrive at something like a consensus of opinion of Rabbinic thought, you go to the Halachah, not to the Aggadah. For instance, on this question of measure for measure, 'tit-for-tat' as Montefiore calls it. Sometimes in the Aggadic literature this is expressed in a way which is bound to be offensive to moderns. Because a person commits this or that sin, therefore he suffers in this or that way. Sometimes even worse. Because he commits this or that sin, his children suffer in this or that way. And the editors are quite right to call attention to the fact that this is not our way of thinking, and it seems offensive to us. But it is interesting that this principle is not found in the Halachah. The *lex talionis* in the Halachah was not taken literally; it was not taken to mean 'an eye for an eye and a tooth for a tooth', but it was taken to mean compensation. And although in the Aggadic literature you do find the offensive doctrine that little children die because of the sins of their parents, the fact is that nowhere in the Halachah is it suggested that anyone should bear guilt or responsibility apart from the person who has committed the crime.

There have been so many discussions on the basic principles of the Jewish faith, and scholars who have discussed this kind of question have gone invariably to the Aggadic literature. The historian Graetz was surely better informed when, in discussing this question, he went to the Halachah and he discovered that the Halachah says that while the Jew is perfectly justified in saving his life at the expense of his observances, there are three acts which he must not commit even in order to save his life: he must not commit murder in order to save his life, he must not bow down to idols in order to save his life, and he must not be guilty of the forbidden degrees of marriage in order to save his life. That is an Halachic ruling, but there you have the quintessence of Rabbinic thought on the articles of the Jewish faith, on the things which really matter. There you have Rabbinic thought crystallized in action.

And, finally, this question of authority. We have the Rabbis and we have their teaching and as Ahad Haam said, 'Whether you like it or not, this *is* our religion.' You may have read Ahad Haam's essay in which he criticizes the Italian Rabbi who says of the Shulchan Aruch that we ought to proclaim in season and out of season 'This is not our religion.' Ahad Haam said, You may proclaim it in season and out of season, and you may disagree, and I disagree, with many of the things in the *Shulchan Aruch*; but if you proclaim in season and out of season that this is not your religion, you are wrong, because we are the heirs of the *Shulchan Aruch* whether we like it or not. We are the heirs of the Rabbis whether we like it or not, and both Montefiore and Loewe recognized this. That is why there are so many stimulating discussions in this book on the question, Where do we go from here? How do we look upon Rabbinic authority? How are the Rabbis, in what way are the Rabbis, *our* authorities, if they *are* our authorities? Now Montefiore as a Liberal Jew virtually rejects – I do not think it is unfair to say this, I think it emerges from the pages of the *Rabbinic Anthology,* and I think it emerges from Montefiore's writings generally – Montefiore on the whole, as a

Liberal Jew, rejects Rabbinic authority. Loewe as an Orthodox Jew accepts Rabbinic authority. Loewe gives his rationale, because the modern Jew requires a rationale for accepting Rabbinic authority, in these words: he says, 'I would say that the combination of ceremonial and moral, which is the aim of Halachah, tends to raise the former, not to cheapen the latter. It is the ceremonial element that is protective: it prevents the disappearance of Judaism in its environment. When David Rahabi came to India and found some people whom he rightly thought to be Jews, though they were scarcely distinguishable from their Indian environment, it was not the Shema which proved that they belonged to the house of Israel, but the fact that they eschewed fish lacking scales and fins. For the discipline of the Torah is so powerful a shield that it could be laid aside only at grave risk. It may not matter to God whether we eat or avoid pig: to us it does matter, just as it matters to us whether we clean our teeth or not. The old gibe at the Breslau school, Think what you like, but carry out the Commands, has always seemed to me to be most unjust. It really means a combination of progress and tradition. It allows intellectual development and freedom of thought, while it safeguards the Jewish life and strengthens the brotherhood of Israel.'

I find myself, if I may be permitted here a personal note, in great sympathy with what Loewe has said; except perhaps to add that much water has flowed under the bridge since the *Rabbinic Anthology* was first published, and there is in the Jewish world, as in the world in general today, a stronger interest in theology. Some of us feel that the Breslau school still has much of value to offer us, but its approach should be tempered with a profounder interest in the theological aspects of Jewish life and thought. Sometimes this kind of argument – I know this would be quite unfair if it were applied to Loewe – but sometimes this kind of argument is used to mean 'Judaism as a way of life', without any reference to the faith on which that way of life is based. 'Do it because your people do it. Never mind if it is true; never mind if your researches into the origins and the development of Jewish institutions convince you that it was not always like this. Do not be too concerned about whether it is true in any objective sense; it is right for you to do it because it is a discipline to which as a Jew you should conform.' Many deeply religious people feel revolted at that approach to religion for they want to look upon the *mitzvot* as *mitzvot,* they want to look upon the observances of Judaism as divine commands. And elsewhere in this book Loewe says that since these institutions of Judaism have survived, then for the observant Jew they become divine commands.

Since the *Rabbinic Anthology* was written two interesting developments have taken place in Jewish life. On the one hand there have been and there are, thank God, Orthodox Jews – I use the term 'Orthodox' here in the sense of observant – who have been prepared to face the problems raised by critical investigation into the sources of Judaism and have not been prepared to accept the obscurantist position. On the other hand, in recent years, many Reform and Liberal Jews have discovered a new interest in the Halachah, and realize, as one of them put it, that religion does not appeal only to the intellect, to the mind, it has to appeal to the whole being of man and has to satisfy psychologically as well as rationally. I doubt whether the leaders of Reform Judaism in the last century would have dreamed that in the mid-twentieth century there would be published Reform Responsa. And so one senses that there is a coming together of the two sections. It would be far too optimistic to imagine that there are no differences; it would be far too optimistic to imagine that in the foreseeable future those differences are going to be completely ironed out. The debate continues, and perhaps it is as well that the debate continues. But the two distinguished authors and editors of the *Rabbinic Anthology,* now in the world of truth, have by their work, by this great work, made it easier for us to engage in the debate and to seek the truth in this world of error.

Part Four
Rabbinics

—15—

Tur: Preface to *Ḥoshen Mishpat*

Jacob b. Asher (d. 1340), compiler of the *Tur,* prefaces the section of this Code which deals with jurisprudence, *Ḥoshen Mishpat,* with a statement on the importance of justice for the social order and the nature of the authority vested in the judges. As a summary of the forms and attitudes which prevailed in the Middle Ages, influencing Jewish life in subsequent ages down to the present, this statement is important for a study of traditional Jewish legal philosophy. The section is here translated into English for the first time (the words in parenthesis, including the source references, are explanatory and are not in the original). The translation is followed by annotations.

The section *Ḥoshen Mishpat* of the *Tur* (and the *Shulhan Arukh*) is different from the other three sections (*Orah Hayyim; Yoreh De'ah* and *Even ha-'Ezer*) not only in the subject matter itself (this naturally differs from section to section) but also in the approach to this subject matter. Although in a general sense all four sections can be said to belong to Jewish law (*Halakhah*), jurisprudence, the topic with which *Ḥoshen Mishpat* deals, is in a category of its own, that of *dine mamonot* (laws of property, 'civil law') and kindred subjects. If the analogy of the tree is allowed, one can say that *dine mamonot* form a separate tree while the topics treated in the other three sections form three branches of the same tree.

The basic difference lies in the place of human reasoning in determining *Halakhah,* conceived of traditionally as divinely revealed law. Human reasoning has a far greater role to play in jurisprudence than it has in other aspects of *Halakhah.* It is true that even in these other areas – those we might refer to as the dogmatic – human reasoning is applied to the revealed law. That this is so is obvious to every student of Talmud and *Halakhah,* as witnessed by some of the hermeneutical principles such as *kal vahomer; binyan av* and the Amoraic *sevara* and, indeed, in the whole idea of debate and discussion. But whereas in dogmatic *Halakhah* the basis is the revealed law, with human reasoning secondary to it and around it, in jurisprudence reasoning is normally the basis of the laws themselves. The details of what is included in a sale and what is not, of contractual obligations, of transfer of property, of mine and thine generally, as discussed in *Bava Kamma, Bava Metsia* and *Bava Batra,* are, with few exceptions, based on human reasoning rather than on the exegesis of Scriptural verses.

It is noteworthy how different are the discussions in the three *Bavot* from, say, the discussions regarding forbidden food in tractate *Hullin.* In the latter, the main role of human reasoning is to discover how the Scriptural laws are to be understood and applied. The laws themselves are in Scripture. The same applies, to give another illustration, to the discussions on what constitutes forbidden work on the Sabbaths and Festivals in tractates *Shabbat* and *Betsah.* In connection with jurisprudence, on the other hand, the laws themselves are based on human reasoning, the Scriptural verses speaking not of the laws themselves but of broad principles such as the eighth commandment and the many injunctions to practise justice and pursue righteousness.

There is a great deal to be said for the solution provided by the famous Rosh Yeshivah, R. Simeon Skopf (*Sha'are Yosher,* Warsaw, 1927, Sha'ar V, chapter 1) to the old problem why a doubt regarding Biblical law is treated strictly (*safek deoraita lehumra*) and yet doubts in cases of ownership are treated leniently in favour of the one who has possession (*safek mamona lekula*). Why should the prohibition 'Thou shalt not steal' be treated more leniently than the prohibition of, say, forbidden food? Rabbi Skopf's reply is that in the case of forbidden food the prohibition comes first and the discussion of the procedural rules afterwards. The prohibition is there in Scripture. It is thus logically significant to discuss which procedure is to be adopted where there is a doubt whether the given law applies, e.g. where there is a piece of meat which may be either permitted meat or forbidden and it is not known which. Here the procedure is stated, that the stricter view is to be followed and the meat is forbidden. With regard to *dine mamonot,* on the other hand, the law follows on the procedural rules. The law here, as in other systems of jurisprudence, depends on the consensus of the authorities. It is logically meaningless to discuss what is to be done where there is doubt as to whether 'Thou shalt not steal' applies since what constitutes 'stealing' has first to be determined and determined, moreover, by the same authorities who lay down the procedural rules in cases of doubt. There cannot, in effect, be any doubt in the matter of 'Thou shalt not steal' since this prohibition cannot be invoked until the authorities have done their work. When the legal authorities have decided in each case then we have either a definite prohibition or no prohibition at all.

The matter is, however, rather more complicated in that the difference between what we have called dogmatic law and jurisprudence is not categorical but one of where the main emphasis lies. There are, after all, Scriptural rules regarding *dine mamonot* too, such as the particular types of fine to be imposed, the disqualification of certain types of witnesses on theological grounds and the different penalties for the goring ox that is otherwise docile and for the goring of the *muad* ox. (That these also have had a history and that their development can be traced to some extent is not germane to our discussion of the laws as they appear in the Codes.) The ordination of judges (*semikhah*) belongs in the category of this dogmatic aspect of *dine mamonot.* No matter how learned in the law a judge may be, he cannot function as a judge unless he has been ordained as such and this rule is considered by the Rabbis to be Scriptural. Here the law of *semukhin* was not invented by the Rabbis (at least, not as it is discussed by the legal authorities rather than among the historians). The discussions of the talmudic Rabbis and their successors on *semikhah* is of the same order as their discussions concerning which food is permitted and which forbidden.

We can see, from the above, that the *Tur* in his preamble to *Ḥoshen Mishpat* considers both these aspects of *dine mamonot.* First, he observes the non-dogmatic basis of the majority of these laws. Justice, truth and peace are necessary if human society is to endure. No appeal to revelation is required. The appeal is to the innate good sense of human beings as human beings, not as Jews who believe in revelation. But he then considers the dogmatic aspect and how human reasoning has operated here to make the law viable. It is perhaps no accident that the *Tur* sees fit to provide this kind of preamble only to *Ḥoshen Mishpat.* All this is strictly relevant to the question that has been aired in issues of this journal, whether there exists such an entity as *Mishpat Ivri* as distinct from other branches of *Halakhah* and whether there is any point in examining *Mishpat Ivri* in isolation from *Halakhah* in general.

TUR ḤOSHEN MISHPAT I

'Rabban Simeon b. Gamaliel says: The world endures by virtue of three things: justice, peace and truth' (*Avot* 1:18). Rabbi Jonah (Gerondi, *c.* 1200–63) of blessed memory comments that this does not mean the world was created for the sake of these three things since, at the beginning of the chapter (*Avot* 1:2), it says, the world *stands* upon three things and they are not the three mentioned here.[1] Rather, first it is said, the world was created for the sake of three things: the Torah, service in the Temple and benevolence. For the sake of the Torah, as it is written: 'The Lord possessed me in the beginning of his way' (*Proverbs* 8:22), the Torah declaring: I have been created before all creatures and they were brought into being for my sake. And so, too, for the sake of service in the Temple; the Holy One, blessed be He, choosing Israel of all the nations and choosing the Temple of all places wherein they should worship Him, from which it follows that for its sake the world was created. And so, too, with regard to benevolence, the attribute of love, which makes men acceptable to God, blessed be He. But here it says 'the world endures', meaning, after it has been created it endures because of these three.[2] The world endures because of the judges who adjudicate between man and his fellow, otherwise whoever is the more powerful would prevail. And so, too, with regard to truth, as the Rabbis say (*Shabbat* 104a): 'Falsehood has no legs', whereas truth is the foundation and the supreme coagulent for all things. And so too, with regard to peace, as the Rabbis say (*Avot* 3:2): 'Pray for the peace of the ruling power for were it not for the fear of the ruling power man would swallow up his neighbour alive.' This is the meaning of the rabbinic saying (*Shabbat* 10a): 'Whoever renders a just and true decision it is as if he had become a partner with God in the work of creation.' For the Holy One, blessed be He, created the world that it might endure and the wicked who rob and plunder destroy it by their deeds, as we find in connection with the generation of the deluge. Their fate was sealed only because of the robbery of which they were guilty, as it is written: 'for the earth is filled with violence through them' (*Genesis* 6:13), the verse concluding: 'and behold, I will destroy them with the earth'. It follows that the judge who shatters the high hand of the wicked, taking from them ill-gotten gains and returning these to their rightful owners, causes the world to endure, thus bringing to fruition the divine will for the world to endure. Thus the judge is a partner of the Holy One, blessed be He.

God only knew Abraham, calling him friend, because he walked in the way of justice and trained his children in that way, as it is written: 'For I know him, that he will command his children and his household after him, and they shall keep the way of the Lord, to do righteousness and justice' (*Genesis* 18:19). Moses our teacher, on whom be peace, master of all the prophets, took Jethro's advice regarding justice, to appoint judges to warn Israel and to command them concerning justice and the Lord concurred with his counsel. Joshua, after having made a covenant with Israel to serve the Lord, concluded his words with the idea of justice, as it is written: 'So Joshua made a covenant with the people that day, and set them a statute and judgement in Shechem' (*Joshua* 24:25), since justice is the foundation and the supreme principle in God's service. After him, every judge judged his people, turning them away from the evil way to the worship of God to walk in the way of Abraham by practising righteousness and justice. As a result they were saved from their enemies; until there arose Samuel, a prophet faithful to God. He judged Israel all the days of his life, travelling around year by year to Beth-El, Mitspah and Gilgal, judging Israel in all these places. The Sages remark (based on *Shabbat* 56a) that he did not journey by the same route each year so that he was able to turn the heart of all the people to the worship of God, to walk in the way of Abraham our father, on whom be peace. He anointed David as king of Israel. David, too, walked in God's way more than any leader before him, as it is written: 'And David executed judgement and justice to all his people' *(2 Samuel* 8:15) 'and Joab repaired the rest of the city' (*1 Chronicles* 11:8), upon which our Sages of blessed memory comment (based on *Sanhedrin* 49a): Joab repaired the rest of the city through the merit of David who practised judgement and justice. There arose in his stead his son, the beloved of the Lord who loved to walk in the statutes of David and his father, asking of the Lord an understanding heart to judge his people that they might understand the difference between good and evil. It was pleasing to the Lord that he had made this request and He gave him so wise and understanding a heart that there was none like unto him before him and none that came after him. And Jehoshaphat, too, who walked in the ways of his fathers and whose heart was lifted up proudly in the ways of the Lord, strengthened himself in the idea of justice by appointing judges. 'And he said to the judges: Take heed what ye do; for ye judge not for man, but for the Lord, who is with you in the judgement' (2 *Chronicles* 19:6). And also of Josiah Scripture testifies: 'And like unto him there was no king before him, that turned unto the Lord with all his heart' (2 *Kings* 23:25), which the Rabbis understood to mean (*Shabbat* 56b) that in connection with every decision he had rendered before he had reached the age of eighteen he returned the money to its owner out of his own pocket. And King Messiah, may he be revealed speedily in our day, is also praised by Scripture in connection with the idea of justice, as it is written: 'But with righteousness shall he judge the poor, and decide with equity for the meek of the land…' (*Isaiah* 11:5).

Corresponding to the great reward for the practice of justice is the punishment of one who sets it aside and perverts it, as we have learnt (*Avot* 5:8): 'The sword comes into the world because of the postponement of justice and the perversion of justice.' And David declared: 'I have done justice and righteousness; leave me not to mine oppressors' (*Psalm* 119:121), implying that one who refrains from practising justice will be delivered into the hands of his oppressors. And Jerusalem would not have been destroyed nor would Israel have been exiled were it not that they had set justice aside, as it is said: 'She that was full of justice, righteousness lodged in her, but now murderers' (*Isaiah* 1:21). And it is written: 'They judge not the fatherless, neither doth the cause of the widow come unto them' (*Isaiah* 1:23), followed by: 'Ah, I will ease Me of Mine adversaries, and avenge Me of Mine enemies' (*Isaiah* 1:24). And it is by virtue of justice that she will be redeemed in the future, as it is written: 'Zion shall be redeemed with justice, and they that return of her with righteousness' (*Isaiah* 1:27). And it is written: 'Seek justice, relieve the oppressed, judge the fatherless, plead for the widow' (*Isaiah* 1:17), after which it is written: 'Though your sins be as scarlet, they shall be as white as snow' (*Isaiah* 1:18). And justice brings near the redemption, as it is written: 'Keep ye judgment and do justice, for My salvation is near to come and My righteousness to be revealed' (*Isaiah* 56:1). And the Holy One, blessed be He, desires justice more than all the sacrifices, as it is written: 'To do righteousness and justice is more acceptable to the Lord than sacrifice' (*Proverbs* 21:3). It does not say more than a burnt-offering or a sin-offering but more than sacrifice (implying more than all the sacrifices).

In many passages we are warned by Moses our teacher to practise justice: 'Ye shall not respect persons in judgment; but ye shall hear the small as well as the great; ye shall not be afraid of the face of man; for the judgment is God's' (*Deuteronomy* 1:17). He furthermore warned us about it in the form of a positive commandment: 'In righteousness shalt thou judge thy neighbour' (*Leviticus* 18:15); 'And ye shall judge righteously' (*Deuteronomy* 1:16). And he commanded that judges be appointed in every place, as it is written: 'Judges and officers shalt thou make thee in all thy gates' (*Deuteronomy* 16:18): the term 'judges' denoting those appointed to judge and the term 'officers' those who stand in the presence of the judges ready with rod and staff to enforce their decisions.

R. Jeremiah said (*Sanhedrin* 7b): 'which thou shalt set before them' (*Exodus* 21:1). The verse should have said: 'which thou shalt teach them' but it refers to the insignia of the judges, the rod, the lash, the shoe (for the ceremony of drawing off the shoe, *Deuteronomy* 25:5–9) and the trumpet. Rav Hai (Gaon of Pumbedita 939–1038) writes that the Court must have ready in the place where the judges sit a rod wherewith to exercise dominion, a strap wherewith to flog offenders and a trumpet wherewith to proclaim the ban. A scroll of the Law must also be present in the Court, as we say (based on *Bava Kamma* 82a, but the reading in current versions is different): It is an enactment of Ezra that the Courts sit on Mondays and Thursdays. And we ask: What is the reason? Because many people are present there (coming into the towns on these market days). If you want I can say: Because it would be too much trouble to take out a scroll of the Law (from the synagogue).

We have learnt in the first chapter of tractate *Makkot* (7 a): 'The law regarding the setting up of a Sanhedrin applies both to the Holy Land and to outside the Holy Land.' The *Gemara* concludes that there is this difference between the Holy Land and outside it: in the Holy Land there is an obligation to have a Sanhedrin in every district and every city whereas outside the Holy Land there is only an obligation to set up a Sanhedrin in every district not in every city. This applies only at a time when there is ordination (*semikhah*) but nowadays, when there is ordination, all the laws regarding the appointment of judges are set aside according to the (strict) laws of the Torah, as it is written 'set before *them*' (*Exodus* 21:1), referring to the judges called *elohim* in this section, namely, those who are ordained, and we expound it thus (*Gittin* 88b) 'before *them*' and not before laymen and we are laymen.[3] Consequently, according to the (strict) Torah law there are no judges but (nevertheless) we act as the agents (i.e. on behalf of) of the earlier (ordained) teachers (*Gittin* 88b). The conlusion is reached (*Bava Kamma* 84b) that we only act on their behalf in matters that occur frequently and which involve financial loss,[4] for example, cases of admission and loans, namely, where A claims money from B supported by the evidence of witnesses that B had admitted his debt in their presence or that B had borrowed from A in their presence. But no judgement is rendered in a case of infrequent occurrence even if financial loss is involved, for example, a case of physical assault. Similarly, no judgement is rendered in a case involving no financial loss, even if it is of frequent occurrence, such as putting a man to shame. The *Rambam* (Maimonides, 1135–1204, in (*Yad, Sanhedrin* 5:10) writes that we do render judgement in cases involving doctor's fees (for recovery from a physical attack) and compensation for loss of work and so did the Geonim rule, stating that it is an everyday occurrence in Babylon to decide such cases. But it would appear from the words of my master and father the *Rosh* (Asher b. Jehiel, *c.* 1250–1327), the memory of the righteous is for a blessing, that no judgement is rendered in such cases. So, too, the case of an ox injuring a human being is of infrequent occurrence and no judgement is rendered but the cases of a man injuring an ox and an ox another ox are frequent and decisions are consequently rendered in these cases. This only applies where the injuries were caused by *shen* ('tooth') or *regel* ('foot'), whether the ox did damage to another animal by rubbing against it (for pleasure, thus falling under the heading of 'tooth') or whether it ate fruit it was its habit to eat and all such cases or whether it did damage to food for which the payment is the full amount. But if it did damage by *keren* ('horn', i.e. malicious damage for which only half damages has to be paid, see *Exodus* 21:35–36) or its derivatives (e.g. kicking or biting) no judgement is rendered. For if the ox is docile *(tam,* i.e. it had not gored more than once before) the ruling is (*Bava Kamma* 15b) that the payment of half damages is in the nature of a fine (not compensation for loss) and no decisions are rendered in cases of fines. And if the ox is a *mu'ad* ('warned', i.e. it has gored three times so that the owner is not obliged to pay the full damages and this is not a fine) there is no law of *mu'ad* in Babylon (obviously not since the law of *tam* cannot be decided there). No decision is rendered even if the animal had been declared a *mu'ad* in the Land of Israel and was then brought to Babylon because such is of infrequent occurrence (*Bava Kamma* 84b).

The claim by a wife of her marriage settlement, the claim of an inheritance and the claim that a gift had been given are treated as similar to cases of debt and decisions are rendered concerning them in order to shut a door against the unscrupulous who would otherwise rely on the inability of the party to find experts (i.e., ordained judges) to try the case.[5] And so, too, decisions are rendered in cases of robbery. But no decisions are rendered in cases of fines. And so did the *Rambam* (*Yad, Sanhedrin* 5:9) write that there is no enforcement of payment for any of the fines imposed by the Sages on one who blows a trumpet to frighten his neighbour or one who smacks his neighbour's face (i.e. causing him no injury but embarrassing him) and so forth. And wherever the payment is that of only half the damage or more than the damage, payment cannot be enforced (since it is not compensation but a fine: *Bava Kamma* 15b) with the exception of the half damage to be paid in the case of *tserurot* ('pebbles', i.e. where pebbles sprang from under the feet of an animal and where the payment is half damage but *is* compensation, *Bava Kamma* 15b) which is in the nature of monetary compensation and not a fine. Outside the Holy Land we can enforce, in cases of robbery and theft, the actual amount stolen but not any addition due to increase in value. Not all cases of admission of guilt can be enforced outside the Holy Land. The law does recognise liability where there is an admission of guilt in cases of depreciation, shame and ransom (*kopher,* paid where a *mu'ad* killed a human being, see *Exodus* 21:30) e.g. where one says 'I have seduced the daughter of So-and-so' or 'My ox has killed So-and-so' but payment in these cases cannot be enforced by judges outside the Holy Land. Where payment is for indirect damage this is not treated as a fine (but as compensation) and can be enforced outside the Holy Land. And so, too, in the case of an informer, though no act was involved, payment of compensation can be enforced.

Now in all these cases where the Courts cannot enforce the law, if the injured party manages to seize property to the value of that which is due to him the property he has seized is not taken from him.[6] But *Rabbenu Tam* (Jacob b. Meir, *c.* 1100–71) writes (Tosafists to *Bava Kamma* 15b, end) that this only applies where the seizure was of that which caused the damage (i.e. the actual animal which gored) and only when the seizure was made at the time when the damage was done but not otherwise. For if seizure were to be effective in all instances where the seizure was made at a later date (lit. 'today or tomorrow') the victim will seize much more than his due and it will be impossible to reclaim the surplus since cases of fine are not adjudicated in Babylon. But my master and father, the *Rosh,* of blessed memory, writes that even if he seized some other property (i.e. not the animal itself) it is not taken from him and if he seized more than his due an assessment is made by the Court and the surplus taken from him. This does not come under the heading of fines (which cannot be enforced by the Court) since the payment for the damages has been made by the enactment of the Sages of blessed memory who have ruled (*Bava Kamma* l5b) that if he seized property it is not taken from him (thus the Court, when making the assessment, is not illegally deciding cases of fines). All the Court does is to sit in judgement for the return of the surplus (i.e. not for the original amount to be paid which is by the prin-ciple of seizure). From the language used by Rav Alfasi (the *Rif*, to *Bava Kamma,* chapter 8, beg.) it appears he holds, where the victim demands of the Court an on-the-spot assessment of the damage so that he may know the amount he is entitled to seize, the Court must pay heed to him. But my master and father writes that this is far from obvious. They must never, in fact, make any assessment for the purpose of collecting the amount due. It is only when the victim has already seized the property that an assessment is made, the Court saying to him: Return suchand-such an amount.

If the victim demands that the Court should accept the testimony of witnesses (to the damage) so that when, at a later date (lit. 'today or tomorrow'), he seizes property it will not be taken away from him, the Court is to pay no heed to him to accept the testimony of the witnesses in anticipation of a later seizure, for since no fines can be imposed in Babylon the Court must not accept the testimony, as we say: There is no *mu'ad* in Babylon (i.e., even though at the time no actual transfer of property is involved and there is a mere acceptance of the testimony). Consequently, the Court must not accept the testimony, even though at the time no money is extracted. But if the victim has already seized the property and then the perpetrator of the damage summons him to the Court for this, the Court instructs the victim to produce his witnesses (that the damage has been done). If the Court then discovers that the seizure has been lawful they say to the perpetrator: We cannot impose the fine but if you wish to redeem that which he has seized give him such-and-such an amount of money. And if he had seized more than the amount due to him he is instructed to return the surplus. If the victim is unable to produce witnesses, they instruct him to return that which he has seized.

R. Abraham b. David (of Posquières, *c.* 1125–98) of blessed memory writes that if the perpetrator of the damage admitted his liability and then witnesses came to testify to his liability we follow the opinion of Rav (*Bava Kamma* 74b) who holds that one who admits to liability in cases of fines is exempt from payment even if witnesses later came to the Court to testify to his liability. If the victim has seized the property and the perpetrator then admitted his liability we still take it away from him and we do not argue that seizure before admission of liability is treated as if witnesses had testified first (i.e., we do not argue that the seizure is accepted as a legal decision, akin to that rendered after witnesses had testified so that a later admission of liability is ignored). But the *Ramban* (Nahmanides, 1194–1270) finds this difficult since admission of liability is only acknowledged as such where it took place in a Court. Nowadays, since we no longer have Courts composed of experts (i.e., ordained scholars) it is as if the admission of liability took place outside the Court, an admission which does not exonerate from the payment of a fine, just as we say that there is no *mu'ad* in Babylon since for this purpose testimony before a Court is required and there are no Courts (in Babylon). Consequently, if he seized property it is not taken away from him whether he seized it before the admission of liability or after the admission of liability.

Rav Alfas writes (*Rif* to *Bava Kamma,* chapter eight, beg.), although fines are not enforced by the Courts, it is the practice of the two Yeshivot (of Sura and Pumbedita) to place the offender under the ban until he appeases his victim (i.e. by compensating him for the damage he has suffered).[7] But as soon as he gives him the amount due to him we remove the ban immediately irrespective of whether or not the victim is appeased. And so, too, writes R. Abraham b. David, adding that where the fine is a fixed amount, the 50 zuz to be paid in cases of rape and seduction (*Exodus* 22:15–16; *Deuteronomy* 22:28–29) for example, we place the offender under the ban until he pays that fixed amount, and so write some of the Geonim. But this is unacceptable to my master and father for there is no greater form of enforcement than this, to hold him by his testicles until he surrenders his cloak (an expression found in *Bava Metzia* 101b, i.e. since the Court is not empowered to inflict fines how can it compel, through the ban the payment of these fines). And R. Sherira Gaon (of Pumbedita, *c.* 906–1006) writes, we do not find in the Talmud that a ban is placed on him unless it be for the purpose of removing that which causes the damage *Bava Kamma* 15b, i.e. the ban is only imposed where the animal is dangerous and its owner refuses to have it put down or placed under strict control). However the later (post-Talmudic) sages and the Heads of the Yeshivot relied on this (i.e. to extend the ban even where there is a refusal to pay as above) for they observed the great harm that is done as a result of the rule that fines cannot be imposed by the Courts. Consequently, they issued an enactment (i.e. although this was illegal in Talmudic times) that the one guilty of the assault be placed under the ban until he appeases his victim approximately For there is no way to be more exact (i.e. to make a real, not an approximate, assessment) by saying: Such-and-such an amount have we fixed for you to pay and we have fixed it to receive this amount. To do that would be to decide in cases of fine. But the Court makes a private (lit. 'in their heart') approximate assessment which they do not reveal to others. They then place the offender under the ban until he appeases his victim and they see whether or not this approximates to the amount they have assessed. If it is approximately the same but the victim is unwilling to accept it they say to him: We have no power to keep him any longer under the ban and he is released from it forthwith. But if the amount he pays is far removed from the amount they had assessed approximately in private the ban is not removed until it does approximate to their assessment.

Also with regard to one who puts his neighbour to shame by insulting him verbally, although the law is that he does not have to pay him any compensation (*Bava Kamma* 91b), R. Sherira writes that he is placed under the ban until he appeases his victim in accordance with the latter's dignity (i.e. the compensation must depend on the dignity of the victim).[8] My master and father, of blessed memory, writes that this is very plausible since greater embarrassment is suffered by the victim of verbal insults than by the victim of a physical assault, for there is nothing worse than the evil talk and libel a man spreads about his neighbour.

The Jerusalem Talmud (*Bava Kamma* 8:6, 6c) records: One who puts a scholar to shame must pay him full compensation. A certain man insulted R. Juda bar Hanina. The case came before Resh Lakish who imposed on him a fine amounting to a pound of gold.[9]

NOTES

1. The earlier Mishnah in *Avot* is in the name of Simeon the Just but R. Jonah assumes that the two statements are complementary since the editor of the Mishnah recorded them both and since in the first the term *omed,* 'stands', is used whereas in the second the term used is *kayyam,* 'endures'. The commentary of R. Jonah is, in fact, on the first statement, of Simeon the Just, not on the second, but the *Tur* is, in any event, paraphrasing R. Jonah not quoting him verbatim. R. Jonah's Commentary to *Avot* is printed in the edition of *Avot* in the Romm, Vilna, edition of the Babylonian Talmud. Although R. Jonah's Commentary does not belong to the halakhic literature, it is used here by the *Tur* because the latter's formulation here is not really halakhic but a kind of homily on the importance of justice for society. A similar semi-homiletical preface is given by R. Mordecai Jaffe (*c.* 1535–1612) to the section of his Code dealing with jurisprudence *(Levush Jr Shushan,* Venice, 1619, 1:1). For the *Tur* and the arrangement of his material see Chaim Tchernowitz, *Toledot haposekim* (New York, 1974, Vol. II, 199–220; and Menahem Elon *Hamishpat ha 'Ivri,* second enlarged edition (Jerusalem: Magnes Press, 1978), 1058–80.
2. Rabban Simeon b. Gamaliel, according to this interpretation, is not concerned with the metaphysical question, discussed by Simeon the Just, of the aim of creation but the more practical question of how society is to *endure* now that the world has been created. He offers a prescription for an ordered society. Justice, truth and peace are the essential ingredients of a viable society. There must be competent judges to administer the law and so prevent oppression of the weak by the strong; truth must be accepted as an abiding value; and society must so order its affairs that peace and harmony reign supreme. The Rabbinic saying that the judge is a partner of God means that the judges share in the divine creativity because without a stable society the world would collapse into chaos and God's purposes would be frustrated. The *Tur* proceeds to give a brief history of the administration of justice from Abraham through the just kings and leaders. Even in the Messianic age there is need for justice to be administered and the Messiah is praised for possessing the ability to see that this is done. Conversely, there are many instances of dire calamities befalling a state in which justice is perverted. The prophets teach that God desires justice more than all the sacrifices.
3. Having stressed the importance of justice and the judges who administer it, the *Tur'* now turns to the great paradox that, according to the rabbinic understanding of the matter, only scholars who have been ordained (who have *semikhah,* the 'laying on of hands', believed to reach back to Moses, who 'ordained' Joshua) can act as judges and in the Diaspora in talmudic times and in the period of the *Tur* everywhere there are no judges with *semikhah.* The history of *semikhah* is fascinating but the details are obscure. (For the whole question and the attempts to revive *semikhah,* as a prelude to the advent of the Messiah, in sixteenth century Safed see the article SEMIKHAH in *Encyclopedia Judaica,* Vol. 14, pp. 1140–47 and Elon, *supra* n. 1, at 18–30). It appears from the talmudic sources quoted here by the *Tur* that the authorities in Palestine in talmudic times, zealous for the honour of the Holy Land, refused to ordain any of the scholars, no matter how eminent, who resided in Babylon. The Palestinian Amoraim have the title 'Rabbi', because they have *semikhah,* whereas the Babylonian Amoraim only have the lesser title 'Rav'. The paradoxical situation prevailed from the beginning of the third century that while Babylonian Jews possessed the full machinery of justice in the Exilarch and his Court, police officers and prisons, their judges had no standing in the eyes of the strict Torah law. In Palestine, on the other hand, the judges had the authority conferred upon them by *semikhah* but possessed little autonomy in the administration of justice. Obviously such a situation was impossible. To cope with it, the Babylonian teachers introduced the legal fiction that in certain cases the Babylonian courts were able to exercise their powers because they were authorized so to do by the Palestinian authorities, whose agents they became and on whose behalf they were authorized to act. (The main talmudic sources are: *Gittin* 88b; *Bava Kamma* 15b; 27b and 84a–b; *Sanhedrin* 2b–5a). The Jewish Courts in the Middle Ages followed the rule laid down for the Babylonian Courts but the details of how exactly the Courts composed of technical 'laymen' were to function is far from clear and the problem aggravated by the ruling (*Bava Kamma* 15b) that even where the Courts had no power, in cases of fines, for instance, the seizure of property by the offended party to the value of the compensation due to him (had there been 'expert' judges to decide the matter) was recognized. It is to these

problems that the *Tur* now addresses himself. Cf. D.M. Shohet, *The Jewish Court in the Middle Ages* (New York: Herman Press, 1931), chapters VI and VII, pp. 120-50; A.Gulak, *Yesode Hamishpat ha'ivri* (Berlin: Dvir, 1922), iv. 24–38.

4. This is not too exact since the Court can compel a recalcitrant husband to divorce his wife where she has good grounds for her divorce petition (*Gittin* 85b) and proselytes are accepted even though a Court of three is required for this purpose *(Yevamot* 46b).Exceptions to the rule are made in these cases because the release of the wife from an intolerable burden and the bringing of a soul 'under the wings of the Shekhinah' are no less praiseworthy aims than the obtaining of financial compensation. See R. Moses Isserles, *Darkhe Mosheh,* ed. H. S. Rosenthal (Jerusalem: *Makhon Yerushalayim,* 1979), 1a and R. Y M. Epstein's *'Arukh hashulan Hoshen Mishpat* (Warsaw: M. Zederbaurn, 1884), Chapter 1.
5. The legal principle in this paragraph is that a Court of 'laymen' is not empowered to impose fines, even where the law demands it, because 'laymen' have no power to try the case. In ancient Jewish law a Court-enforced payment could be either for the purpose of compensating a victim (*mainon*) or as a fine to the perpetrator (*kenas*). In the latter case the purpose of the payment is not to compensate the victim but to punish the offender, except that since the punishment has to be inflicted the money is not paid into the Court, as, say, in English law, but to the victim. But, since the basic aim in these cases is not that of compensation, the Court of 'laymen' is not empowered to act on behalf of the 'experts'. The *Tur* here discusses whether or not certain border-line cases fall under the heading of 'fines', which cannot be administered in Babylon and hence everywhere else in the period of the *Tur*.
6. In this paragraph and the next the *Tur* discusses the extent to which the law recognises seizure of property in cases of fines, etc. The *locus classicus* is *Bava Kamma* 15b where the conclusion is reached that although the payment of half-damages for an ox that is a *tam* is in the nature of a fine, which cannot be imposed in Babylon, yet 'if he seized it, it is not taken away from him'. *Rabbenu Tam* finds it hard to accept that the Talmud allows seizure of property by a man whose case the Courts have no power to decide. Such a carte-blanche admission of seizure into the law can so easily lead to abuse. Consequently, *Rabbenu Tam* is compelled to interpret the Talmudic passage in a forced manner, namely, that the reference is only to seizure of the ox itself and only if the seizure is made at the time. The *Rosh* disagrees and allows seizure of any property to the value of the claim. But the *Rosh* is then faced with the problem of who is to decide whether the amount seized is accurate. The only way this can be determined is by the Court sitting in judgement on the case and this would involve trying cases of fines in 'Babylon'. The *Rosh*'s neat solution is that since seizure is a legal right the amount seized to the value of the claim is not in dispute at all so that all the Court has to do is ascertain whether there is a surplus and, if there is, to assess its value. The decision here is not one of fines but of compensation, i.e. to the offender.
7. The powerful weapon of the ban was used by the Courts in the Middle Ages for the enforcement of the law (see Shohet, *supra* n. 3, at 133–50). The *Tur* discusses here whether the use of the ban to enforce payments of fines is contrary to the rule that these cannot be enforced by Courts of 'laymen'. The eventual decision is that, though this is illegal according to talmudic law, the post-talmudic teachers are empowered to enact new legislation since otherwise justice will not be done. In all this the tension is clearly to be observed between the need for the Courts to have coercive powers and the opposite need to preserve the continuity of the law. The post-talmudic authorities never went so far as to abolish entirely the talmudic rules against enforcement of fines by a Court of 'laymen' but they did not scruple to endow these Courts with the terrible power of the ban.
8. In talmudic law there is no redress for slander or, 'insulting words' i.e. defamation of character. Here, too, the power of the ban is invoked. At a later stage the Courts, by special enactments, *takkanot,* intervened more directly, compelling the man guilty of character assassination to pay full compensation to his victim, see *Shulhan Arukh Hoshen Mishpat* 420:38.
9. There is some evidence that scholars tended to abuse the scholar's privilege mentioned here, even encouraging others to insult them so as to lay claim to the 'pound of gold'. Thus while the *Shulhan Arukh, Yoreh De'ah* 243:7 records the rule that the Court is to impose a ban on anyone who insults a scholar, *Isserles* (ad loc.) states that 'nowadays there are no scholars' so that the law of the 'pound of gold' no longer applies.

—16—

Historical Thinking of the Post-Talmudic Halakhists

From the close of the Babylonian Talmud in the sixth century C.E. down to the period of the Emancipation (late eighteenth century), the preponderance in Jewish studies was in the Halakhah, the legal side of Judaism. Of course, in this period, too, many works were produced on other aspects of Judaism – Biblical exegesis, Hebrew grammar, liturgical and general poetry, mysticism and the Kabbalah, and, especially, Jewish philosophy and theology – but the main emphasis everywhere was in the direction of Halakhic studies.

Every legal system is to some extent indifferent to history. The law pursues its own way, with a life of its own, as it were, impervious to notions of historical development. This is true *a priori* of the Halakhah, conceived of, at least on the surface, as a complete, self-contained system reaching back to the Torah given to Moses at Sinai. Even later Rabbinic legislation is thought of as part of the same process, unchanging and with ultimate Biblical sanction, so that, so far as Jewish practice is concerned, the origins of the laws become irrelevant. The key-note is sounded in the Talmudic expression, used when a law is discussed of only past application: 'What difference does it make? What has been has been.'[1] Moreover, mediaeval Jewish philosophy tended towards a meta-historical view of the whole Torah, to see the Torah as beyond the flux of time. The greatest of the mediaeval philosophers and also the most distinguished Halakhist, Moses Maimonides (1135–1204), could calmly say of works of general history that they are of no practical consequence so that to read them is a sheer waste of time.[2] In addition, real historical study, as opposed to mere chronology, is largely the product of modern Jewish learning. It is, consequently, a little precarious to speak at all of historical thinking in the post-Talmudic Halakhah. For all that, such thinking can be detected as it entered through the back door, so to speak.

It was the Karaite rebellion against the authority of the Talmud at the beginning of the eighth century that gave the impetus to the followers of the Rabbis, the Rabbinites, to investigate the history of the Talmud itself. To face the Karaite challenge, the Rabbinites felt the need to demonstrate that there was a continuous chain of tradition from the Bible through the Talmud to the mediaeval representatives of Rabbinism. Furthermore, once the Talmud had become, as it did, the final court of appeal – in Maimonides' words, 'to it nothing must be added and from it nothing subtracted'[3] – the Talmud achieved the status of a sacred text, second only to the Bible, and the study of the lives of the Talmudic sages as much part of the religious obligation to study the Torah as the study of the lives of the Biblical heroes. But unless one knew which of the Talmudic sages lived earlier and which later, many Talmudic passages remained opaque, and the rule was laid down that from the time of the fourth-century teacher, Rava, and onwards, the law – the Halakhah in the sense of practical decision – always followed the opinions of the later sages. (The rationale for this rule is that presumably the later sages knew of the opinions of the earlier sages and yet took issue with them.)[4] It was consequently essential for those rendering Halakhic decisions to have some knowledge of Talmudic chronology.

The works of Talmudic methodology produced in our period usually consist of an exposition of terms used in the Talmudic debates together with chronologies of the Talmudic Rabbis who feature in the debates. As Gerson D. Cohen has noted, these chronological works exploited, in their defence of Rabbinism, the Muslim technique of *isnad*: that is, the authentication of a tradition or practice by scrutinizing the process of its transmission.[5] The earliest of these methodologies is the anonymous *Seder Tannaim ve-Amoraim* ('The Order of the Tannaim and Amoraim'), compiled probably in the year 885 according to Cohen,[6] thus coinciding with the period when the Karaite challenge was particularly acute. (The Tannaim are the teachers, mentioned in the Talmudic literature, who flourished in the first two centuries of the present era; the Amoraim are their successors in both Palestine and Babylon.) The *Sefer ha-Qabbalah* ('Book of the Tradition') by Abraham Ibn Daud (*c.* 1110–80) treats the history of the tradition from Bible times down through the Talmudic sages to the Rabbinic contemporaries of the author.[7] Ibn Daud's arrangement of the Talmudic teachers generation by generation (for example, second generation Tanna, third generation Amora, and so forth) was followed by practically all historians of the Halakhah. The other main works of the genre (in addition to the famous Letter of Sherira Gaon and the work of Maimonides, both to be noted presently) are: *Mevo ha-Talmud* ('Introduction to the Talmud') attributed to Samuel ha-Naggid (d. 1055);[8] *Sefer Keritut* ('Book of the Covenant'– a loose translation of the title but conveying its meaning) by Samson of Chinon (end of the thirteenth century);[9] *Halikhot olam* ('Paths of the World' or 'Eternal Paths') by Joshua of Tlemcen (compiled in Toledo ca. 1467);[10] *Sheney Luḥot ha-Berit* ('The Two Tablets of Stone') by Isaiah Horowitz of Prague (d. *c.* 1630);[11] and *Yad Malakhi* ('The Hand of Malachi') by Malachi ha-Kohen of Leghorn (early eighteenth century).[12] To be noted is that all these works belong firmly in the Halakhic tradition and have as their aim both the elucidation and application of that tradition.

The most influential work of Talmudic chronology is the *Iggeret de-Rav Sherira Gaon* ('The Letter of Rabbi Sherira Gaon'). The Geonim ('Excellencies') were the spiritual heads of the colleges of Sura and Pumbedita in Babylon, looking upon themselves, and accepted as such by the majority of Jews, as the legitimate heirs to the Talmudic sages of Babylon and, therefore, since the Babylonian Talmud had become more authoritative than the Palestinian, as the authorities of Jews everywhere. In response to a question put by Jacob b. Nissim of Qairawan, Sherira, Gaon of Pumbedita, composed in 986 his Letter in which he sought to explain how the Mishnah and the Talmud, the great commentary to the Mishnah, were compiled.[13] The Talmud is notoriously obscure on the matter of its own compilation. The questions Sherira seeks to answer are: who edited the Mishnah and the Talmud and by which process?

Sherira describes the manner in which, as he sees it, the Mishnah was edited by Rabbi Judah the Prince towards the end of the second century. Much of the material found in the Mishnah, Sherira suggests, goes back to the Men of the Great Assembly, the originators, in the immediate post-Biblical period, of the 'Rabbinic' tradition, and contains all the doctrines, teachings, and laws delivered to Moses at Sinai in the form of the Oral Torah. At first, there was little debate on the laws; the material was simply handed down intact from generation to generation. The great debates arose among the Tannaim during the first two centuries, a time when many details of the original revelation had been forgotten. Various attempts were made to compile a *Mishnah* (the word means 'a teaching') that would provide a record both of the Oral Torah as a whole and of the debates which took place around its meaning and application. One such Mishnah was compiled by Rabbi Akiba, another by Rabbi Meir. Rabbi Judah the Prince, acknowledged Patriarch of the Jewish community in Palestine, was best equipped to compile his own Mishnah, soon afterwards accepted universally as *the* Mishnah. The Amoraim based all their teachings on the Mishnah of Rabbi Judah the Prince, discussing it and elaborating on it in both Palestine and Babylon. The deliberations of the Palestinian Amoraim are contained in the Palestinian Talmud, those of the Babylonians in the Babylonian Talmud – 'our' Talmud, as the Geonim refer to it. The editors of the Babylonian Talmud were Rav Ashi and Ravina towards the end of the fifth century. The scholars known as the Savoraim added glosses to the Babylonian Talmud and some little additional material of their own. Sherira records a tradition, for instance, that the opening passage of tractate *Kiddushin* is Savoraic. The Geonim of Sura and Pumbedita were the successors of the Savoraim and Sherira proceeds to give a history of the Gaonate down to his own day, thus seeking to demonstrate that the Rabbinic tradition represented by Rabbinic Judaism, with the Geonim at its head, is the authentic tradition of Judaism as taught throughout the ages since the days of Moses.

The whole matter is complicated in that we are in possession of two distinct versions of Sherira's Letter. According to the Talmud itself there existed a prohibition against recording the Oral Torah in written form.[14] Since, however, the Talmud, the repository of the Oral Torah, was eventually written down, this, though illegal, must have been tolerated as an emergency measure 'lest the Torah be forgotten from Israel'. The French scholars in the Middle Ages piously refused to believe that Rabbi Judah the Prince and Rav Ashi and Ravina would have disregarded a clear prohibition or that the emergency that would have required the dispensation existed in Talmudic times. The Spanish scholars, on the other hand, held that the emergency measure was both required and adopted as early as the time of Rabbi Judah the Prince. Consequently, in the Spanish version of Sherira's Letter, Rabbi Judah the Prince is said to have recorded the Mishnah in writing and Rav Ashi and Ravina the Babylonian Talmud. In the French version of Sherira's Letter, Rabbi Judah the Prince only compiled the Mishnah, Rav Ashi and

Ravina the Talmud, in verbal form; the whole corpus received its written form at a later date. It is difficult to know which version of the Letter is the authentic one. Scholars still discuss this question.[15]

Sherira's sources are twofold. The main source, naturally, is the Talmud itself. Sherira has pieced together observations found scattered throughout the Talmud to form some kind of coherent picture. But, as the successor to the Geonim, Sherira relies, too, on traditions preserved by them. The tendency among modern historians of the Halakhah is to acknowledge the value of Sherira's attempt while questioning some of his conclusions, arguing that, on occasion, he has read Geonic patterns back into the Talmudic period, much as, say, a historian writing in a thousand years' time might imagine that the conditions of university life in the twentieth century accurately reflect conditions in sixteenth-century Oxford. The problem of the Savoraim and their contribution to the Babylonian Talmud has also been a source of contention in modern Talmudic scholarship.[16] It is hard to accept at face value the view of Sherira that Rav Ashi and Ravina are the final editors of the Talmud, since there are numerous Talmudic passages in which these Amoraim feature as heroes of the story with what appears to be later discussions of their views. The tendency is, nowadays, to insert a period of anonymous editors of the Talmudic material between the Amoraim (including Rav Ashi and Ravina) and the Savoraim.[17] Thus, instead of Sherira's Tannaim, Amoraim, Savoraim, and Geonim, we have Tannaim, Amoraim, the anonymous editors, Savoraim, and Geonim. In short, the apologetic nature of Sherira's account cannot be overlooked. Sherira's intention was to demonstrate the unbroken chain of tradition, contrary to the Karaite rejection of that tradition. In the process it is hardly to be expected that he worked with complete objectivity, an ideal virtually unknown in Sherira's day.

Like Sherira, but with greater elaboration, Maimonides gives a summary of the history of the tradition, from Moses down to his own day, in his Commentary to the Mishnah, compiled in his youth.[18] In the Introduction to his great Code of Law, the *Mishneh Torah*,[19] Maimonides repeats this history in capsule form, basing himself as did Sherira on statements found in the Talmud. For all his comparative indifference to general history, Maimonides, like Sherira, feels obliged to support the tradition by recording the chain from Moses onwards. In fact, he lists forty bearers of the tradition, working backwards from Rav Ashi through the

Amoraim and Tannaim back to Ezra and the Prophets and then to Joshua, who received the tradition from Moses himself.

Maimonides continues:

All the sages mentioned are the great ones of their generation – some of them heads of Yeshivot, some Exilarchs, some members of the Great Sanhedrin – and together with them in each generation there were thousands and tens of thousands who heard it from them and with Ravina and Rav Ashi there were the final sages of the Talmud. Rav Ashi compiled the Babylonian Talmud in the Land of Shinar after R. Johanan, about one hundred years earlier, had compiled the Palestinian Talmud.[20] The nature of the two Talmuds is commentary to the words of the Mishnah and an exposition of its profundities together with all those topics that had been newly introduced by our holy master [Rabbi Judah the Prince] up to the compilation of the Talmud. From the two Talmuds, the Tosefta, the Sifra, and the Sifre [other Tannaitic works], from all these there emerges an exposition of that which is forbidden and that which is permitted; that which is unclean and that which is clean; that for which there is liability and that for which there is no liability; that which is fit and that which is unfit, as was received from one to another reaching back to our teacher Moses at Sinai.

It can be seen that Maimonides' reconstruction is an artificial one, all extremely neat and tidy. Like his mediaeval contemporaries Maimonides was not bothered by anachronisms, seeing, for example, the institution of the Sanhedrin reaching back to the Biblical period. What we have here is not history but simple chronology with an avowed purpose. The need to verify the sources and test their reliability, a major concern for the historian, simply did not exist for Maimonides and his contemporaries. For all that, Maimonides often gives the history of particular laws in his Code, of which the following is a typical example.[21]

Prefacing the section in his Code dealing with marriage,[22] Maimonides writes:

Before the Torah had been given, if a man met a woman in the market place and both he and she agreed to marry, he would bring her into his house, have intercourse with her in the privacy of the house, and she would then become his wife. Once the Torah had been given, Israel was commanded that if a man wished to marry a woman he must first acquire her [to be his wife] in the presence of witnesses and [only] then does she become his wife, as it is said: 'If any man take a wife, and go in to her' [Deuteronomy 22:13]. To take a wife in this way is a positive precept of the Torah. By one of the following means a woman is acquired [as a wife]: by the delivery of a sum of money; by the delivery of a marriage document [*shetar,* a document in which it is stated: 'Be thou my wife'] or by intercourse; by intercourse or by the marriage document according to the Torah and by money according to the words of the Scribes [*mi-divrey soferim*]. These methods of acquiring [a wife] are referred to everywhere [in the Rabbinic sources] as *kiddushin* ['designation'] or *erusin* ['betrothal'] and a woman acquired by one of these methods is known as a *mekuddeshet* or *meoreset*. Before the Torah had been given, if a man met a woman in the market place and both he and she agreed to have intercourse, he would pay her fee, have intercourse with her by the wayside and then go his way. Such a woman was known as a harlot [*kedeshah*]. Once the Torah had been given, the harlot *[kedeshah]* was forbidden, as it is said: 'There shall be no harlot of the daughters of Israel' [Deuteronomy 23:18]. Consequently, whoever fornicates with a woman without *kiddushin* is liable to the penalty of flogging by Torah law since he has had intercourse with a harlot.

It is abundantly clear what Maimonides is trying to do in this 'historical' introduction to the laws of marriage. He is concerned to demonstrate that the methods, found in the Rabbinic sources, of acquiring a wife are the only methods and that extramarital sex is forbidden by the Torah. In obedience to these aims, Maimonides, aware that from the Biblical narrative of Judah and Tamar (Genesis 38) a less restrictive attitude prevailed (since Judah is not condemned for associating with a harlot) and also aware that in the earlier period, too, the institution of marriage existed (since there are references in the early narratives of the Bible to married women), reconstructs the history to fit in with his understanding of the law as recorded by the Rabbis in the Talmud. According to Maimonides, marriage in the pre-Torah age was optional. Casual sex with a harlot was not forbidden (that is, by the Noahide laws). There were also permanent marriage arrangements in which a woman consented to be a man's wife and she was then forbidden to all other men. This relationship could only be established by the two living together as man and wife in the privacy of their home. Once the Torah had been given, the laws, as recorded in the Rabbinic literature, came into operation for the Israelites. One of the three methods of acquisition had to be adopted in the presence of witnesses. The legal formalities had to precede the physical union.

All this is Maimonides' own reconstruction to which he subordinates his sources, which is why other Halakhists take issue with his formulation. Abraham Ibn David, Maimonides' great critic, remarks on Maimonides' ruling that for a man to live with a woman without *kiddushin* is harlotry: 'The word *kedeshah* means 'one who is ready', that is, one who is ready to abandon herself to all and sundry, but when a woman devotes herself to one man there is neither the penalty of flogging nor even a negative precept. This is the *pilegesh* referred to in Scripture.'[23] Elsewhere in his Code,[24] Maimonides states explicitly that the *pilegesh* ('concubine') is only permitted to a king, never to a commoner. And in his *Guide for the Perplexed* Maimonides inveighs against concubinage,[25] stating that there is no way to engage in permitted sexual intercourse than through singling out a woman and marrying her in public. Maimonides refers with approval more than once[26] to the Aristotelian dictum that the sense of touch is shameful. Here in his Code he reconstructs the history to be in accord with his philosophical and ethical predilections.

Maimonides does not, however, yield entirely to anachronism. In his *Sefer ha Mitzot* ('Book of the Commandments'), for instance, while he holds that the right of later sages to introduce new laws is sanctioned by the Torah, he understands this in a very general sense. Take the law introduced by the Rabbis that, in celebration of the victory of the Maccabees over Antiochus, the Hanukkah lights must be kindled and the benediction recited: 'Who has sanctified us with His commandments and has commanded us to kindle the Hanukkah lights.' This only means, Maimonides is at pains to point out, that the sages in Maccabean times had Biblical warrant to introduce the new observance. He ridicules the notion that the Biblical sanction involves a direct anticipation of events that were to happen in two thousand years' time – that, in the time of Moses, God informed him that one day the Maccabees would be victorious and the sages of the day would introduce a new practice, here and now meeting with God's approval.[27]

Maimonides refers to the two Talmuds, the Jerusalem (or Palestinian) Talmud and the Babylonian, stating that the latter was compiled about one hundred years after the former. This historical question of when the two Talmuds were compiled had implications for the post-Talmudic Halakhah. Since the principle, referred to above, is accepted, that the later teachers are to be followed where they are in disagreement with earlier teachers, the rulings of the Babylonian Talmud, where they differ from those in the earlier Palestinian Talmud, are the ones adopted by the post-Talmudic Halakhah. This was stated explicitly by R. Isaac Alfasi (1013–1103), known as the *Rif,* in his famous Halakhic compendium, *Sefer Halakhot,*[28] where he observes, regarding a certain Sabbath law on which the two Talmuds disagree, that the Babylonian ruling is adopted. The Babylonian Talmud, declares the *Rif,* must have known of the ruling in the Palestinian Talmud and yet departs from that ruling. As modern scholars note, there is no evidence that the editors of the Babylonian Talmud had before them the text of the Palestinian. Nowhere do they refer to the earlier work.[29] Yet the statement in the *Rif* resulted in the preference, on the part of the later Halakhists, for the Babylonian Talmud as the basis of the Halakhah.[30] This is as good an illustration as any of how the Halakhah follows its own rules whatever the historians have to say.

The French glossators to the Talmud known as the Tosafists (eleventh through to the thirteenth century), whose opinions enjoy a good deal of authority among the later Codifiers, evince a keen interest in historical matters. Their historical glosses are of two kinds. First, where the Talmud refers to past events and there is a degree of uncertainty about these, the Tosafists generally note the problem. Scores of such historical observations are found in the Tosafists, though their sources are exclusively Rabbinic.[31] Second, where a law is said in the Talmud to be based on certain conditions and these no longer obtained in the time of the Tosafists, they generally note this, arguing that the law can be changed when the original circumstances in which it was promulgated are no longer relevant. Many Halakhists take issue with the Tosafists, and hold that once the law is accepted in the Talmud it is irrevocable, even when the original conditions no longer obtain.[32] The Tosafists, however, do accept the principle of change so that a further reason emerges why some knowledge of history is required for Halakhic decision making.

For example, the Talmud is very strict regarding washing the hands after, as well as before, meals. In mediaeval France, the practice of washing hands after the meals was no longer in vogue. Defending their countrymen's neglect of a law stated in the Talmud, the Tosafists point out that the reason for the law given in the Talmud is that every trace of a certain salt must be removed from the hands after a meal because, if this came in contact with the eyes, it could cause blindness.[33] 'Nowadays,' remark the Tosafists, 'we no longer use this kind of salt and the law has justifiably fallen into abeyance.'

The Mishnah rules that dancing or even clapping the hands in joy is forbidden on a Festival and yet this rule was ignored by the French Jews. The Tosafists point out that the reason for the prohibition, stated in the Talmud, is to prevent the fashioning of a musical instrument; that is, in the joy of the dance people might forget that it is a holy day and they might fashion an instrument to assist the merriment. 'Nowadays,' say the Tosafists again, 'we lack the skill to fashion a musical instrument so there is no reason for the original prohibition to stand.'[34]

The Talmud is opposed to a father exercising the right, given to him in the Bible, of marrying off his minor daughter before she is old enough to choose for herself the man she wishes to marry. Here, too, the French Jews ignored the law. In their defense, the Tosafists remark that while such marriages are valid they are, indeed, illegal; yet, in the harsh conditions obtaining at the time it is essential to permit these marriages. If child marriages were to be disallowed, the opportunities for marriage may not arise later and the poor girls would remain unmarried all their lives.[35]

In these and similar instances history is invoked by the Tosafists as a *post factum* defence of a prevailing practice apparently at variance with the law. The Tosafists are certainly not engaged in objective historical investigation. Nevertheless, historical factors are allowed a voice in determining the Halakhah, as they are when the Tosafists refer to a ruling of the Geonim.[36] In Talmudic times, a widow could only claim her *ketubah,* the marriage settlement, from the real estate of her husband. It could not be claimed from movables, on which there was no lien. In Geonic times, however, when ownership of real estate was far less frequent, it became imperative to introduce new legislation according to which movables were also held in lien for the *ketubah.* The change in the historical circumstances is duly noted to allow changes in the law.

Another far-reaching change in the Geonic period was in connection with the strict Talmudic prohibition of Gentile wine. The Geonim relaxed some of the restrictions on the grounds that the Gentiles among whom they resided were Muslims and the more severe Talmudic restrictions applied only to the Gentiles in Talmudic times who were idolators.[37]

Here a number of further instances of historical factors having a say in how the Halakhah develops can be quoted. The Talmud states that a married woman need not recline at the Passover Seder since she is in awe of her husband, unless she is a 'woman of high rank' (*ishah ḥashuvah).* But a famous German Halakhist argued that in Talmudic times class distinctions were more pronounced, but 'all *our* women are of high rank'.[38] According to Talmudic law a man who profaned the Sabbath in public was to be treated as a non-Jew.[39] He could not, for example, help to form a quorum for prayer. Yet R. Jacob Ettlinger (1798–1871) of Altona argued that in Talmudic times the Jew who publicly profaned the Sabbath had cast himself off thereby from the Jewish community. Nowadays conditions are different. Many Jews profane the Sabbath out of ignorance; the law was historically conditioned and no longer has force.[40] In Talmudic law the deaf-mute (*ḥeresh*) is treated as an imbecile. R. Simhah Bunem Sofer of Pressburg (1842–1906) argues that this was because in Talmudic times, in the absence of schools for the deaf, there was no way for him to be educated.[41] Nowadays such schools exist and there is no longer any reason for treating a deaf-mute as if he were an imbecile.

The Halakhists at times show an interest in past events not so much because these have any relevance to the Halakhah in practice, but because they seem to show the ancients acting in an illegal manner, which in turn seemed to challenge the doctrine of the immutability of the Torah. R. David Ibn Abi Zimra (1479–1573), known as *Radbaz*, was asked how Adam could have disobeyed God to eat of the fruit of the tree of knowledge;[42] why Mordecai put the whole of his people in danger by refusing to bow to Haman when he could have avoided it by leaving Shushan to live elsewhere;[43] how Jacob could have married two sisters since, the Rabbis say, the patriarchs kept the Torah before it had been given;[44] and how Jonah could have avoided the direct command of God for him to go to Nineveh.[45] *Radbaz* defends the Biblical heroes by demonstrating that, in the particular circumstances in which they found themselves, they could not have acted otherwise than they did. R. Hayhim Jair Bacharach (1638–1702) was asked how he would defend the insulting behaviour of some of the Talmudic Rabbis in their debates.[46] Bacharach proceeds to examine all the Talmudic passages in which it is said that such unworthy conduct took place and tries to explain them away. There is an opinion in the Talmud that the Torah was originally written in the present square script, but a questioner wrote to R. Moses Alashkar (1466–1552) that he had in his possession an ancient coin with an inscription in the old Hebrew script, showing this to have been the original script. Alashkar replies that it does not follow from the inscription on the coin that the Torah was originally written in the script on the coin, only that the coin-makers used this script.[47]

While it can be seen from the above that it is not too anachronistic to speak of historical thinking in the Halakhah, the majority of the great Halakhists had little interest in history as a subject of study, and their methods, from the point of view of modern scholarship, were lacking in both objectivity and critical assessment. Historical critical method was not employed in the study of the Halakhah until the rise of the *Jüdische Wissenschaft* movement in the nineteenth century, when Krochmal, Rapoport, Frankel, and I. H. Weiss used the recently developed tools and were followed, in this century, by Saul Lieberman, Louis Ginzberg, Louis Finkelstein, Chaim Tchernowitz, J. N. Epstein, and a host of others. Yet important links were provided to the moderns in the work of a handful of traditional Halakhists who anticipated the new approach, albeit in rudimentary form. Prominent among these was the famous Moravian Halakhist, Yom Toy Lippmann Heller (1579–1654).

Heller seems to have possessed a keen sense of history, extremely rare until the modern period. In his Commentary to the Mishnah, *Tosefot Yom Tov,*[48] Heller is bold enough to suggest that the Mishnah is a work independent of the Talmud and that a student of the Mishnah is consequently entitled to read the Mishnah on its own terms, even if his interpretations are at variance with the interpretations of the Mishnah recorded in the Talmud. He did add, however, that this activity can only be a purely academic exercise. In actual practice the law must follow the interpretations given in the Talmud. In his Commentary to the Code of Asher b. Jehiel, entitled *Leḥem Ḥamudot,*[49] Heller surveys historically the two methods of Halakhic codification among the earlier Codifiers. The Codes of Maimonides and Jacob b. Asher's *Tur* follow the concise method of the Mishnah, while the Codes of the Rif and Asher b. Jehiel follow the more discursive methods typical of the Talmud. In his Introduction to his Commentary to the Mishnah,[50] Heller discusses the Rabbinic saying that God showed to Moses at Sinai all the later laws that were to be expounded by the Scribes and the Rabbis. This cannot possibly be taken to mean that everything was already given at Sinai for that would mean a complete abolition of human history. The teaching of the Scribes and the Rabbis were their own original teachings. These were not *given* to Moses. He was only *shown* them, God providing Moses with a miraculous glimpse into the future.

Links with modern scholarly methods were also supplied in two famous compendiums of Halakhic biography and bibliography.

Jehiel Heilprin (1660–1746) compiled his monumental *Seder ha-Dorot* ('Order of the Generations'), as he states in the Introduction to the work,[51] because only Halakhic confusion results from ignorance of Talmudic and Halakhic chronology. He provides a detailed list of textual errors which a knowledge of history can correct. To give only one illustration, many students of the Halakhah often identify incorrectly references to Rabban Gamaliel, failing to appreciate that there were three Rabban Gamaliels living at different times. Heilprin, out of his great knowledge, has astonishingly presented in this work a wealth of material culled from the sources for the reconstruction of the life and activities of the Talmudic and later Rabbis. All subsequent biographers have used Heilprin's work as the basis of their own researches, although, naturally, they view some of his sources with a more critical eye than a scholar living in eighteenth-century Russia could have possesssed.

Heilprin was followed by the Palestinian Halakhist, Hayyim Joseph David Azulai (1724–1806), known as *Ḥida. Ḥida's Shem ha-Gedolim* ('The Names of the Great Ones')[52] is in two parts. In the first the names and biographies of all the famed Halakhists (and other saintly teachers) are given; in the second are listed all the works they compiled. *Ḥida,* a great traveller, visited European libraries, where he consulted hundreds of manuscripts and early editions. Despite his uncritical acceptance of a good deal of purely legendary material, *Ḥida* can be seen as the forerunner of the moderns to whom in a real sense he belongs. In his detailed and colourful accounts of their lives, *Ḥida* brought the Halakhists to life as real human beings, each with his own individual temperament, instead of, as in the older view, mere abstract legal cyphers. From this it was but a step to seeing the Halakhah itself as governed by external conditions and a proper history of the Halakhah became possible.

NOTES

1. *Yoma* 5b; *Ketubot* 3a. Cf. the remarks of Menahem Meiri of Perpignan (1249–1316) in his *Bet ha-Behirah,* ed. I. Ralbag (Jerusalem, 1974), 44, to the passage in tractate *Sanhedrin* 15b in which the question is raised how many judges were required to sentence an ox to be stoned that had strayed on to the mountain (Exodus 19:13). Meiri, desperate to discover some practical Halakhic application, suggests the instance where a man makes a solemn promise to provide as many poor men with clothes as there were judges in that far-distant event. On the general subject of Talmudic chronology see Daniel Sperber's

'Studies in Talmudic Chronology' (Hebrew) in *Mikhtam le-David,* Memorial Volume for Rabbi David Ochs, ed. Y. Gilat and E. Stern (Ramat-Gan, 1978), 77–85.

2. *Commentary to the Mishnah,* ed. J. Kapah (Hebrew) (Jerusalem, 1963), to *Sanhedrin* 10:1; *Nezikin,* 140–141.
3. *Commentary to the Mishnah,* Introduction, 25 (my translation): 'After the demise of all the sages, on whom be peace, the last of whom were Ravina and Rav Ashi, the Talmud was complete so that whoever rose afterwards had no other purpose than to understand the words that had been compiled [i.e., the Talmud]. To it nothing must be added and from it nothing subtracted. Consequently, the Geonim composed commentaries to the Talmud but to the best of our knowledge none of them managed to compile a commentary to the whole of the Talmud.'
4. This rule is post-Talmudic but quite early. One of the sources in which it occurs is the *Sefer Keritut* of Samson of Chinon (Hebrew), ed. J. Z. Rotha (Brooklyn, 1961), Part 4, section 3:6, 263; ed. S. B. and J. M. Sofer (Jerusalem, 1983), 185. The reasoning behind the rule is given in the Response of Joseph Colon (d. 1480), the *Maharik* (Warsaw, 1884), No. 84, p. 92. Cf. the Responsa of Moses Alashkar (1466–1552) (Jerusalem, 1959), Nos. 53 and 54, for the conservative view that the rule has no application after the Geonic period.
5. Gerson D. Cohen, *The Book of Tradition Sefer ha-Qabbalah by Abraham Ibn Daud* (London, 1967), Introduction, p. 1.
6. *Ibid.,* lii. *Seder Tannaim ve-Amoraim,* ed. and transl. into German by K. Kahan (Frankfurt a.M., 1935).
7. Cohen, *The Book of Tradition.*
8. Printed with Commentaries in the Vilna, Romm editions of the Babylonian Talmud, after tractate *Berakhot.*
9. *Idem.*
10. Warsaw, 1883, with Commentaries.
11. Amsterdam, 1649, section *Torah she-be-al Peh.*
12. Jerusalem, 1976.
13. *Iggeret de-Rabbenu Sherira Gaon,* with Commentary, *Patshegen ha-Ketav,* by Aaron Hyman (London, 1911). The best edition is that of B. M. Lewin, *Iggeret Ray Sherira Gaon* (Jerusalem, 1972).
14. *Temurah* 14a; *Gittin* 60b. See the discussion in detail in Hermann L. Strack, *Introduction to the Talmud and Midrash* (Philadelphia, 1945), 12–20.
15. See especially Lewin's Introduction and J. N. Epstein, *Introduction to Amoraitic Literature* (Hebrew), ed. E. Z. Malammed (Jerusalem-Tel-Aviv, 1962), Appendix, 610–615. Epstein casts doubt on whether the two different versions have anything to do with the question of writing down the Mishnah and the Talmud.
16. See the literature cited in my *The Talmudic Argument* (Cambridge, Eng., 1984), 18–19 and David Weiss Halivni, *Midrash, Mishnah, and Gemara* (Cambridge, MA., 1986).
17. The much discussed key passage is *Bava Metzia* 86a: 'Rav Ashi and Ravina the end of Horaah'. The best analysis of the whole question is still Julius Kaplan, *The Redaction of the Babylonian Talmud* (New York, 1933). See especially Kaplan, 31–2, for the uncertainty about Sherira's view. On Sherira reading back Geonic institutions into the Talmudic period see David Goodblatt, *Rabbinic Instruction in Sassanian Babylon* (Leiden, 1975).
18. *Commentary to the Mishnah,* ed. Kapah, Introduction, 1–31.
19. Ed. S. Z. Rubenstein, *Rambam la-Am,* Introduction, and in various editions. The passage listing the forty sages is in Rubenstein, 10–11.
20. This view that R. Johanan (d. *c.* 270) was the editor of the Palestinian Talmud appears to be original with Maimonides and is probably based on the fact that this teacher is mentioned more often in the Palestinian Talmud than any other Amora. But clearly the present text of the Palestinian Talmud must have been edited at a much later date; see *Encyclopedia Judaica,* vol. 10, 146 and J. J. Greenwald, *Harau Messaderey ha-Bavli et ha-Yerushalmi?* (New York, 1954), 9–11.
21. See e.g. *Eruvin* 1:1–2; *Ḥametz u-Matzah* 1:8–9; *Taanit* 1:1–4; *Megillah ve-Ḥanukkah* 1:1; 3:1–3 and frequently in Maimonides' Code.
22. *Ishut* 1:1–4.
23. *Rabad* to *Ishut* 1:4.
24. *Melakhim* 4:4.
25. Guide, III, 49.

26. *Guide*, II, 36, 40; III, 8, 49.
27. *Sefer ha-Mitzvot* (Warsaw, 1883), *shoresh rishon*, 3b.
28. Vilna, Romm edition, 35b.
29. On this question see Epstein, *Introduction to Amoraitic Literature*, 290–2, and Greenwald, *Harau Mesadderey ha-Bavli et ha-Yerushalmi?*
30. See Malachi ha-Kohen, *Yad Malakhi* (Jerusalem, 1976), 'Rules Regarding the Two Talmuds', No. 2, 177a.
31. See e.g. Tosafists to *Betzah* 5b; *Megillah* 5b; *Gittin* 80b; *Bava Kama* 3b and *passim*.
32. On this see the survey in I. H. Weiss, *Dor Dor ve-Doreshav* (Berlin, 1924), II, 61–6.
33. Tosafists to *Ḥullin* 105a.
34. Tosafists to *Betzah* 30a.
35. Tosafists to *Kiddushin* 41a.
36. Tosafists to *Ketubot* 5la.
37. See Maimonides, *Mishneh Torah, Maakhalot Asurot* 11:7.
38. Mordecai b. Hillel (d. 1298) *Sefer Mordekhai, Pesaḥim* No. 128, quoted by Isserles in *Shulhan Arukh Orah Ḥayyim* 472:4.
39. See Ḥullin 51.
40. Responsa *Binyan Tzion*, New Series (Vilna, 1878), No. 23.
41. Responsa Shevet Sofer (Jerusalem, 1974), Even ha-Ezer, No. 21.
42. Responsa *Radbaz* (Warsaw, 1862), No. 256.
43. Responsa *Radbaz*, No. 284.
44. Responsa *Radbaz*, No. 696.
45. Responsa *Radbaz*, No. 842.
46. Responsa *Ḥavvot Yair* (Frankfurt, 1699), No. 152.
47. Responsa *Maharam Alashkar* (Jerusalem, 1959), No. 74.
48. *Tosefot Yom Toy* (various editions) to *Nazir* 5:5.
49. Introduction to *Leḥem Ḥamudot* in *Sefer Rabbenu Asher* (beginning) printed in Vilna, Romm edition of the Babylonian Talmud immediately after the text *of Berakhot*.
50. Introduction to *Tosefot Yom Tov*, discussing the Talmudic passage, *Megillah* 19b. In this same Introduction, Heller remarks that while the tradition in general goes back to Moses at Sinai, many of the details were forgotten in the course of time and hence the debates among the Rabbinic teachers are attempts at rediscovering the original Mosaic teaching.
51. *Seder ha-Dorot*, ed. Naftali Maskil le-Etan (Warsaw, 1877), photocopy with many supplements (Jerusalem, 1985).
52. *Shem ha-Gedolim*, ed. Menahem Mendel Krengil (Podgora-Cracow, 1905–30). I. A. Benjacob's *Otzar ha-Sefarim* (Vilna, 1880), the standard tool for Rabbinic bibliography, consists of the second part of *Ḥida*'s work with further elaborations and notes.

—17—

The Responsa of Rabbi Joseph Hayyim of Baghdad

Rabbi Joseph Hayyim (1833 or '35–1909) was the acknowledged spiritual head of the Baghdad Jewish community. The only official rabbinic position he occupied, however, was that of preacher, succeeding his father in this exalted office, which he held for fifty years until his demise, attracting, it is said, thousands of people to his discourses. Rabbi Hayyim was also a great authority on the Kabbalah, though, unlike conventional Kabbalists, who received the doctrines from an adept, he was self-taught in the subject. At the end of each volume of his legal Responsa there is a section entitled *Sod Yesharim* ('Secret of the Upright') in which he treats purely Kabbalistic questions, and he is not averse to introducing Kabbalistic themes into his legal decisions. Rabbi Hayyim was a man of enormous wealth. His critic Dr. Jacob Obermayer, the famous geographer of Babylonian Jewry and teacher of French in the palace of the Persian Prince 'Abbas Mirza, wrote disparagingly of the rabbi's alleged neglect of the spiritual needs of his community as he studied in seclusion while his four brothers attended to the family's vast commercial interests. For his pains Obermayer was placed under the ban until he had appeased the sage.[1]

Rabbi Hayyim's fame as a legal authority spread far beyond the confines of Baghdad. Halakhic questions were addressed to him from the Sephardi communities of Bombay, Calcutta, Rangoon, Singapore, Shanghai, Salonika, Constantinople, Ismir, and Jerusalem. He was known to the Ashkenazi Halakhists of his day and was himself thoroughly familiar with the works of the Ashkenazi authorities of former times. Rabbi Isaac Herzog reported that when he was a boy in London, he heard the renowned Lithuanian Rabbi Jacob David Willowski (1845–1913) deliver a funeral oration over Rabbi Hayyim in which this fiery preacher, no respecter of persons, referred to the departed rabbi as 'head of all the sons of the Diaspora,' a title generally reserved for the most outstanding Halakhist of the age.[2] Rabbi Hayyim's Responsa collections, *Rav Pe'alim* ('Mighty in Deeds', after II Sam. 23:20), was published in Jerusalem in four volumes (1901–12). In the reprint (Jerusalem, 1962–64) the editors remark:

> This work is a guide and a means of illumination to those who sit in judgment [i.e., who have to render decisions in Jewish law]. In addition this work serves as a splendid example of how to write legal decisions [*pesakim*] and how to solve complicated legal problems. All practising rabbis as well as those studying for the rabbinate will learn from the work how one proceeds to solve legal problems. They will note how the author examines every detail with profound penetration, analysing everything and diving into deep waters until he arrives at his decision.

Historians of Eastern Jewries will find in this collection a wealth of fascinating material.[3] Students of Jewish theology will also find much here of interest to them. But the aim of this article is to study Rabbi Hayyim's Halakhic approach as revealed in these Responsa. A number of the Responsa will be noted so as to observe how the actual process of rendering Halakhic decisions is engaged in and how the classical sources are used in arriving at the actual law in practice.

The author's Introduction to Volume I contains a survey of the methods used by Halakhic Respondents. First there are the two different types of the merely selective scholar and the one who uses deductive reasoning. The former, when asked to render a decision, consults all the sources, talmudic and post-talmudic, weighing up all the pros and cons until he finally arrives at the rule to be followed. But in this process of carefully sifting the material there is little originality, and the final decision is not, in fact, the Respondent's own but that of the authority, or authorities, on whom he relies. Such a Respondent can justifiably lay claim to the title of 'Sage' *(Ḥakham)* but hardly qualifies as a 'rabbi'.[4] The latter type is far more original. This Respondent applies his knowledge of the law and brings into play his intellectual skills in order to arrive at a decision even in cases about which the sources are either silent or ambiguous. Capable of discovering new rules and applying the old rules to new situations not envisaged in the sources, this Respondent deserves to be called 'Rabbi' as well as 'Sage'.

Another habit to be observed among Respondents is that some of them preface their written decisions with protestations of their basic unworthiness. It is true that many of the great Respondents do this but, Hayyim says, he personally prefers the attitude of those who proceed bravely and immediately to the task in hand. If a Respondent really believes himself to be unworthy to the task, by stating it in writing and later in print, he is guilty of parading his modesty. If he does not really believe himself to be inadequate, he is guilty of the even worse offence of laying claim to a virtue he does not possess. If a man doubts his ability to render decisions, he ought to leave the work to others better qualified. If he is confident that he can bring the task to a successful conclusion, let him get on with it, refusing to pander to what has unfortunately become a mere convention and one that borders on the ridiculous. It none the less must be appreciated that the great Respondents were never formally appointed to be such. It was simply that their peers considered them to be competent. This is no doubt why, despite Hayyim's objection, some of them did feel that professional etiquette demanded that they protest too much.

A more significant distinction is between the Respondent who is content to examine the basic sources of the law, proceeding to render his decisions without having any recourse to the works of the later Halakhists, sternly independent, convinced that he has nothing to learn from his contemporaries or near contemporaries; and the Respondent who will first feel obliged to read all that has been written on the subject. On the whole the first approach is that of the Ashkenazi Respondents, the second that of the Sephardim. Naturally Hayyim sides with the Sephardim. Why should even the most brilliant of jurists refuse to examine at all what others have said, even if only to disagree with them? He may come across a fresh argument or novel application that had not occurred to him. Even when he encounters theories that seem absurd to him, the topic will receive further clarification in the very process of refutation and in defence of his own position. The third-century Palestinian teacher R. Johanan, the Talmud informs us,[5] was far more pleased with the colleague who tried to refute his arguments than with the colleague who merely quoted authorities in their support. Finally, there are the Respondents who calmly dismiss the arguments of the earlier Halakhists if they find them inadequate, using, at times, extremely harsh expressions, accusing them of ignorance or stupidity. And there are those other Respondents, again represented chiefly by the Sephardim, who may also at times disagree with earlier authorities but who do so in a deferential manner and with the respect due to the sages of former times. Posterity generally gives the accolade to the victim of the critic, let it be remembered, rarely to the critic himself. Note what happened to the famous critic of Maimonides, Abraham Ibn David! He seized every opportunity to offer critiques of Maimonides' decisions in his great Code, the *Mishneh Torah,* and yet Maimonides' reputation is still as secure as ever, after over seven hundred years of diligent study of the gigantic work in which the critic has himself been refuted by generations of keen scholars who sprang to their hero's defence. Hayyim points to a number of gross errors perpetrated by noteworthy Ashkenazi authorities of recent times in their critical zeal and disrespectful attitude towards the giants of the past.[6] This exercise, Hayyim protests, is not solely for the purpose of exposing the Ashkenazim. If that were his aim, he would have been guilty of the same fault he attributes to them. No, his aim is to demonstrate how easy it is for the later scholars, with all their preoccupations and distractions, from which the mediaeval teachers were more or less free, to overlook simple statements of fact and occasionally lapse into ignorance of laws clearly formulated and known to all.

Many of the Responsa in *Rav Pe'alim* are concerned with religious law. Hayyim is, on the whole, very strict with regard to Sabbath observance, following the authorities who hold that one who profanes the Sabbath in public is to be excluded from the Jewish community.[7] On the other hand, he permits the riding of a bicycle on the Sabbath, where there is an *'eruv* so that 'carrying' is not involved, and on the Festivals.[8] On the use of artificial methods of contraception, Hayyim follows the strict Ashkenazi authorities of the nineteenth century in forbidding these even where a pregnancy may result in danger to the wife.[9] On the question of abortion Hayyim is very circumspect.[10] The case he considers is that of a married woman who became pregnant as a result of her adultery. Is she permitted to abort her five-month-old foetus? Hayyim remarks, unusually for him, that he is unwilling to give a definite decision one way or the other but will content himself by quoting the Halakhic authorities who deal with the question. These are: the German Rabbi Jair Hayyim Bacharach (1638–1703), who, in a similar case, argues that while in Jewish law foeticide is not treated as homicide, it is still forbidden for the married woman to abort the foetus; Rabbi Jacob Emden of Altona (1697–1776), who forbids it in the case of a single girl who becomes pregnant, yet not only permits it in the case of a married woman, but goes so far as to suggest that it may be meritorious; and the Turkish Rabbi Joseph Trani (1568–1639), who is even more permissive wherever there is strong benefit to the woman. Hayyim remarks, therefore, that a case can be made out to permit the abortion if a failure to have it performed will result in disgrace to the family concerned. Yet Hayyim repeats that he refuses to add his own decision or even to disclose his own opinion in the matter. The questioner should show Hayyim's summary of the opinions to a sage who will then be able to render a decision.

The Sephardi rabbis normally enjoyed complete autonomy in their administration of family law, unlike their Ashkenazi counterparts in Europe. As a result, the Sephardim were bolder in their efforts to introduce new legislation in the sphere of marriage law[11] in order to cope with the problem of the *'agunah,* the wife bound to a husband who refuses to divorce her or the widow bound to the levir (Deut. 25:5–10) who refuses to participate in the ceremony of loosing the shoe (*ḥalitzah*) in order to release her to marry another. The problem was particularly acute where the husband or levir had become converted to another faith and therefore refused to participate in the Jewish rites of *get* or *ḥalitzah.* The particular difficulty here is that no court is empowered to grant the *get* or release the woman from the levirate bond without the consent and participation respectively of the husband or the levir. A remedy with talmudic antecedents was for the marriage to be conditional in the first instance so that, in the event of the husband's or the levir's apostasy, the marriage is retrospectively annulled. Hayyim persuaded the Persian rabbis to introduce, as standard procedure in every marriage, the conditional clause that in the event of the husband converting to another faith, the marriage is null and void from the beginning.[12] In a case that came before him of a childless couple who were in great distress because the husband's brother was an apostate, Hayyim advised the husband formally to divorce his wife and then remarry her on the condition that if he later dies without issue, the marriage is null and void from the beginning.[13]

Polygamy was practised by the Babylonian Jews since the ban of 'Rabbenu Gershom' did not apply to the Sephardim. It was the practice, however, from the Middle Ages, for the wife's family to stipulate, if they saw fit so to do, that no other wife be taken. A number of the Responsa in *Rav Pe'alim* deal with legal problems arising out of polygamous marriages." In talmudic times there were normally two stages in the marriage process. The first of these was the betrothal (*kiddushin*); the second, the consummation (*nisu'in*). The betrothed woman was a married woman in law, and she required a *get* to release her to marry another. During the Middle Ages,[15] in Ashkenazi communities as well as in the majority of Sephardi communities, the two events took place simultaneously, and this is the common practice among Jews today. But in Babylon, the home of the Babylonian Talmud, the old talmudic procedure was still followed. We learn from *Rav Pe'alim*[16] that there was, indeed, a special rabbinic official – the *mekaddesh* – whose function it was to supervise betrothals in order to see that the requirements of the law were satisfied. The Baghdadi court, headed by the Chief Rabbi, Hayyim Elisha Nisim, consulted Hayyim[17] regarding a breach of promise case, a legal problem particularly acute in the Baghdadi situation since once *kiddushin* had been given the girl required a *get*. The husband can release her, but she would then acquire the status of a divorcée. Her future marriage prospects would be diminished considerably in that a divorcée cannot marry a priest (*kohen:* Lev. 21:7), and, in any event, 'it is notorious that in this city [Baghdad] a divorcee is cheap in people's eyes'. The particular case presented to Hayyim was that of a young man who betrothed a girl in the usual public ceremony, presided over by the *mekaddesh,* but later refused to consummate the marriage on the grounds that the girl's father was a mere schoolteacher and he wished to marry into a more 'respectable' family. The court cannot possibly accept the young man's plea. The status of the girl's father was known to him before he betrothed her. His refusal now to consummate the marriage can only be because he has in the meantime fallen in love with someone else. Assuming that the court cannot compel him to consummate the marriage, when he divorces the girl, is he obliged to compensate her for the extreme embarrassment she suffered through his unworthy behaviour? Hayyim quotes earlier authorities who treat breach of promise cases under the general heading of *boshet* ('embarrassment'), the compensation due to one who has been put to shame by another even where there has been no physical injury.[18] The practice of the courts is to award damages even for damage to a person's reputation. Consequently, Hayyim rules, the Baghdadi court must impose a heavy fine on the man to be paid to the girl as compensation for the shame he caused her to suffer. If he refuses the court must resort to coercion. Strictly speaking, they should place him under the ban (*ḥerem*), cutting him off from all social intercourse in the community until he agrees to pay, although, Hayyim admits, there are difficulties in adopting, nowadays, this drastic measure upon which the Gentile authorities frown. Other methods of coercion are available to the court, however, and, in any event, it is obvious that the young man must not be allowed to marry anyone else until he has done his duty by the girl. To clinch the argument Hayyim quotes a Responsum of the famous Ashkenazi authority R. Moses Sofer of Pressburg (1762–1839), known as *Ḥatam Sofer.* A man invited a *mohel* to his village for the purpose of circumcising his newly born son whereas in reality the child was a girl. When the *mohel* arrived at the village, all prepared to perform the circumcision, he was exposed to the ridicule of the villagers. The *Ḥatam Sofer*[19] decided that the victim of this practical joke is entitled to damages although the *Ḥatam Sofer* also remarks that the court cannot avail itself of the *ḥerem* in order to enforce payment since this was illegal in Hungary.

Another problem of marital law was addressed to Hayyim from the town of Shiraj in Persia.[20] A wife demanded that her husband divorce her because he is impotent and she wants children. The husband does not deny that he is impotent but refuses to divorce his wife. Can he be compelled to divorce her? Hayyim quotes the *Shulḥan 'Arukh,*[21] where the rule is laid down that if the wife claims her husband is impotent and he denies it, some authorities hold that he is obliged to divorce her, but since he denies it, she has no claims on the marriage settlement, the *ketubah.* The seventeenth-century commentator to the *Shulḥan 'Arukh,* Samuel Uri Shraga Phoebus, observes[22] that it follows, if the husband admits that he is impotent, that the husband is not only obliged to divorce her but he must in addition pay her the *ketubah.* Hayyim also quotes the decision[23] of R. Ezekiel Landau of Prague (1713–93): 'Concerning the case of the wife who claims that her husband is impotent and he admits it, the law is obvious that he must divorce her and pay the *ketubah.'* But since the later authorities disagree as to whether this also applies to the additional amounts voluntarily entered into the *ketubah* or only to the basic, minimum amount fixed for all, Hayyim rules that this constitutes a doubt in law and the husband's possession of the additional amount cannot be disturbed.

On the general question of the court compelling a husband to give a *get* to his wife where there are grounds for divorce, Hayyim states that while this procedure is stated in the Mishnah,[24] the post-talmudic authorities are reluctant to engage in coercion except in cases stated explicitly in Mishnah and Talmud.[25] But in the particular case considered, a wife's claim that she requires to have children is stated in the Talmud to be a legal claim.[26] Hence Hayyim concludes:

> This is the law as it has emerged from all that has been said, with God's help. In this case, where the husband is impotent and unable to carry out his marital duties at all and he admits this, and, moreover, the wife advances a claim referred to in the Talmud, that she wishes to have a child upon whom she can lean for she has no son at all, in these circumstances one should rule that every means of coercion be resorted to in order to compel him to give the *get,* and she must not be allowed to remain an *'agunah* all her days without ever enjoying her marital rights.

However, Hayyim quotes many authorities who rule that if the husband is willing to consult physicians who may cure him of his impotence, he is to be given reasonable time to allow him to seek such a cure before being compelled to divorce his wife.[27]

A number of Hayyim's Responsa deal with questions of legal procedure. The general legal principle in civil cases is that doubt cannot disturb possession so that the benefit of the doubt is given to the defendant if, as is usually the case, he has possession.[28] This does not only apply to where the doubt is about the facts of the case but even where the doubt is due to uncertainty as to what the law is.[29] Thus where the authorities disagree as to what the law is in a particular case, the man who has possession can claim that he is convinced that the law is with those authorities who side with him. This is known as *kim li,* 'It is established for me,' i.e., that the opinion of such-and-such an authority is correct.[30] For some of the Sephardi communities, however, including those of Palestine and Baghdad, the authority of R. Joseph Karo (1488–1575), author of the *Shulḥan 'Arukh,* was so great that no plea of *kim li* was allowed if the teacher quoted disagreed with Karo's ruling.[31] Karo's authority was sufficient even to disturb possession. The members of the communities in which this principle had been adopted are obliged by social contract to honour it. Now in addition to the *Shulḥan 'Arukh,* Karo was the author of Responsa.[32] Would the exception to the *kim li* rule apply even where Karo's opinion is only found in his

Responsa or does it only apply to Karo's opinions in his standard Code? Hayyim neatly argues that since there are at least three prominent Sephardi authorities who hold that the exception only applies to Karo's opinions in the *Shulḥan 'Arukh,* and there is a fourth Sephardi authority who is in doubt as to whether it applies even to Karo's opinions in his Responsa, this in itself constitutes a doubt whether or not *kim li* applies, and this is obviously to be treated like any other case of doubt. The man in possession can claim *kim li,* and it would be begging the question to invoke Karo's opinion in the Responsa since this is itself in doubt, whether Karo's opinion in the Responsa can be invoked. If, however, Hayyim concludes, neither the plaintiff nor the defendant has possession, i.e., where the dispute concerns property in the possession of neither, then the court is justified in following the opinion of Karo against other authorities even if that opinion is only found in Karo's Responsa.

Hayyim discusses this problem of juristic ethics.[33] If two members of a court of three in a civil case decide for the defendant and one for the plaintiff, the majority opinion is followed. If, however, the third judge declares that he does not know who is in the right, i.e., he cannot decide one way or the other, then two further judges are to be added and the five judges retry the case.[34] Supposing the third judge is convinced that the defendant is liable, may he, none the less, state that he cannot come to a decision in the hope that when the further two judges are added they will manage to convince their colleagues of the defendant's liability? Hayyim quotes earlier authorities who discuss this very question, largely in terms of whether such a white lie is permissible. Hayyim seeks to prove from a number of talmudic passages that it is permitted to adopt such a subterfuge, a lie for the sake of peace or the sake of truth and justice being no lie.

The Baghdadi Court addressed this question to Hayyim.[35] After three judges had decided a case in favour of A and against B, B, believing the chief judge to be the one responsible for the adverse decision, insulted that judge, who retaliated by slapping B's face twice. The case met with further complications, and the judges had to sit once again. B now declares that the affair has rendered the judge his 'enemy' who cannot serve as a judge. Is there any substance in B's plea? Hayyim produces a number of authorities, including R. Meir of Rothenberg (d. 1293), from whose writings it appears that the judge is not disqualified as an 'enemy'. In any event, Hayyim continues, it is notorious that in Baghdad, in former times as well as nowadays, some of the people who come before the courts and are dissatisfied with the verdict do insult the judges, and yet it is the common custom for the judges nevertheless to proceed with the case. At the very least, therefore, there is a consensus in the Baghdadi community that a judge who has been insulted and retaliates is not thereby disqualified as an 'enemy' of the man who insulted him, and consensus in these matters is binding upon the members of the community.

Attempted suicide is not a criminal offense in Jewish law. But the *Shulḥan 'Arukh*[36] rules that the near relatives of a suicide are not to carry out the usual mourning rites of rending the garments and of *shiva'* (the seven days of mourning). What of the other religious rites, such as prayers for the repose of the soul, the recital of *kaddish,* and the kindling of a memorial light? Hayyim[37] quotes the views of the Ashkenazi authority *Ḥatam Sofer,*[38] who, says Hayyim, is also quoted by the Sephardi R. Hayyim Palagi of Smyrna (1788–1869), both of whom hold that prayers and the like on behalf of the suicide do not fall under the heading of the mourning that is forbidden. They are means of atonement to which the suicide is also entitled. Hayyim quotes further the work *Besamim Rosh,*[39] which takes a very lenient view of suicide, but the *Ḥatam Sofer* has cast serious suspicions on this work. After quoting further opinions, Hayyim rules that the memorial prayers, etc., should be recited, and he refers to the recently published compendium of Jewish law, *Sedey Ḥemed,* by Hayyim Hezekiah Medini, who gives a comprehensive account of all the laws regarding a suicide.[40] In another Responsum on suicide,[41] Hayyim considers the case of a girl who took poison because she had had a dream in which she was told that she would die on a certain day, on which day she did, in fact, commit suicide. Hayyim is convinced that the *kaddish,* etc., can be recited for her. In addition to the authorities he has quoted in the previous Responsum, he refers to Eliezer Fleckeles of Prague (1754–1826), who states[42] that the saying 'A suicide has no share in the World to Come' is false. There is no such saying in any of the classical Jewish sources.

Although Hayyim is seldom at a loss in discovering some analogous case to the one he considers, even where there is no explicit statement in the sources, he tries unsuccessfully to discover an exact analogy in the following.[43] A made a wager with B that B would not succeed in solving a riddle he would set him before nightfall. B, knowing of his inability to solve the riddle, consulted a sage who told him the answer. Is B entitled to his winnings, and is the sage at all culpable? Hayyim cannot discover any Halakhic ruling to guide him in this matter, but embarks on a general discussion on the legality of gambling and the collection of gambling debts.[44]

Hayyim has a number of Responsa on promises to give to charity.[45] This case came before him.[46] Reuben (i.e., 'A') used to sup with unworthy companions, and whenever he visited the home of his mother-in-law she used to flirt with him. At the urgent request of his father, Reuben took a solemn oath that he would give a gold coin to charity if he visited in the future his father-in-law's house or supped with his companions. Reuben was, however, unable to keep away from his companions or his mother-in-law, visiting each a number of times. The charity treasurer now demands a gold coin for each separate visit, but Reuben claims that in the absence of a direct promise to give a gold coin for each separate visit, he is only obliged to give two coins, one for all the visits to his mother-in-law, and one for all the occasions on which he supped with his companions. Hayyim refers to a similar case in the Responsa of the German Rabbi Jacob Popers (d. 1740).[47] A community issued a proclamation to the effect that a fine of twenty-five gulden be imposed for the benefit of the poor on whoever departed from the communal practice to have a private *minyan* for prayers. A man offended against this communal regulation a number of times. Does a single payment of twenty-five gulden suffice for all the times he offended? Popers declares that it seems obvious to him that a single fine suffices and he seeks to prove it from a talmudic passage.[48] Here it is stated that a Nazirite who drinks a quarter of a *log* of wine is liable to be flogged provided he has been previously warned that this penalty awaits him and yet he persists. If he drank a large quantity of wine, and he was warned before he drank each quarter of a *log,* he is to be flogged separately for each quarter of a *log* he drinks, but if he was given only one warning at the beginning, he is only liable to a single flogging no matter how much wine he drinks. Hayyim demurs that the two cases are not at all analogous. In the case of the Nazirite the penalty is conditional on the prior warning, and there had only been one warning. But the communal fine is for the offence itself, and since there have been a number of separate offences, it seems obvious to Hayyim that there ought to be a separate fine of twenty-five gulden for each. Moreover, Popers has overlooked the talmudic rule that no procedural rules can be derived in civil cases from cases of religious law.[49] The Nazirite case is one of religious law, whereas the claims of the poor are to be treated like other cases of monetary claims. Furthermore, there is a reference in the Talmud to a man who insulted another by slapping his face twice and the court ordered him to pay a separate fine for each slap.[50] After drawing further analogies of a somewhat casuistic nature, Hayyim comes to the conclusion that Reuben is obliged to pay a gold coin for each separate offence.

The Ashkenazi rabbis of Jerusalem turned to Hayyim for his ruling[51] in connection with the *Ḥalukkah,* the charity distribution in the Holy Land.[52] The poor of Jerusalem were supported by the donations sent by various groups in the Diaspora. The overseers of the various groups (*kolelim*) in Europe collected the amounts from generous donors and forwarded these to the overseers in Palestine, who distributed them among the poor. The question addressed to Hayyim by the Jerusalem rabbis was which of the two *parnasim* is the main *parnas,* the European *parnas* who collects the money, the Palestinian *parnas* being only his agent for distribution, or the Palestinian *parnas,* who, after all, is the one responsible for the distribution? This is not a purely academic question. According to Jewish tradition, a *parnas* must be elected democratically by the people he is appointed to serve. He must be elected by the community. Moreover, which is, in fact, the 'community' for this purpose, that of Europe or that of Palestine?

Both the questioners and Hayyim himself refer to the relevant talmudic passage[53] that a leader (*parnas*) must not be appointed over a community without first consulting the community, just as Moses consulted the people before appointing Bezalel (Exod. 35:30). Although Maimonides does not record this in his Code, this, says Hayyim, is because in his codification Maimonides generally ignores purely Aggadic, nonlegal passages. For all that, it remains a piece of advice found in the Talmud and so should be followed. Karo also does not record it in the *Shulḥan 'Arukh,* but he does refer to it as a rule in his Responsa.[54] Now since the proof-text is that dealing with Bezalel, it follows that it only applies to a *parnas* who resembles Bezalel, whose right it was to decide which gifts were acceptable for the Tabernacle. This gave Bezalel a degree of power and control over the affairs of others, and here it is only just that those over whom the power is to be exercised should first be asked for their consent. The communities in the Diaspora who donate the amounts have fulfilled their obligation as soon as they have contributed. Their *parnasim* have similarly fulfilled their obligations as soon as they have sent the money off to Palestine. The community of the poor in Palestine are, on the other hand, in the power of the Palestinian *parnasim.* There is, consequently, no doubt at all that it is the *parnasim* in the Holy Land who are the real *parnasim* and the community of the poor in the Holy Land that has to elect these *parnasim.*

A number of Hayyim's Responsa deal with cases of misrepresentation. One of these concerns Reuben who bought a crate of European crockery from a Gentile.[55] Reuben sold the crate to Simeon, a retailer. It then became known that the crockery had been used by another Gentile at the wedding feast of his son. Since the crockery had been used for forbidden food Simeon can only sell it to Gentiles. Simeon claims that Reuben has been guilty of misrepresentation, and he wishes to cancel the sale. Hayyim, on the basis of similar rulings in the *Shulḥan 'Arukh,*[56] rules that since it has been established that Simeon does sell his wares to Gentiles as well as to Jews, and since Reuben made no declaration to the effect that the crockery was *kasher,* then it all depends on whether or not Simeon has paid Reuben for the crockery. If Simeon had not yet paid, he can revoke the sale. This is a straightforward case of doubt, and Simeon has possession. But if the money has been paid, then it is Reuben who has possession, and this cannot be disturbed by doubt. Even if the majority of Simeon's customers are Jews, this rule would still apply since possession cannot be disturbed in cases of doubt even where the laws of probability favour the plaintiff.[57]

In a curious Responsum Hayyim deals with a case of misrepresentation in marriage.[58] The questioner provides, incidentally, a vivid picture of marriage customs in the Baghdadi community. The talmudic practice was followed of having two stages in the marriage process:[59] the betrothal, *kiddushin,* and the consummation, which took place at a later date. But the bride was considered as married from the time of the *kiddushin,* and she required a *get* before she could remarry. On the first night, the female relations of the bride and groom and occasionally two or three males as well would wait in an adjoining room. When the groom opened the door after having put on his clothes, a female relative would enter to inspect the sheet. After the *kiddushin* had taken place, the parents of a girl discovered to their horror that she had previously had an affair and was no longer a virgin. Fearful that the groom would accuse the bride of being unfaithful, i.e., of having had the affair after the *kiddushin,* the parents arranged by subterfuge for the sheet to be stained. The matter became known to a relative of the bride, but this man held his peace. It so happened that a day or so later this man was studying tractate *Ketubot,* where he came across a passage in which it is implied that if a man marries a woman on the understanding that she is a virgin, the marriage is invalid if, in fact, she is not.[60] This led the relative to feel somewhat guilty in keeping silent. Perhaps he is now obliged to expose the trickery so that the groom can, if he so wishes, remarry the girl; otherwise they will be living together in sin for all their days without knowing it. On the other hand, to expose it will almost certainly result in the most serious quarrels, and who knows what the outcome of these will be? Perhaps, therefore, discretion is called for. A further mystical question addressed to Hayyim in the matter is whether the souls of the children of the marriage will be affected through 'confusion', i.e., because the girl had previously lived with another man.

Hayyim is convinced that the relative must hold his peace. He argues the case for silence brilliantly. The couple are committing no sin by living together. The authorities are divided on whether the marriage is valid where a man stated explicitly that he only marries his bride on the understanding that she is a virgin. Some authorities hold that even then the marriage is valid, since whatever the groom's stipulation at the time of the betrothal, his unconditional consummation of the marriage must mean that he has cancelled out his original condition. Otherwise his act of intercourse would be with a woman to whom he is only doubtfully married, since at the time when he comes to perform the act he does not know whether or not his condition has been satisfied. A man would not willingly do this, so it can be assumed that he cancels out his original condition. Again, the authorities argue that where no explicit condition had been made, it is possible that the groom is not too insistent that his bride be a virgin. There is thus in our case a double doubt – *safek safeka.*[61] There is the doubt whether the groom is sufficiently concerned in the first instance that his bride be a virgin. But even if he is the kind of person who would invalidate the marriage if he knew at the time of the *kiddushin* that his bride was no virgin, this is no better than an express stipulation to that effect, and here there is the further doubt that, possibly, those authorities are followed who hold that since he consummated the marriage without any stipulation, he has cancelled out his objection as implied in the condition. In religious law, our concern here, a double doubt is sufficient to permit an act even where the possible offence is biblical. True, continues Hayyim, a double doubt cannot succeed in disturbing possession in a civil case,[62] and in the event of her becoming divorced or widowed the wife will have no claim to a virgin's *ketubah,* yet at the moment this question does not arise. The girl's relatives should, however, quietly agree among themselves that if at a later date there is a claim on the husband or on his estate for the *ketubah,* they should only allow her to claim as for a nonvirgin.

As for the Kabbalistic question regarding the souls of the children, it is true that in some Kabbalistic works the idea is found that the first man to have intercourse with a woman provides, as it were, the 'spirit',' *ruḥa,* which becomes the base of the souls of all the children she will subsequently bear, but many other Kabbalists find this whole notion bizarre, for if it were true it would mean that the children a widow or a divorcée has from her second husband would have something in them of her first husband, which is the height of absurdity. In any event, Hayyim concludes, this notion would not apply to our case, where the girl's relations with her lover were unlawful. Whatever 'spirit' her lover did succeed in imparting to her will have been removed by the act of legal *kiddushin* by the husband. Hayyim concludes, as he does all his Responsa, with the prayer: 'May the Almighty in His abundant mercies illumine our eyes with the light of His Torah. Amen. So may it be His will.'

In another Responsum on misrepresentation in marriage,[63] Hayyim considers this case. A man, whom Hayyim refers to as 'a scholar and an exceedingly God-fearing man', had a match proposed to him by marriage brokers who told him that the girl they suggested for him was of good family and her brother, a well-known scholar. When he inquired of the brokers the girl's age, they told him that she was twenty-four years old, and he betrothed her, performing the act of *kiddushin.* He then discovered that the girl was in fact thirty-two years old. This recalled to him the passage in the Talmud[64] that if a woman marries before she is twenty, she can have children until she is sixty, but if she marries after she is twenty, she can only have children until she is forty. This caused the man much grief, since it would mean that his bride, who is now thirty-two, will only be able to give him children for another eight years and no more. He upbraided the brokers for misleading him, but they protested that it was not their fault at all, the girl's relatives having assured them that she was only twenty-four. The man was minded to have the *kiddushin* annulled on the grounds of misrepresentation. Even if they had given him a large sum of money, he would never have consented to marry a woman who is capable of giving him no more than eight years of childbearing. Being, however, of a shy disposition, and learning that the girl's brother was determined to create a fuss if he tried to back out of the marriage, the man resolved to go ahead with the *nisu'in* but first asked his friends to find out whether the *kiddushin* was valid in Jewish law. These friends returned with the decision of a certain sage that the marriage was perfectly valid, although they admitted that they had not referred the sage to the talmudic passage and the sage himself was evidently unaware of it. The friends also informed him that the girl's sister was married after she had reached the age of twenty and yet she continued to have children until she was fifty, so the man thought to himself, perhaps 'nature has changed' since talmudic times.[65] The man, therefore, went ahead with the *nisu'in,* and the woman bore to him two sons and a daughter but had no further pregnancies once she had reached the age of forty, and two years afterwards had her menopause and ceased having her periods. The man is now distressed that perhaps this shows that his fears were not groundless, and perhaps, therefore, they were never validly married. He is afraid to cohabit with her because, not being married, this would be an illicit act. Furthermore, being an extremely pious man, he is minded to ask whether he is allowed to cohabit with her even if they are validly married since it can possibly be held that the marital act is forbidden or is at least unworthy if it cannot lead to procreation, and here the woman is beyond childbearing age.

In his reply Hayyim states categorically that the marriage was valid and the man need have no qualms about living with his wife. That this is so can be seen from the Mishnah,[66] which rules that if a man marries a woman whom he imagines to be of priestly stock and she turns out not to be, or whom he imagines to be rich and she is really poor, the marriage is still valid 'because she did not mislead him'. As Rashi to the passage explains it, he allowed himself to be misled, and since he made no express stipulation at the time that he only marries her if she is what he imagines her to be, it is a case of 'words in the heart' (*devarim she-be-lev*), i.e., it is a mere mental reservation, which the law disregards. This is the law as recorded in both Maimonides and the *Shulḥan 'Arukh.*[67] Now in our case the man made no express stipulation at the time of the *kiddushin* that he only marries her if she is twenty-four years of age and no older. The girl herself did not mislead him in any way. It is not as if he had asked her at the time of the *kiddushin* how old she is and she replied that she is twenty-four. She herself had not spoken to anyone about her age. Although, according to the brokers, the girl's family did state that she was only twenty-four, the girl herself knew nothing of this. From the question, continues Hayyim, he has learned the identity of the girl, and he is quite certain that the circumstances were such in that family that she was not consulted at all until after the match had been arranged. Consequently she herself was not guilty of misrepresentation, nor had she instructed anyone else to engage in misrepresentation on her behalf. The man allowed himself to be misled by relying on the word of the brokers instead of investigating the matter, which he should have done if he was really concerned, and he would then have discovered her real age.

It can perhaps be argued, continues Hayyim, that the Mishnah only refers to where there had been no prior indication of the man's wishes, but that where there had been some such indication, i.e., where it was known that he really thought the girl to be of priestly stock or rich, the marriage would be valid even without any express stipulation to that effect at the time of the *kiddushin.* If this is correct, then in our case the marriage would have been invalid, since in his prior discussion with the brokers the man did make it quite clear that he imagined the girl to be no older than twenty-four and would not have married her had he known that she was thirty-two. But Hayyim rejects this on two counts. First, the man had made no explicit statement to the brokers to the effect that if the girl is more than twenty-four he does not wish to marry her. Although, as became clear from subsequent events, he certainly had it in mind, it is still only a mental reservation and, as such, of no consequence. Secondly, even if the man had declared explicitly to the brokers that he only wants her if she is no older than twenty-four, the marriage is still valid since the girl herself did not mislead him, which is, after all, the reason given in the Mishnah. That this is so is stated by R. Nissim b. Reuben Gerondi (*c.* 1310–*c.* 1375), the *Ran,* who is quoted by the Commentary *Tosefot*

Yom Tov to the Mishnah by R. Yom Tov Lipmann Heller (1575–1654). The *Ran* observes that whenever the woman herself did not actually mislead the man the marriage is valid, even if the man has previously shown his intention to be otherwise. Relying on the *Ran,* the famous Commentator R. Joshua Falk (1680–1756), in his *Peney Yehoshua',*[68] goes even further to suggest that the Mishnah deals, in fact, with the case where the man had previously declared openly his true preference and yet the marriage is valid. Falk argues that if this were not so, the Mishnah would be stating the obvious. In our case, Hayyim says, he knows with certainty that the girl was not informed at all of the matter, not even by her relatives and her mother. It was only after the match had been arranged that the girl was told that she was to be married to So-and-so, who would shortly be arriving for the purpose of the *kiddushin.* She was sent to change into her best clothes, and shortly afterwards the groom arrived to perform the *kiddushin.* The brokers were in no way the agents of the girl. She was totally unaware of their existence. Nor were her relatives, who did discuss the match with the brokers, the girl's agents. She knew nothing of the whole affair until she was told that the groom would shortly arrive. There was not the slightest degree of misrepresentation on her part, and since there was none, the rule of the Mishnah is that the marriage is perfectly valid.

Hayyim refers to a Responsum of R. Simeon b. Zemah Duran (1361–1444), rabbi of Algiers. Here the following case is discussed.[69] A man put it around that he was a rich man and then proposed to and married a woman, allowing her to believe that he really was rich whereas, in fact, he was poor. Duran rules that there are, nevertheless, insufficient grounds for dissolving the marriage, and he relies on the ruling given in the aforementioned Mishnah. True R. Moses Sofer is uneasy about Duran's ruling,[70] but the doubts expressed by this late authority are quite inadequate when weighed against the great authority and certainty of Duran. Moreover, it is likely that in our case even R. Moses Sofer would have no doubts. In the Duran case, the man was himself responsible for letting it be known that he was rich when in fact he was nothing of the kind. He was the one who did the misleading, the woman relying on what she had heard about him, for which rumours he himself had been responsible. In our case, on the other hand, not a single word had come from the girl herself, who knew nothing of the whole matter until it was all over. Furthermore, in our case the man himself was perfectly aware that the girl knew nothing of it at the time. There is no doubt whatsoever, concludes Hayyim, that the marriage was a valid one and had been blessed by God with children so that no more need be said, especially since the questioner demanded an answer on the self-same day.

As for the general question of whether there is anything at all improper in a man having intercourse with his wife when she can no longer have children, Hayyim states that it is obvious not only that it is permitted but that it is an obligation. Man's duties to his wife do not cease because she can no longer bear him children. The famous Kabbalist Isaac Luria is quite emphatic about it, that in addition to the duty of procreation there is high value in the marital act, even, as in the case of a nursing mother or a woman who is already pregnant, when the act cannot possibly lead to conception. This is because the sex act in marriage has cosmic significance, influencing the harmony of the realms on high. But apart from the Kabbalistic mysteries involved, all the Codes are perfectly clear that man's marital duties are to his wife whether or not she is capable of having children. Hayyim clinches the argument with a quote from the Talmud.[71] Here it is said that if the Israelites had not sinned by worshipping the Golden Calf, they would have attained immortality at the time when the Torah was given, and there would have been no further need for them to procreate since they themselves would live for ever. In fact, had they not have sinned, by a miracle there would have been no more childbearing. And yet the Israelites were, none the less, instructed to repair to their tents after the Torah had been given because of 'the joy of fulfilling one's marital duties'. Hayyim understands this to be in line with Luria's views that the sole purpose of intercourse in marriage is not procreation, but there is also the high cosmic purpose of which Luria speaks. 'Now this was said to all Israel, wise men and men of understanding, among whom were prophets. It follows, therefore, that even a saint and a holy man must not separate himself from his wife even when she has had her menopause and is no longer able to become pregnant. This is as clear as can be.'

According to talmudic law,[72] a father can marry off his daughter, if she is a minor, without her consent, and it appears that this was common practice in Baghdad in Hayyim's day. But once the girl has attained the stage of *bogeret,* i.e., when she has reached the age of twelve and a half and has, in addition, acquired the signs of puberty, she can only be married of her own free will. The particular case sent to Hayyim for his decision by the court[73] was of a man who lived in another town, his daughter living in Baghdad, and who sent a telegram to his relatives that he had betrothed, with *kiddushin,* his daughter to a certain man. When the girl heard of it, she was so distressed that she threatened to commit suicide if her father persisted in forcing her to marry that man. There was some uncertainty about the girl's actual age, but all the evidence went to show that she was a *bogeret.* Thus the only ground for requiring a *get* from the man was that she may have appointed her father an agent to marry her to that man (which, in fact, she and father both denied) or that she may later have acquiesced in the marriage, and this may have had the effect of her father becoming her agent retrospectively. It so happens that the girl was the daughter of a *kohen,* and there was a marked aversion, in any event, in Baghdad for an ordinary Israelite to marry a woman of priestly stock. She could only marry, therefore, a *kohen,* who may not marry a divorcée. Hayyim has to find a way out without having recourse, therefore, to a *get.* (He remarks that apart from this it is doubtful whether the man in question would be willing to give the *get.*) This he succeeds in doing by invoking the principle of the 'double doubt', *safek safeka.*[74]

In fact, he states, in this case there are no fewer than four doubts. Thus: first, the law may be in accordance with those authorities who hold that even if it can be assumed that the girl later acquiesced in the father's choice, there is no validity to the marriage since she has not appointed the father to be her agent, and her acquiescence later is not construed as a retrospective appointment of him as her agent. Secondly, even if the other authorities are followed, who hold that her consent does succeed in making the father her agent retrospectively, there are still other authorities who hold that this only applies where it is known that she had eventually given her consent, not here, where it would seem she never consented. And even if the law follows those who assume consent, there are still other authorities who apply it only where the father and the girl both live in the same city. And even if this is disregarded, in our case the girl eventually did protest, so that the authorities can be followed who hold in cases of this sort that her later protest is clear evidence that she never consented, even if she did not protest immediately. Hayyim quotes all the relevant authorities and builds up his case to permit the girl to marry another without requiring a *get*. Hayyim concludes: 'So it seems that one can rely on all these doubts to permit her to remarry without requiring a *get*. For if we would demand a *get* in order to be absolutely certain [i.e., even though it is not really required by law], you cause her much harm because if she receives a *get* she will be unfit to marry a *kohen,* and in this our city of Baghdad the Israelites keep themselves far from the daughters of *kohanim,*[75] and how much more so if, in addition, she is a divorcée. So by demanding a *get* you cause her great harm. Furthermore, according to the questioner, the groom will certainly refuse to grant the *get* and it will cause her to become an *'agunah.* Again, according to the questioner, the girl has become ill because of this unfortunate episode, and she has demonstrated to the court that in no circumstances can she ever accept the situation. And may Almighty God illumine our eyes with the light of His Torah. Amen. May it so be His will.'

Hayyim emerges from his Responsa as a Halakhist of note, true to his methodology, as stated in his Introduction, of summarizing all that has been written on a given question but reserving for himself the right to decide by his own reasoning and sense of justice. Like other famous Respondents, he tries hard to be completely objective, working always as if there is a pure science of the Halakhah that is free from all external influences, whether personal or due to the social background. Of course, in reality, there is no escaping one's background. Hayyim's approach is coloured by the conservative and very 'Oriental' society in which he lived. To recognize this is to cast no aspersions on Hayyim's great ability. There is, after all, a history of Jewish law, and even the most noteworthy of the Respondents do not operate in a spiritual vacuum.

NOTES

1. For Hayyim see *EJ,* vol. 10, pp. 242–3; David Solomon Sassoon, *A History of the Jews in Baghdad* (Letchworth, 1949), chap. XXVI, 149–56; Abraham Ben-Jacob, *A History of the Jews in Iraq* (Heb.), (Jerusalem, 1965), chap. 6:5, 190–200; Solomon B. Freehof, *The Responsa Literature* (New York, 1973), 44–45; Louis Jacobs, *Theology in The Responsum* (London, *1975),* 261—74. Obermayer's account is in the periodical *Ha-Maggid,* vol. XX (Lyck, 1876), 58, 65–6, 76–7, 84–5, 103, 146–7.
2. For this and the following, see the note by the editors of the new edition of *Rav Pe'alim,* printed at the end of vol. I, no pagination.
3. Ben-Jacob, op. cit., has made use of some small portion of this material, but cf. Hayyim's description of the turban worn by him and by most Jews in former times, vol. I, *OH,* no. 26; the many references to polygamy, e.g., vol. I, *YD,* no. 31; vol. II, *EH,* nos 13 and 26; superstitions, vol. I, *YD,* nos. 42 and 43; vol. II, *YD,* nos. 29 and 31; the practice of women wearing special garments during their periods, vol. I, *YD,* nos. 32 and 37; business affairs, vol. III, *HM,* no. 5; vol. IV, *HM,* nos 2 and 3; communal taxation, vol. II, *HM,*

no. 10; vol. IV, *YD*, no. 1; and many more. In these notes the following abbreviations are used: *OH* = *'Oraḥ Ḥayyim; YD* = *Yoreh De'ah; EH* = *'Even ha- 'Ezer; HM* = *Ḥoshen Mishpat.*

4. Based on *BT Bava Metzi'a* 85b and 86a: 'Samuel Yarbina'ah will be called *Ḥakham* but will not be called *Rabbi,*' i.e., he will not be fully ordained to render decisions in all branches of the law. Hayyim, unlike the majority of his contemporaries, published his works without any rabbinic approbation; see Obermayer, op. cit., p. 58, who criticizes Hayyim for this. Hayyim also refused to give his approbation to books; see Ben-Jacob, op. cit.,p. 194.
5. *BT Bava Metzi'a* 84a.
6. Hayyim is particularly incensed with the great Polish authority R. Solomon Luria (d. 1574), who in a Responsum on procedure where the Kabbalah differs from the Codes (Responsa *Rashal* [Fuerth, 1768], no. 98), boldly rejects the Kabbalistic ruling and goes on to state that R. Simeon ben Yohai, the traditional author of the Zohar, is not followed in his legal decisions, so that even if he came back to earth, we would be obliged to ignore his rulings. Hayyim protests that for all his immense learning, Luria had no right to treat R. Simeon as if he were a colleague of his. Luria had evidently overlooked the saying of the Rabbis *(BT Shabbat* 112b): 'If the ancients were like angels, we are like human beings; but if the ancients were like human beings, we are like donkeys.' Hayyim understands this to mean that if we treat the ancients as if they were angels, then we ourselves are human, but if we persist in treating the ancients as if they were mere human beings like ourselves, then we are like donkeys who lack the capacity to appreciate the high rank of the saints of old. Luria (*Yam shel Shlomo, Ḥullin* [Cracow, 1615], Introduction) is similarly critical of the decisions of R. Joseph Karo in his *Bet Yosef* and *Shulḥan 'Arukh.* And yet the whole Jewish world has accepted the authority of the *Shulḥan 'Arukh* and not alone the Sephardim, but also the Ashkenazim, except in the matter of Ashkenazi custom as recorded by R. Moses Isserles in his glosses to the *Shulḥan 'Arukh.* Hayyim continues that, having pointed out the errors of an early Ashkenazi authority, Luria, he will proceed to point out an error of a later Ashkenazi scholar, R. Jacob Emden (1697–1776), who was similarly critical of the great ones of the past. No one is immune from error, states Hayyim, not even an Ashkenazi Gaon whom he professes to admire greatly, R. Joseph Saul Nathanson of Lemberg (1810–75), author of Responsa *Sho'el U-Meshiv,* 5 vols (Lemberg, 1865–90). 'All these observations I made in haste,' continues Hayyim, 'as one treads on glowing embers. I mention these only in order to demonstrate that such errors are to be found even among the greatest of the later scholars and even though they were so vastly learned in the Torah. For who is greater than Joseph, the aforementioned Gaon [Nathanson], a storehouse of learning, the lion of his group, keen and expert in all the halls of learning and with clear reasoning powers to boot, yet in his sharpness and as he proceeded swiftly, he failed to note these things. Consequently, let not the critic vaunt himself over the great scholars, neither in holding up their errors such as these nor by accusing them of ignorance. For this is no new thing and is no fault of the scholars of our day, when the troubles of the age cause a diminution of the heart. Only where the law and the Halakhah are concerned is it fitting to express criticism in print, and then only on the condition that the critic be not overhasty and allow his words to be in humility and with all due deference.'
7. Vol. II, *OH*, no. 11, and vol. III, *OH*, no. 12. Cf. the proclamation signed by many rabbis in Ben-Jacob, op. cit., against Sabbath profanation, to which Hayyim appended this note: 'I, too, the undersigned, concur with regard to one who profanes the Sabbath in public that no one should officiate at his marriage; no one should call him up to the reading of the Torah for the Sabbath day or allow him to make up the *minyan* for prayer; no one should allow his sons to be circumcised or allow him to be buried in a Jewish grave.'
8. Vol. I, OH, no. 25, and supplement printed after the Introduction. Even where there is no *'eruv,* Hayyim permits it if the town is small, on the grounds that a rabbinic (as opposed to a biblical) offense can be set aside for such a great *mitzvah* as attending synagogue. (For the history of the idea that a 'public domain' for the biblical prohibition of 'carrying' has to have 600,000 people passing through it, so that 'nowadays' there is no 'public domain' [*Shulḥan 'Arukh, OH 345:7*], see S. H. Kook, *Sinai,* 15 [1952], 370—73.) Cf. Obermayer, op. cit., 58, who says of Hayyim: 'While in some respects he behaves like a Polish Hasidic Rebbe, there is in him, too, a goodly measure of the [reformist]

tendencies of a Geiger,' though Obermayer seems to be referring to Hayyim's liturgical innovations.

9. At least as far as a precoital device is concerned; see David M. Feldman, *Birth Control in Jewish Law* (New York, 1968), 198, n. 22, who lists the nonpermissive authorities.
10. Vol. I, *EH,* no. 4. On the whole subject see Feldman, op. cit., pt 5, 251–94, where a comprehensive survey is given of the opinions of the authorities quoted here by Hayyim.
11. See A. H. Freimann, *Seder Kiddushin U-Nesu'in* (Jerusalem, 1964), 223; on Baghdad and on Hayyim's legislation in particular, 294–98.
12. Ben-Jacob, op. cit., 193, from *Sinai,* vol. I (1938), 434.
13. Vol. II, *EH,* no. 6. Hayyim quotes in support a long list of authorities, both Sephardim and Ashkenazim, who, as he remarks, utilized this procedure. The first to introduce this procedure was, as Hayyim notes, the fifteenth-century German Rabbi Israel Bruna, whose opinion is recorded by Isserles in his gloss to *Shulḥan 'Arukh, EH* 157:4.
14. Vol. I, YD, no. 31; vol. II, *EH,* nos 13 and 26. On the history of monogamy, see Z. W. Falk, *Jewish Matrimonial Law in the Middle Ages* (Oxford: Clarendon Press, 1966), 1–34.
15. See Falk, op. cit., 35ff.; Freimann, op. cit., 29–31 and 294 on the continuation of the older talmudic practice in Baghdad and in Iraq generally.
16. Vol. II, *EH,* nos and 7. See Freimann, op. cit., that the office of *mekaddesh* in Baghdad was a hereditary one.
17. Vol. II, *EH,* no. 3.
18. *M. Bava Kama* 8:1; *T. Bava Kama* 9:1; *BT Bava Kama* 83b; Maimonides, *Yad, Ḥovel U-Mazzik* 2:2; *Shulḥan 'Arukh, Ḥoshen Mishpat* 600:3 and 8.
19. Responsa *Ḥatam Sofer, HM* (Vienna, 1872), no. 176.
20. Vol. IV, *EH,* no. 12.
21. *EH* 154:7.
22. *Bet Shemuel* ad loc.
23. Responsa *Noda' Biyudah* (Jerusalem, 1969), *Tinyana, EH,* no. 89.
24. *Ketubot* 7:10.
25. *Shulḥan 'Arukh, EH* 154:21.
26. *BT Ketubot* 64a and *Yevamot* 65b, given incorrectly as *Yevamot* 64b.
27. Hayyim refers to the Responsum of Ezekiel Landau quoted earlier and that of Samuel di Medina (1506–89) of Salonika, Responsa *Maharashdam* (Salonika, 1797–98), *EH,* no. 103.
28. *BT Bava Kama* 46a–b.
29. *Tur, HM* 25, and Isserles' gloss to *HM* 25:2.
30. For the rule of *kim li,* which dates from the thirteenth century, see the list of authorities quoted in Isaac Lampronti's *Paḥad Yitzhak,* photocopy *Mekor* (Jerusalem, 1970), vol. VII, s.v. *kim li,* 193–200; the later summary by Jacob Lorberbaum (d. 1832) printed in editions of the *Ḥoshen Mishpat* after chap. 25; Menahem Elon, *Ha-Mishpat ha-'Ivri,* vol. II (Jerusalem, 1973), 1062–3; and, for an account in English, Isaac Herzog, *The Main Institutions of Jewish Law* (London, 1965), vol. I, 265–73. J. M. Epstein (1829–1908), in his huge digest of Jewish law, *'Arukh ha-Shulḥan,* has only a single very brief passage on *kim li* (*HM* 25:13), in which he states that the rules and opinions on this matter are so complicated that there is no point in dealing with them, i.e., *kim li* is hardly ever applied. Cf. the comprehensive essay by H. Ben-Menahem in *Diney Yisrael,* vol. III (1972), 89–96.
31. On this see Hayyim Hezekiah Medini's (d. 1904) compendium *Sedey Uemed,* ed. Friedman (New York, 1962), *Kelaley ha-Posekim,* 13:31, vol. IX, 166–7.
32. These have been published in two collections: *Responsa Yosef Karo* (Salonika, 1598); *Responsa 'Avkat Rokhel* (Salonika, 1791). Hayyim's views are to be found in vol. II, *HM,* no. 2. Cf. no. 3.
33. Vol. III, *HM,* no. 1.
34. *HM* 18:1.
35. Vol. II, *HM,* no. 1.
36. *YD* 345:1.
37. Vol. III, *YD,* no. 29. See Ben-Jacob, op. cit., 143, that in 1880, as a result of the worsening situation in Baghdad, there was a severe outbreak of suicides, whereupon the rabbis felt obliged to have proclaimed in all the synagogues the seriousness of the offense and that 'a suicide has no share in the World to Come'.
38. Responsa *Ḥatam Sofer, EH,* no. 69, and *YD,* no. 326.

39. *Besamim Rosh*, 2d ed. (Cracow, 1881). On this notorious forgery by Saul Berlin (1740–94), see Saul Berlin and the "Besamim Roah"', in my *Theology in the Responsa*, 347–52.
40. *'Avelut*, nos. 118–23, ed. Friedman, vol. 5, 54–55.
41. Vol. III, *YD*, no. 30.
42. Responsa *Teshuvah me-'Ahavah* (Kassa, 1912), no. 345.
43. Vol. IV, *HM*, no. 5.
44. Very skilfully Hayyim does quote the stories of the wagers in *Midrash Lam. R.* 1:4–19, but states that these are not strictly analogous to his case. The general question of whether gambling debts are enforceable is discussed by Hayyim as falling under the heading of *'asmakhta;* see *ET*, vol. II, s.v. *'asmakhta,'* 108–15.
45. Vol. I, *YD*, nos 39–45; vol. IV, *YD*, nos 26 and 27.
46. Vol. I, *YD*, no. 41.
47. Responsa *Shav Ya'akov* (Frankfort, 1741–42), vol. II, *HM*, no. 25.
48. *BT Makkot* 20b; *Nazir* 38b, wrongly given as *Nazir* 20b.
49. *BT Betzah* 38b.
50. *BT Bava Kama* 37a.
51. Vol. IV, *YD*, no. 26.
52. On the *Ḥalukkah* see *EJ*, vol. 7, 1207–16.
53. *BT Berakhot* 55a.
54. Responsa *'Avkat Rokhel*, no. 137.
55. Vol. II, *HM*, no. 12.
56. *HM* 232:20–23.
57. Based on *BT Bava Kama* 27b and 46b, see supra, n. 28.
58. Vol. I, *EH*, no. 2.
59. See supra, p. 179.
60. *BT Ketubot* 12b.
61. See *BT Ketubot* 9a.
62. See supra, p. 186.
63. Vol. I, *EH*, no. 8.
64. *BT Bava Batra* 119b, given incorrectly as 19.
65. Cf. Rabbi Isaac Herzog, *Hekhal Yitzḥak, EH*, vol. I (Jerusalem, 1960), nos 6, 54, who remarks that this saying in *B.B.* is one of those of which the Codes say that 'nature has changed', i.e., it is not in accord with the facts of medicine as we now know them. Neither Maimonides nor the *Shulḥan 'Arukh* quotes the passage. Rabbi Herzog adds that since some rabbis do rely on the passage, he saw fit to consult medical experts, who informed him that it is quite possible for a woman married after the age of twenty to have children until she is around forty-five. On the idea that "nature has changed," and its application in practical law, see Tosafists to *BT M.K.* 11a and Hull. 47a and *Sedey Ilemed* 9:5.
66. *M. Kidd.* 3:5, *BT Kidd.* 62a.
67. Maimonides, *Yad, 'Ishut* 8:6; *Shulḥan 'Arukh, EH* 38:24.
68. Novellae *Peney Yehoshua'*, var. editions, to *BT Kidd.* 50.
69. Responsa *Tashbetz* (Amsterdam, 1738–41), Pt I, no. 130.
70. Responsa *Ḥatam Sofer, EH*, no. 82.
71. *BT A.Z.* 5a.
72. *M. Kidd.* 2:1. nl, fo 73. Vol. IV, *EH*, no. 4.
74. See supra, p. 187.
75. This Baghdadi custom was evidently based on talmudic opposition to a non-*kohen* who is not a scholar marrying the daughter of a *kohen* (*BT Pes.* 49a). Cf. Responsa *'Avney Tzedek* (Lemberg, 1888), *EH*, no. 8, of R. Jekuthiel Judah Teitelbaum (1808–83) that this talmudic rule is no longer operative.

—18—

Objectivity and Subjectivity in Jewish Law: The Debate on AID

(A lecture given at the Institute of Advanced Legal Studies on 18th June 1991, sponsored by the Oxford Centre for Postgraduate Hebrew Studies and the Institute of Advanced Legal Studies)

When a new situation gives rise to a Halakhic problem, the usual procedure in the Responsa literature is to use analogy in order to discover a precedent in the law. The subsequent debates on the correctness or otherwise of whatever decision is given will depend on whether the analogy is sound and therefore to be accepted or whether it is inexact and the decision based on it to be rejected or, at least, remain unsupported.

A good illustration of the process is provided by the contemporary Halakhic debate, to be examined in this lecture, on the question of the artificial insemination of a married woman by a donor other than her husband – AID. The recently discovered method of impregnating a woman by means of artificial insemination was obviously unknown in ancient times but the Talmud (*Ḥagigah*) does know of a woman who became pregnant through bathing in a bath (*ambati*) into which a man had previously deposited his semen. (Whether this is medically sound has been discussed by the commentators[1] but is irrelevant for a discussion of the law. Even if such a thing could never actually take place, the fact remains that the Talmud has a view on what the law would be if it could take place and the Talmud is the final court of appeal for Orthodox Jewish law.)

Moses Lima (d. 1658) discusses[2] whether the child of a woman impregnated in this manner, by bathing in the *ambati*, is treated in law as the son of the man who had deposited therein his semen. Is the child counted as his, for instance, for the purpose of the fulfilment of the duty of procreation? Lima argues that the child is the child of the 'donor' for all purposes of the law. He bases his opinion on the curious legend[3] that the prophet Jeremiah was compelled by his enemies to deposit his semen in a bath, after which the prophet's daughter bathed therein and became impregnated, giving birth, as a result, to Ben Sira! Since Ben Sira is declared to be the son of the prophet it follows that a son born in this manner is the legal son of the 'donor'.

Samuel b. Uri Shraga Phoebus (second half of the seventeeth century), in his commentary to the *Shulḥan 'Arukh,* entitled *Bet Shmuel,* seeks to prove it from another source. He refers to a source quoted by Joel Sirkes (1561–1640, author of *Bayit Ḥadash,* abbreviated *Baḥ);* the *Baḥ*[4] gives as his source R. Perez of Corbeil (d. *c.* 1295) in his notes to the work of his teacher, Isaac of Corbeil, the *Sefer Mitzvot Katan* (the *Semak*). Perez discusses why a menstruant (*niddah*) is permitted to sleep on sheets on which her husband had previously slept and yet married women do take care not to sleep on sheets on which a man other than their husband had previously slept. Perez replies that even in the very unlikely event of the menstruant becoming pregnant as a result of sleeping on the sheets no harm is done. A menstruant is forbidden to have intercourse with her husband but here no intercourse had taken place. In the case of the married woman, on the other hand, although here, too, it is only the act of intercourse that is forbidden, yet if she does become pregnant from the semen of a man other than her husband that man may have children from his wife and when the child grows up he may inadvertently marry his sister. This fear, that a brother might marry his sister, is found in the Talmud (*Yevamot* 37b) where it is stated that a man should not marry a woman in one country and another in a different country 'because this might result in a brother marrying his sister'.

Turning now to the AID question, we must first note the views of the famous Orthodox Rabbinic authority, R. Moshe Feinstein (1895–1986) who argues for a permissive attitude.

Rabbi Feinstein's Responsum on the subject,[5] dated *Rosh Ḥodesh Adar* 5721 (= 1960) is headed: 'Concerning a woman into whose womb a doctor injected the semen of another man. Is the woman forbidden to her husband and are there any doubts regarding the status of the child?' The basic legal issue is this: a married woman who had relations with a man other than her husband, while she was married to him, is forbidden henceforth to her husband and the child born of her union with her lover is a *mamzer.*[6] Do these rules apply where, as in AID, there had been no sexual act, only insemination of the woman? In the actual case considered by Rabbi Feinstein the wife did not consult her husband. When the doctors had informed her that her husband was infertile she had recourse to AID and presented her husband with a *fait accompli.*

Rabbi Feinstein begins his reply that the desire of a woman to be a mother is normal and perfectly legitimate. This desire is acknowledged in the Talmudic ruling (*Yevamot* 65b) that a wife whose husband had failed to give her children can petition for divorce on these grounds. Even though the duty of procreation does not devolve on a woman[7] she can still demand that a divorce with full legal settlement be granted on the grounds that she needs a child to take care of her in her old age. From the Biblical narratives, too, we can see how passionately the matriarchs longed for children.

In the case he considers, Rabbi Feinstein states categorically that the wife is permitted to her husband and the child is not a *mamzer.* It is the sexual act with a man other than her husband that renders a married woman forbidden to her husband and the child a *mamzer,* not the injection of the semen. That this is so can be seen from the fact that where the act has taken place even without any ejection of semen or where anal intercourse took place the woman still becomes forbidden to her husband. This demonstrates that it is the adulterous act of intercourse that renders her forbidden and whether or not there was an emission of semen is irrelevant. Intercourse without emission of semen renders her forbidden. Conversely, the insertion of the semen of another man does not render her forbidden. By the same token the child is only a *mamzer* when conceived as a result of the sexual act. True the child is a *mamzer* even if the act was done under coercion (say, where the couple were forced to have intercourse under the threat of death) and without any pleasure in the act. But in that case there had been an adulterous act, albeit one for which there is no culpability. Where, on the other hand, there has been impregnation without intercourse, as in the case of the *ambati* and in the case of AID, the fact that the semen of a man other than the husband has been injected into the wife does not render the child conceived as a result a *mamzer.* That this is so can be demonstrated from the case of Ben Sira. A child born of an incestuous union is a *mamzer* so why is it nowhere suggested that Ben Sira was a *mamzer*? This can only be because there was no act of intercourse. As for those who argue[8] that a child born as a result of AID must be considered to be a *mamzer* since even when a child is born as a result of adulterous intercourse where there is no pleasure in the act that child is a *mamzer,* Rabbi Feinstein dismisses such an argument as 'nonsense' (*hevel*). Even where there is no pleasure in the act it is still an adulterous act, whereas in the case of AID there is no act at all.

Rabbi Feinstein adds that where the identity of the donor is known the child born as a result of AID would not be allowed to marry one of the donor's other children since, in law, the donor is the father of the child. But where the identity of the donor is unknown the fear 'that a brother might come to marry his sister' can safely be disregarded. His argument here is based on the accepted ruling that the child of a Jewish mother and Gentile father is the child of the mother not of the father and he may consequently marry another child of his natural father from another Jewish woman. Since the majority of citizens in the USA are non-Jews the principle of *rov* ('probability') comes into operation so that the fear, mentioned in the Talmud, of a brother marrying his sister is non-existent. However, Rabbi Feinstein concludes, where, as in the case he is considering, the wife resorted to AID without first informing her husband, the husband has no legal obligation for the child's maintenance or for any expenses incurred in the birth and hospital treatment.

Rabbi Feinstein deals with the question at greater length in another Responsum[9] dated *Rosh Ḥodesh Nisan* 5719 (=1959) and with the heading: 'Concerning the law where a woman has been inseminated as practised nowadays by the doctors'. Rabbi Feinstein repeats his argument that it is intercourse alone that renders the woman forbidden to her husband. And, as he remarks in the other Responsum, the fear, mentioned by Perez, that a brother might come to marry his sister, does not apply since the majority of donors are Gentiles. The authority[10] who writes: 'Heaven forbid that a Jewish woman should be so abandoned as to engage in the form of mechanical adultery which the doctors have nowadays introduced', is way off the mark. There is no question of adultery with regard to AID since there is no intercourse. The only possible objection is because of the fear of a brother marrying his sister and, for the reason stated, this does not apply to AID.

In yet another Responsum[11] Rabbi Feinstein replies to the lengthy critique of his position by Rabbi M. H. E. Bloch. This

Responsum, dated *Sivan* 22,5722 (=1962) begins: 'I have received your lengthy missive full of rebuke, taking me to task because of what I wrote in Responsa Nos. 10 and 71, which, in your opinion, will bring about some breach in the purity and sanctity of the genealogical pride of the Jewish community. The truth is, however, that there is nothing in all I have written and decided to bring about, Heaven forfend, any desecration of Israel's purity and sanctity but it is all based on the true Torah of our early teachers. ' Rabbi Feinstein repeats his arguments. But evidently Rabbi Bloch had put forward a new argument against Rabbi Feinstein to which the latter now addresses himself.

Of a married woman's adultery Scripture (Leviticus 18:20) uses the expression 'lying for seed' (*zera'*) which can be interpreted to mean that the prohibition does apply to insemination even where there is no intercourse since, after all, the woman has the 'seed' of a man other than her husband in her womb. But, Rabbi Feinstein points out, Abraham Ibn Ezra, in his commentary to the verse, castigates those who stress the word *zera* to yield this interpretation since it might then be concluded that the offence of adultery depends on whether the woman became pregnant. The Talmud (*Yevamot* 55b) understands the word *zera* to exclude intercourse with an inert member or, according to those who hold that this, too, constitutes adultery, to exclude an act of necrophilia. And the Talmud (*Yevamot* 49a) states emphatically that a child has the status of a *mamzer* through his having been born as a result of the forbidden act of intercourse, not because he has been born of foreign 'seed'. It follows that when Nahmanides[12] comments: 'It is possible that when Scripture says *lezera'* there is a hint at the reason for the prohibition for it will not be known to whom the seed belongs', Heaven forfend that we should understand him to be giving the real reason, thereby giving sinners, as Ibn Ezra says, an opportunity to limit the scope of the prohibition. How can this possibly be the true reason since the laws regarding identification of progeny – *havḥanah*[13] – are Rabbinic not Biblical? Nahmanides can only mean that in the case of a married woman committing adultery there is the additional reason to which he refers. But it is obviously not the true reason and Nahmanides could never have intended to give it any Halakhic status. If he were not afraid to do so, states Rabbi Feinstein, he would suggest that this whole passage in Nahmanides is not the great teacher's but an interpolation by an ignorant disciple of the master. All the authorities who quote Perez agree that if the woman did have a child through sleeping on the sheets, that child would not be a *mamzer* since no illicit act of intercourse had taken place. Even though, Rabbi Feinstein continues, he had described the view that the child is a *mamzer* as 'nonsense' it was only in the heat of the moment without any disrespect being intended. But it remains true that it is only in the first instance that the Talmud frowns on a man having wives in different countries out of the fear that a brother might marry his sister. If a man did have wives in different countries his children would be allowed to marry without having to take into account the extreme improbability that of all the prospective candidates for marriage they would come up with a sibling. And in the case of AID it is permitted even in the first instance for the reason stated, that the majority of donors are Gentiles.

Rabbi Feinstein now turns to the question of *havlyanah.* This law is stated in the Talmud (*Yevamot* 42a–b) according to which a man must wait three months of her widowhood before marrying a widow, otherwise the child born to her after seven months of the second marriage would be of doubtful parentage – either a nine-month child from the first husband or a seven-month child from the second husband. Various reasons are advanced for why it is essential to establish with certainty the child's parentage – *havḥanah* means 'distinguishing' i.e. establishing who is the real father of a child. Now, on the face of it, as Rabbi Bloch had evidently argued, this law would preclude resort to AID since people will assume that the child is that of the woman's husband whereas, in fact, he is the natural child of the donor. Rabbi Feinstein has no difficulty disposing of this objection. In the case of *havḥanah* it cannot be known which of the two is the father but here it is known that the child is the donor's. No one has ever suggested that it is forbidden for a man to adopt an infant on the grounds that people will imagine the child to be his natural child.

At this stage Rabbi J. Breisch of Switzerland enters the fray; in his Responsa collection, *Ḥelkat Yaakov,*[14] where a number of Responsa are devoted to a critique of Feinstein's view, giving Feinstein the opportunity to reply, which the latter does in a letter dated *Kislev* 24, 5725 (=1965). Here Feinstein, while repeating his arguments, takes issue with new objections voiced by Breisch.

The *Sefer Ḥasidim*[15] writes that if the Gentiles refrain from eating a certain food (the example given is the meat of an animal with which a human being had committed bestiality) Jews should not eat that food even though it is permissible in Jewish law. The reason for this strictness is because it is wrong for Jews to give the impression that they have lower standards of sanctity and morality than Gentiles. Since, Breisch argues, the Catholics forbid resort to AID and are very severe in their condemnation of the practice, it would constitute a profanation of the divine name if the Jewish authorities were to permit it. Surely, retorts Feinstein, the *Sefer Ḥasidim* cannot possibly mean that Jews are obliged to base their standards of morality on those of Christian dogma. The *Seferljasidim* refers only to matters reprehensible on general universal standards of morality. But with regard to AID the Catholic objection is on doctrinal grounds, the point at issue being precisely this question of whether Scripture forbids the act of adultery *per se* or because of the emission of semen. As Ibn Ezra has noted, the Jewish understanding is morally superior in that it strictly forbids the act whether or not there is an emission of semen. To apply the principle stated in the *Sefer Ḥasidim* to AID is to make nonsense of the stern warning that Jews must not adopt practices based on the dogmas of a faith other than Judaism.

Breisch mentions a further reason for the prohibition of AID. According to the Talmud (*Yevamot* 42a) the law of *havḥanah* mentioned above applies also to a Gentile couple who became converted to Judaism. They must wait three months after their conversion before having marital relations so as to distinguish between a child conceived in 'holiness' and one conceived while they were still Gentiles i.e. it can be established at three months whether or not the woman is pregnant. Why is it important to know whether or not the child was conceived in 'holiness'? Breisch understands it to be on the grounds that a child conceived while its parents were Jews is superior in holiness to a child conceived while the parents were Gentiles. If this is so, Breisch argues, *a fortiori* it should be forbidden for a Jewish woman to allow herself to become impregnated with the 'seed' of a Gentile in AID. Feinstein reacts vehemently against such a 'racialist' interpretation. Where is it suggested, he asks, even remotely, that a convert to Judaism is racially inferior? The Talmud certainly does not mean to suggest that the child conceived while the parents were Gentiles is inferior, only that there must be no confusion regarding the child's parentage i.e. there must be no confusion regarding whether or not the child was 'sown in holiness'. It is purely a matter of accurate definition. In the case of AID there is no confusion since, on the probability principle, it is established that the child has certainly been 'sown' by a Gentile. There is not the slightest suggestion that a child whose mother is Jewish and his father a Gentile is racially or spiritually inferior to a child both parents of which are Jews.

We turn now to the chief opponent of Rabbi Feinstein, the Sotmarer Rebbe, Rabbi Joel Teitelbaum (1887–1979). In the Sotmarer's Responsa collection, *Divrey Yoel,* there are lengthy Responsa attacking the Feinstein position[16] In the biography of Rabbi Feinstein, published soon after his death,[17] it is told that a delegation of Rabbis made its way to Feinstein to persuade him to retract. Before leaving, the members of the delegation sought the Sotmarer's blessing on their enterprise. The Rebbe, noted for his sense of humour, said to them: 'But what will you do if he seeks to engage you in a discussion of Torah?'

The Sotmarer prefaces his remarks[18] by expressing his astonishment that Feinstein should have given such a perverse ruling as to permit AID. He goes on to present the arguments against Feinstein most of which the latter had already demolished. Some of the Sotmarer's arguments are less than convincing. For instance, he suggests that the reason why the child is not a *mamzer* in the Perez case or the Ben Sira case is because in these cases the semen had been injected automatically without any action whatever on the part of the woman, whereas in AID the semen is actually inserted into her womb. This distinction is obviously forced and it is clear from the Sotmarer's Responsa that he believes AID to be so obviously morally reprehensible that the flimsiest Halakhic arguments are admissible. On the argument from Nahmanides' interpretation, the Sotmarer admits that the question of 'seed' cannot be the main reason but it is none the less a reason and one advanced by one of the greatest Halakhic authorities and this is sufficient to ban the practice even though there is no actual intercourse.

The 'racist' motif appears in a particularly offensive form in the strange book published by Rabbi Yom Tov Halevi Schwartz, *Maaneh le-Iggerot.*[19] Schwartz's stated aim in this book is to demolish Feinstein's standing as a posek, seeking, on the whole quite unsuccessfully, to show that Feinstein is often in error in his Halakhic decisions. To the unbiased reader Schwartz cannot hold a candle to Feinstein in Halakhic expertise and Talmudic learning. Schwartz takes issue with Feinstein's views on AID in the body of the work but in the Introduction to the book the Feinstein position is attacked particularly in these terms:

'For it is well-known that the reason why we Jews are compassionate is because we are the children of compassionate parents. We have inherited this quality from our remote ancestors reaching back to Abraham and Sarah ... The only reason we have succeeded in this long, bitter exile in preserving our capacity for compassion, modesty and benevolence is because we have preserved our racial purity so that no foreign seed should be mixed with ours to destroy our character ... So how can we now agree with the torah of Rabbi Moshe which allows kosher Jewish daughters to mix clean blood with unclean, to contaminate the whole house of Israel, Heaven forfend, with unclean blood and with the corrupt qualities of the seed of Amalek, may his name be blotted out. And who can guarantee that this kosher woman who follows Rabbi Moshe's decision will not have the merit of bearing a son to one of the murderers at Auschwitz who murdered the father or one of the other relatives of that woman.'

As for the ruling that the child of a Jewish mother and a Gentile father is a Jew, Schwartz admits that this is the law where it is a *fait accompli* but how can anyone suggest that it is permitted, as in AID, in the first instance. Although in his reply to Breisch[20] Feinstein protests that he never intended for his decision to be acted upon, yet to the end of his long life he remained firmly convinced that his ruling was correct. In Volume Four of his Responsa[21] he replies to ten questions put to him by Rabbi E. Ellinson, in a Responsum dated *Marcheshvan* 5743 (=1982) i.e. when Feinstein was eighty-seven years of age. Evidently, Ellinson had asked Feinstein whether, in the light of all the opposition to his views, he had retracted. Feinstein replies: 'It is all true and perfectly clear and I have no need to retract. There are no objections to artificial insemination where the donor is a Gentile'. For all that, Feinstein concludes, he has never given a permissive decision in such a case. (He probably means a direct decision given to a woman who consulted him. The first two Responsa on the subject are in the form of replies put to him by other Rabbis so that, whatever he writes, the actual decision is theirs alone.)

'However, I have never given any actual ruling since it is of no avail to the husband so far as the duty of procreation is concerned and the wife does not have this obligation. It can easily result in the husband becoming very jealous. Consequently, it is not good counsel. To those who have disagreed with me I have given clear replies but none of these have been published except for the reply

I had given to the Gaon Rabbi M. Breisch of blessed memory. I have no desire to write any more on this subject even as a theoretical exercise. To be sure one should not advise the adoption of this procedure for the reason I have given. But if anyone did have recourse to it the child is kosher and, if a daughter, she may marry a priest.'

It would be too much to say that Feinstein has climbed down here. He repeats that his decision is correct according to the law. Yet he seems to have become tired of the whole matter and nothing further is heard of the desire of a woman to become a mother, the extra-Halakhic motif with which he began the whole discussion. To be sure Feinstein operates more within standard Halakhic categories than his opponents but he, too, is swayed by extra-legal considerations; at first in his appreciation of the strong desire of a woman to become a mother, and, in the end, by fearing to cause the husband to be jealous.

Feinstein's opponents hardly seek to hide their extra-Halakhic motivation, using Halakhic arguments and the Halakhic process in order to demonstrate what to them is axiomatic on the grounds of general morality. Especially, the appeals to prevent a profanation of the divine name, the extravagant advocacy of 'racialism', and the use of expressions like 'abomination', 'artificial adultery', show that for Feinstein's opponents there is the strongest conviction that AID is so intrinsically reprehensible that if the Halakhah appears to countenance it, the Halakhah must be understood, come what may, so as to condemn the practice.

In my book *A Tree of Life* I argue that the great Halakhists are often influenced by their general view of Judaism so that, even when they operate within the Halakhic process and with Halakhic-style argumentation, they are not only saying what the law is but also determining what the law must be if other Jewish values, as seen by them, are to be upheld. There can be few better examples of this than the contemporary Halakhic debate on the legitimacy or otherwise of AID.

From all this, and from the many other examples I have given in my book, it is clear that the great Halakhists are governed in their decision making by considerations other than those of pure Halakhah. Consciously or unconsciously, the Halakhists.are not only asking what the law is but also determining what the law should be if the general values of Judaism, as they see these, are to be realized. You no doubt recall the famous Clerihew:

The art of Biography
Is different from Geography.

Geography is about maps,
But Biography is about chaps.

So far as the Halakhists are concerned, the 'chaps' are conditioned, if that is not too strong a term, by their 'maps'. They are what they are, in part, at least, by where they live, by their particular Jewish environment. And being what they are they can do no other than be true to their own vision of Judaism and decide accordingly; all of which makes for variety and flexibility in Halakhic decision making. Like it or not this is how the Halakhic process operates. Meredith said:

Ah, what a dusty answer gets the soul
When hot for certainties in this our life.

There is no area of Jewish life and thought where greater certainty is to be had than in the Halakhah, with its great precision and strong sense of continuity. Yet even here, since the Halakhists are human beings of differing temperaments, while the actual decisions may be delivered with an air of certainty and finality, it remains true that, especially on matters of profound moral concern, certainties are not to be had. This is the answer the sincere inquirer gets when he asks what the Halakhah is on this or that complicated moral question. A 'dusty answer' maybe but the only answer possible in the circumstances.

NOTES

1. See the sources quoted in *Otzar ha-Posekim,* Vol. 1, Jer., 1970, par. 1 No. 42 and the articles on the subject in *Noam,* Vol. 1, Jer., 1958, pp. 111–6. Cf. Immanuel Jakobovits *Jewish Medical Ethics,* sec. ed. New York, 1975 pp. 244–50, Fred Rosner: 'Artificial Insemination in Jewish Law' in *Jewish Bioethics,* ed. Fred Rosner and J. David Bleich, New York, 1 979 pp. 105–11.
2. *Ḥelkat Meḥokek, Even ha-'Ezer* 1 note 8.
3. For this legend see Louis Ginzberg *Legends of the Jews,* Philadelphia, 1946, Vol. 6, pp. 400–2.
4. *Baḥ* to *Tur, Yoreh Deah* 195, quoted also by *Taz. Yorez Deah* 195 note 7. The *Bet Shmuel* source is *Even ha-'Ezer,* op. cit. note 10.
5. *Iggerot Moshe, Even ha-'Ezer,* New York, 1974, Responsum No. 10.
6. On the law of *mamzer* see my *A Tree of Life,* OUP, 1984, Appendix B, pp. 257–75.
7. Mishnah and Gemara *Yevamot* 65b.
8. Quoted in *Otzar ha-Posekim, loc. cit.*
9. *Iggerot Moshe, Even ha-'Ezer*, New York, 1974, Responsum No. 71.

10. Quoted in *Otzar ha-Posekim, loc. cit.*
11. *Iggerot Moshe, Ḥoshen Mishpat* etc., New York, 1964, *Even ha- 'Ezer,* Responsum No. 11.
12. *Perush ha-Ramban 'al ha-Torah* ed. C. D. Chavel, Jer., 1960, p. 105. For the lbn Ezra passage see *Ibn Ezra 'al ha-Torah,* ed. A. Weiser, Jer., 1977, to verse Leviticus 18:20, Vol. 3, p. 57.
13. See *Entziklopedia Talmudit,* Vol. 8, s.v. *havḥanah,* pp. 102–119.
14. Vol.3, Bene Berak, 1966, Nos 45–52 Nos 45 and 46 contain the critique Breisch sent in a single letter to Feinstein. No. 47 is a later letter in reply to the defence Feinstein had sent him. Nos. 48–-52 contain Feinstein's reply together with Breisch's critical notes.
15. *SeferḤasidim,* ed. R. Margaliot, Jer., 1973, No. 829.
16. *Divrey Yoel,* Brooklyn, New York, 1983, Nos. 107–110, Responsa dated 1964–65.
17. *Rabbi Moshe Feinstein* by S. Finkleman and R. Schirman, Jer., 1987, p. 1921.
18. No. 107, the first Responsum in Vol. 2 of the *Divrey Yoel.*
19. *Maaneh le-Iggerot,* New York, 1973. This book is a curiosity, too, because Schwartz had resort to the same publisher as the one who published Feinstein's works and the work at a superficial glance, looks like an additional Feinstein volume since exactly the same format, type and binding is used for both. See the biography of Feinstein, op. cit. p. 192 that the embarrassed publisher consulted Feinstein before publishing the Schwartz book but Feinstein told him to go ahead since his living depended on it.
20. *Helkat Yaakov,* op. cit. No. 48, beg.
21. *Iggerot Moshe,* vol. 6, Bene Berak, 1985, No. 32.

Index

Please note that, where applicable, names of Rabbis are filed under 'bar', 'ben', or 'Ibn'